Project Management
for Healthcare
Information Technology

Project Management for Healthcare Information Technology

Scott Coplan, PMP

David Masuda, MD

New York Chicago San Francisco
Lisbon London Madrid Mexico City
Milan New Delhi San Juan
Seoul Singapore Sydney Toronto

The McGraw-Hill Companies

Cataloging-in-Publication Data is on file with the Library of Congress

3 4 5 6 7 8 9 0   QVS/QVS   1 7 6 5 4 3

ISBN 978-0-07-174053-1
MHID 0-07-174053-8

Sponsoring Editor
Judy Bass

Copy Editor
Julie Searls

Editing Supervisor
Stephen M. Smith

Proofreader
Kalpona Moitra

Production Supervisor
Pamela A. Pelton

Indexer
Robert Swanson

Acquisitions Coordinator
Michael Mulcahy

Art Director, Cover
Jeff Weeks

Project Manager
Manisha Singh, Glyph International

Composition
Glyph International

McGraw-Hill books are available at special quantity discounts to use as premiums and sales promotions, or for use in corporate training programs. To contact a representative, please e-mail us at bulksales@mcgraw-hill.com.

This book is printed on acid-free paper.

About the Authors

Scott Coplan, PMP, is a project manager, educator, author, and speaker on project management best practices. He is the founder and president of COPLAN AND COMPANY, a project management software and services firm. Mr. Coplan helped Milwaukee Children's Hospital build its HMO and oversaw implementing more than nine financial, administrative, and clinical applications at three separate Los Angeles County, California, hospitals in both in-patient and ambulatory settings. He holds faculty positions at the University of Washington Schools of Public Health and Medicine, where he teaches healthcare project management.

David Masuda, MD, is a physician and educator at the University of Washington. During the past 10 years, he developed and delivered courses in clinical care and applied clinical informatics for certificate, masters, and doctoral programs in health administration, medicine, and nursing. He currently develops distance-learning approaches for healthcare higher education.

Contents

Acknowledgments

For:

- My co-author Dave, who gave life to both this book and my teaching. I am forever in your debt.
- My wife Elizabeth, who is a gifted writer and provided endless support, edits, and insights. Most important, she has always known what matters. Thank you for reminding me when I went astray while writing this book. You are my soul mate.
- My partner John Litzenberg, who is technically an employee, but is actually the source of all my good ideas and willing to put up with my shenanigans. You have never-ending creativity.
- My parents, who do not know what I do for a living, but hopefully this book will help them understand.

Scott

My deep appreciation goes to Scott—despite the trials and tribulations of the past few months as we brought this together, I can say I both learned a great deal and found satisfaction in the process. And to my wife Sarah, my thanks for the encouragement and for the nudging when my energy was low.

David

Project Management
for Healthcare
Information Technology

CHAPTER 1

Introduction

In this chapter, we will:

- *Review the current healthcare crisis and the solution healthcare information technology (HIT) can provide*

- *Explain how HIT, itself in crisis, is part of the problem instead of contributing to the solution*

- *Define project, information technology (IT), and change management as an integrated methodology that can help solve the healthcare and HIT crises*

Virtually anyone involved in healthcare over the last several years would agree that healthcare information technology (HIT) is among the top—if not *the* top—strategic and operational challenges facing healthcare leadership today. As well, it is clearly known that implementing HIT, whether it is the electronic health record (EHR), telemedicine, a personal health record (PHR), or any of the other myriad healthcare applications, is fraught with obstacles and pitfalls. Rarely does a hospital or clinic complete this HIT journey within scope, on time, and within budget.

Our book explores the challenges faced by healthcare delivery organizations (HDOs) in this process of moving from the paper to the electronic medical record. (We refer to *HDOs* throughout as a generic healthcare provider instead of addressing the differences associated with community hospitals, teaching hospitals, physician groups, ambulatory centers, and so on.) This is particularly important given the highly complex nature of healthcare organizations as well as the fundamentally transformative nature of HIT. To avoid as many failures as possible, to maximize the efficiency of their available project resources, and to streamline their path toward digital medicine, we integrated project, IT, and change management together as a single methodology that organizational leaders, managers, and clinicians should follow. We believe that while individually these methodologies have critical key success factors, HIT project leaders will perform best with this integrated approach.

The Challenge

It should come as no surprise to the reader that healthcare in the United States currently faces several crises—a crisis in the costs of care, a crisis in the quality of care, and (despite the enactment of health insurance reform in 2010) a crisis in access to care for millions of Americans. The data supporting these claims are well-known. The United States spends almost $7,500 per capita annually on healthcare, nearly twice the amount of other Organization for Economic Cooperation and Development (OECD) countries.

We consume 17% of our GDP in healthcare. For this roughly $2.3 trillion each year, we get what many would call second-class care.[1] The Institute of Medicine's (IOM) 1999 publication, *To Err Is Human*,[2] reports that 44,000 to 99,000 people die annually due to preventable medical errors costing between $17 and $29 billion yearly. The average time it takes physicians to adopt clearly proven and effective diagnostic and therapeutic interventions is 17 years.[3] A large national study by the RAND Corporation in 2003 found that a patient walking into a clinic or hospital anywhere in the country has a 55% chance of getting the right medical advice.[4]

In the same way we face major societal challenges in healthcare cost, quality, and access, individual HDOs face equally complex and demanding challenges. The environment is extremely complex, influenced by constantly shifting political, social, technical, and financial trends. U.S. healthcare provides fragmented services that include simultaneously competitive and cooperative participants. For example, in many hospitals the physicians who admit patients function as independent contractors of the hospital and as such are not employees of the hospital. In addition, the range of services these physicians provide in their private practices may overlap with those offered in the hospital so the incentives faced by the hospital and the physicians may at times be at odds.

By and large, in the United States medical practice remains a cottage industry. As of 2008 almost one third of private practices were groups of one or two physicians, with another 12% in practices of three to five physicians.[5] Commonly these practices have an arm's-length relationship with the hospital. In many cases this relationship puts them at odds over HIT projects.

> *Healthcare IT implementations are just projects like any others, on one level. There's technology you need to implement, and then shepherding people through the changes. At the same time, there are unique aspects in healthcare that make these implementations more challenging. Namely, the doctors rule the roost, for better or worse, and in many instances the doctors might not even be employed by the healthcare entity where they are providing care. That adds a significant wrinkle. You hear about these nightmare implementations where the doctors just refuse to participate. You wonder, how can they refuse? Don't they ultimately report to someone in the organization that is trying to do this? In some cases, that answer is "no," they're not employed by the institution where they're providing care, they're independent. It is these aspects that make healthcare IT projects even more complex than in other industries.*
>
> —Dan Nigrin, MD, MS, CIO, Children's Hospital, Boston

In addition to the role of physicians, information exchange requirements amplify the unique characteristics of the U.S. healthcare industry. There are literally millions of codes associated with the human body, disease, diagnosis, procedures, and reimbursement that HIT must interchange amongst providers, insurance carriers, and patients. Some examples of data exchange standards are:

- Code sets, such as International Classification of Diseases, Volume 10 (ICD-10), and the American Medical Association's Current Procedural Terminology (CPT). ICD-10, a numeric list of diseases arranged alphabetically by disease name, helps systems render a patient's chart to a series of coded conditions. Clinicians use CPT descriptive terms and identifying codes to report medically performed procedures to payers for reimbursement.

- Languages, such as the Systemized Nomenclature of Medicine (SNOMED) designed by the College of American Pathologists, represent clinical information in an electronic medical record, including signs, symptoms, diagnoses, and procedures. Nursing Interventions Classification (NIC), a standardized language, describes treatments nurses perform. Nursing Outcomes Classification (NOC) provides standardized language that describes patient outcomes from a nursing perspective.

- Data exchange protocols, such as Health Level 7 (HL-7), are a standard series of messages packaged for data exchange among administrative, financial, and clinical systems. Digital Imaging Communications in Medicine (DICOM) is a digital format and exchange protocol for images and related information.

Finally, the individuals who are at the core of healthcare—patients—face challenges of their own. In early 2010, one out of seven U.S. citizens was uninsured or underinsured—roughly 45 million people.[6] In addition, uninsured medical costs are the number one cause of personal bankruptcy.[7]

Without a doubt, healthcare is currently in a quality, safety, and cost crisis—one that exhibits symptoms at the individual, organizational, and societal level. However, we must acknowledge that this sense of crisis is not new. You can find newspaper reports decrying the *healthcare crisis* in virtually every decade of this past century. In fact, it may well be that healthcare is an industry that will always be *in crisis*. It is an industry that affects everyone because it deals in life and death. As such, it is one in which emotions play an equal role to pragmatism.

We believe one factor that did not exist in past decades now affects the current healthcare crisis in a grand way, which is the exponential growth of IT. Granted, during the past six decades the healthcare industry used computing and communications technologies, but it is only in the last two decades that the capabilities of IT expanded at a phenomenal rate.

IT affects every aspect of society and personal life, for example, the Internet, e-mail, texting, cell phones, and handheld computing. Healthcare is no exception. Many say healthcare is relatively slow to accept IT. The IOM called for nationwide adoption of the computerized patient record within ten years as far back as 1990. The IOM reiterated this call in 1999 and again in 2003 with the issuance of the two landmark reports *To Err Is Human* and *Crossing the Quality Chasm*. Yet, progress in this direction is painfully slow.

Key events have effectively accelerated this pace. First, there was the election of the Obama administration in 2008 on a platform that emphasized healthcare reform. Second, there was the contemporaneous global economic meltdown and the subsequent enactment of the American Recovery and Reinvestment Act (ARRA), including the section entitled Health Information Technology for Economic and Clinical Health (HITECH). HDOs, as well as state and federal legislative and regulatory agencies, are now entrants in an HIT compliance race. Current federal law directs the Centers for Medicare and Medicaid Services (CMS), to begin a fundamental redefinition of reimbursement for healthcare services by effectively mandating all healthcare providers install and *meaningfully use* HIT (primarily by using electronic health records that share information freely through health information exchanges or HIEs).

Nearly a decade of research outlines the ways in which HIT can address cost, quality, and access problems; however, the adoption rate of HIT in HDOs remains lower than one might hope. The *New England Journal of Medicine's* (NEJM) July 3, 2008, article,

Electronic Health Records in Ambulatory Care—A National Survey of Physicians,[8] indicates that only 4% of physicians report having extensive, fully functional EHR systems. On March 29, 2009, the NEJM article *Use of Electronic Health Records in U.S. Hospitals*[9] stated, "only 1.5% of U.S. hospitals have a comprehensive electronic-records system (i.e., present in all clinical units), and an additional 7.6% have a basic system." The reasons for this slow rate of adoption are myriad and well-known, and include very high capital costs, an immature and rapidly evolving vendor market, and unconvincing evidence on the return on an HIT investment as well as major failures with acquisition and implementation efforts.

The passage of ARRA/HITECH is a game changer. With significant financial and regulatory incentives, it is likely that HDOs will move quickly to electronic clinical care systems over the next several years. A recent study suggests the global market for health information technology applications will grow to $18 billion over the next five years. Electronic health records represent the largest segment of this growth, but related applications such as practice management systems, pharmacy systems, lab systems, and radiology systems, also play a role.[10] As we enter a decade in which effectively all HDOs, from the 1000-bed tertiary care hospital to the two-person primary care clinic, begin the transition from paper to fully interoperable HIT foundations, it is unfortunately predictable that many of these organizations will find the path a very rocky one. This transition requires understanding, support, and commitment from all levels of the organization over a multi-year period to avoid failures. Of these factors, one that is exceedingly clear is a critical organizational capability for HIT project management.

Of the few good IT project management resources, only a limited number address HIT. This makes resolving the healthcare and HIT crises challenging. This book is about HIT project management and dedicated to helping solve these crises. Our intent in this book is to better define the role of IT project management in healthcare settings, using a methodology that encompasses standard models from project, IT, and change management.

Definitions

A *project* is a short term endeavor to achieve specific objectives. *Project management* is the discipline devoted to planning, organizing, and coordinating resources to successfully achieve the objectives of a short term endeavor. For example, project management focuses on managing scope, time, and cost processes that produce outputs to achieve project objectives. While much of the work that goes on in an HIT project is indistinguishable from projects in other industries there are several distinct and unique factors involved in an HIT project as described above.

In other industries, formal project management methodologies are highly effective in controlling scope, time, cost, and quality. There are many approaches to formalizing project management and arguably the most well-known is the Project Management Institute, *A Guide to the Project Management Body of Knowledge (PMBOK® Guide)—Fourth Edition,* Project Management Institute, Inc., 2008, the formal methodology of the Project Management Institute (PMI).[11] The *PMBOK® Guide* defines a structured framework that catalogs the knowledge, skills, and competencies as well as the tools and techniques important to project management success. While healthcare has a growing understanding of the value of this project management methodology, we believe unique healthcare aspects may make this methodology insufficient for successful HIT acquisition and implementation. We argue that HIT projects will substantively benefit by integrating concepts, methods, tools, and techniques from two additional, and often overlapping, disciplines:

- *Product Management*—Product management is the discipline devoted to planning, organizing, and coordinating resources to analyze, design, develop, deliver, maintain, and retire a product. It is important to distinguish between product management and project management. Product management focuses on what the project produces. Project management focuses on the processes, for example, scope, time, cost, etc. For example, construction management focuses on building a product like a bridge, while project management addresses the schedule and cost. Because the product in this book is HIT, we refer to product management as Information Technology Management. It generally relies on tangible or hard skills (e.g., requirements definition, building an IT infrastructure, and security management). IT management is codified in a fashion similar to project management. Perhaps the best known of these is the Software Engineering Body of Knowledge (SWEBOK), authored by the Institute of Electrical and Electronics Engineers (IEEE). When one reviews formal methodologies such as PMBOK and SWEBOK, it is apparent there is a good deal of similarity in their models and methods. There are also differences. Perhaps the best way to appreciate the subtle difference between these two is to consider the fundamental focus of each. In IT management models, the primary focus is the technology itself—the *product*. In project management, on the other hand, the primary focus is on the *project* as opposed to the product. In other words, project management focuses on the process of leading various people and teams that design, build, test, and deploy the product—HIT. Subsequent chapters make clear how these two methodologies intersect.

- *Change Management*—As any HDO that went through the process of implementing an EHR will tell you, having the most skilled and able project and technology managers in the world may well result in unacceptable IT solutions resoundingly rejected by users, the front-line clinicians who care for patients. Multiple experiences with failing HIT projects over the past decade make it clear that success requires equal measure of attention to managing the people in the organization who will use the product of the project. Change management is the discipline devoted to planning, organizing, and coordinating the resources necessary to transition individuals and groups in an organization from the current to a future state. The outcome is human behavioral change, which relies on intangible or soft skills, such as sponsorship, training, and optimization. In the case of HIT, it is increasingly obvious that the *human issues*—and not the technology or project issues—are key to success. Change management, unlike project and IT management, does not yet have a clearly defined or broadly understood formalized methodology. The principles of change management are, however, based on well-developed theories and practices from such fields as organizational behavior and organizational development.

Standards

As noted, there are numerous resources available for IT project management used successfully in many industries and settings. This book relies on the following standards or widely recognized reference works:

- *A Guide to the Project Management Body of Knowledge (PMBOK® Guide)*[12]—The generally accepted project management standards defined by the Project Management Institute (PMI).
- *A Guide to the Software Engineering Body of Knowledge (SWEBOK)*[13]—The generally accepted software engineering standards defined by the Institute of Electrical and Electronics Engineers (IEEE).

This book relies on change management best practices because there are no formal standards.

Integrating the Methodologies

Project, IT, and change management are not entirely distinct disciplines or methodologies. The concepts, activities, and outputs in one discipline have parallel—and sometimes identical—features in the other two. We argue that to optimally plan and execute HIT projects in HDOs requires all three adopted in concert. In this book, we combined these standards and best practices to create an integrated project, IT, and change management methodology.

Success with HIT projects is never a guarantee. There is no management methodology that guarantees an HDO will complete its HIT projects within scope, on time, and within budget. Projects undertaken without the judicious and conscientious use of *some* formal methodology are far more likely to suffer setbacks and perhaps complete failure. Therefore, it is imperative that organizational leaders and managers who choose to adopt one or more methodologies fully understand the limitations therein. Effective implementation of our integrated methodology requires consideration of the following caveats:

- *Guidelines, Not Rules*—Many formalized management methodologies can give the impression that success simply requires following a set recipe or stringently enforcing rules. Nothing could be further from the truth. Because every organization, project, and Project Manager is different, methodologies must be employed as guidelines. All three methodologies of project, IT, and change management have a myriad of tools and techniques; knowing which to use when is core to good management. The Project Manager should always be asking, *Will the tool or technique I am considering really add value to my project?* Managers need to avoid a sense that they must use every single part of our integrated methodology. Doing so may result in an unruly exercise, significant overload, and possible failure. At the same time, one should also recognize that some HIT projects are of sufficient scope and complexity such that the tools and techniques described in this book may be insufficient. Our book is not an exhaustive coverage of the disciplines of project, IT, or change management (e.g., we do not cover the use of project management software). It should be clear from this caveat that there is no substitute for experience in good project management.
- *Conciseness*—Many project management resources focus on the goal of enabling the reader to sit for and pass examinations, such as the Project Management Professional (PMP®) certification. Instead of defining and applying every conceivable project, IT, and change management process, technique, and output

required for an exam study guide, this book describes and applies selected best practices we believe help HIT projects succeed.

- *Selectivity*—Our book *derives from* instead of *adheres to* standards. This book relies on selective standards to fully exploit them for their best potential. For example, the *PMBOK® Guide* outlines requirements definition as the first step in scope management. This poses two problems:

  1. Which comes first: requirements definition that cannot come without scope definition, or a scope definition that cannot come without requirements definition? Anyone responsible for the requirements definition will tell you that you must clearly define the project scope if you ever expect to finish the requirements definition. This involves a preliminary scope definition and follow-up adjustments.

  2. PMBOK outlines the requirements definition, i.e., documenting system needs, as a requirement to fulfill rather than as one of the most important parts of an IT project.

  We resolve both of these issues by addressing requirements management as a completely separate part of IT management, rather than embedding it in project scope management. While this violates standards compliance, it resolves critical requirements management issues, thus increasing the likelihood of project success.

- *Complexity*—Our book includes varying complexity levels associated with each part of the methodology. This variability is not a measure of importance. It simply reflects the intricacy of each part of the methodology and the amount of information and number of examples required to explain it.

Solving the HIT and Healthcare Crises

Project management was an absolute critical aspect of our CHAMPS [Children's Hospital Application Maximizing Patient Safety] implementation. Unless you have sufficient and tuned in project management for a large-scale clinical systems initiative, it's bound to fail. That's not just the management and technical components, obviously that's important and necessary. Change management, for example, includes user training, understanding user existing workflow and how those workflows might change with the implementation. I think those aspects are equally if not more important than the project and technical aspects of the implementation.
—Dan Nigrin, MD, MS, CIO, Children's Hospital, Boston

We believe the application of our integrated methodology increases the prospect of HIT project success—and with the successful implementation and ongoing meaningful use of HIT, will help end the healthcare crisis. However, success, particularly in healthcare, is not measured only by an *event* or point in time, such as system cutover, when a project completes all activities within scope, schedule, and cost constraints. Instead, this project event marks the beginning of a transition or a series of events where users learn about how to employ HIT in a live environment. Because projects are by definition short term endeavors, there is a point in time when the project ends after testing and final acceptance. This begins the transition where an HDO's operations make a long-term commitment to optimize use of their EHR. This book addresses what we need to do during the project transition phase to sustain and enhance project benefits after the cutover event.

Who Should Read This Book

Our book offers management solutions for the HIT challenge. While we targeted healthcare professionals in project management, IT, medicine, and nursing when we wrote this book, we know lessons learned in HIT project management also benefit their counterparts in other industries. Equally important is what this book is not—it is not a study guide for people looking to pass certification exams in any one discipline. It is also not an exhaustive catalog of project management, technology management, or change management tools and techniques. Numerous good texts on those subjects are available to the interested reader.

How We Organized This Book

This chapter (Chapter 1) introduces the reasons we felt compelled to write this book. Healthcare is in crisis. IT is part of the cure, and we want this cure to work. Chapter 2 is an overview of the three management disciplines we review—project, technology, and change management—and describes at a conceptual level how to use these disciplines synergistically. In Chapters 3 through 5, we examine each of these three management disciplines in detail. We define each discipline as a set of knowledge areas that the Project Manager and team must understand, a set of processes or activities they must undertake and complete that are specific to that knowledge area, and a set of outputs or products that are the end result of each knowledge area process. Because all projects evolve over time, we grouped these knowledge areas, processes, and outputs into a basic set of categories that help clarify particular project stages. In essence, these stages are *planning, executing,* and *closing* the project. In each of these three chapters, the format for the chapter is to first define underlying principles of that knowledge area and to then describe a set of the core processes that take place within that knowledge area in the planning, executing, and finally the closing stage. We chose a concise number of processes, generally five to seven for each knowledge area, with an eye toward describing those we felt are most crucial for HIT project success. These are by no means the only processes and outputs that we might consider in each project stage, but given that our goal for this book is to enable HIT project success, we believe that this subset of core processes is a better approach.

In each chapter, you will also find quotes from project leaders at HDOs around the country, who took the HIT journey—with successes and challenges—identifying how our integrated methodology enabled these organizations to reach their HIT project objectives.

These contributors include:

- Florence Chang, CIO, Multicare, Tacoma, Washington
- Robert Greenless, PhD, former CIO, Rancho Los Amigos National Rehabilitation Center (RLANRC), Los Angeles, California
- Ernie Hood, CIO, Group Health Cooperative (GHC), Seattle, Washington

- Beatha Johnson, Director, Clinical Information Systems, Virginia Mason Medical Center (VMMC), Seattle, Washington
- Daniel Nigrin, MD, MS, CIO, Children's Hospital, Boston, Massachusetts
- Michael H. Zaroukian, MD, PhD, FACP, FHIMSS, CMIO, Michigan State University (MSU), Lansing, Michigan

The end of this book includes a model of our fully integrated HIT methodology and a Glossary. The model is a graphical framework of the methodology. Please refer to this model while reading the book and afterwards as a reference tool on each component of our methodology and how they relate to each other throughout an HIT project.

Supplemental Information

Separately, a companion website is available at www.mhprofessional.com/coplan (user name—coplan11; password—instructor). It includes:

1. An interactive version of our integrated methodology with definitions of terms and concepts.
2. A syllabus for instructors.
3. A PowerPoint® presentation for each section included in this book.

Conclusion

We maintain that HIT projects require more than project management to increase success. While PMBOK focuses on project management, our methodology adds IT and change management to help healthcare reduce costly failures, including loss of life.

The next chapter introduces the components of this integrated methodology, exploring how the process group framework offered by PMBOK provides a foundation for also managing IT and change.

Endnotes

1. Goldman, D., and McGlynn, E. A. (2005). *U.S. Health Care: Facts About Cost, Access, and Quality*. Santa Monica: Rand and The Communications Institute. Retrieved from www.rand.org/pubs/corporate_pubs/2005/RAND_CP484.1.pdf.
2. Kohn, L. T., Corriga, J. M., and Donaldson, M. (eds.) (2000). *To Err Is Human: Building a Safer Health System*. Washington DC: Committee on Quality of Health Care in America, Institute of Medicine, National Academy Press.
3. Balas, E. A., and Boren, S. A. Managing clinical knowledge for health care improvement. In J. Bemmel and A. T. McCray (eds.), *Yearbook of Medical Informatics 2000: Patient-Centered Systems*, 65–70. Stuttgart: Schattauer Verlagsgesellschaft GmbH.
4. McGlynn, E. A., Asch, S. M., Adams, J., Keesey, J., Hicks, J., DeCristofaro, A., and Kerr, E. A. (2003). The quality of health care delivered to adults in the United States. *New England Journal of Medicine, 348*, 2635–2645.
5. Boukus, E., Cassil, A., and O'Malley, A. (2008). 2008 Health Tracking Physician Survey, Center for Studying Health System Change. Retrieved July 8, 2010, from www.hschange.com/CONTENT/1078/#fig1.

6. McGlynn, E. A., Asch, S. M., Adams, J., Keesey, J., Hicks, J., DeCristofaro, A., and Kerr, E. A. (2003). The quality of health care delivered to adults in the United States. *New England Journal of Medicine, 348,* 2635–2645.

7. Himmelstein, D. U., Thorne, D., Warren, E., and Wollhandler, S. (2007). Medical bankruptcy in the United States: Results of a national study. *The American Journal of Medicine, 122,* 741–746.

8. DesRoches, C. M., Campbell, E. G., Rao, S. R., Donelan, K., Ferris, T. G., Jha, A. K., Kaushal, R., et al. (2008). Electronic health records in ambulatory care—a national survey of physicians. *New England Journal of Medicine, 359,* 50–60.

9. Jha, A. K., DesRoches, C. M., Campbell, E. G., Donelan, K., Rao, S. R., Ferris, T. G., Shields, A., Rosenbaum, S., and Blumenthal, D. (2009). Use of electronic health records in U.S. hospitals. *New England Journal of Medicine, 360,* 1–11.

10. Millard, M. (2010). Big Growth Projected for HIS Market. *Healthcare IT News.* www.healthcareitnews.com/news/big-growth-projected-his-market.

11. Project Management Institute (2008). *A Guide to the Project Management Body of Knowledge* (4th ed.). Newtown Square, PA: Project Management Institute.

12. Project Management Institute (2008). *A Guide to the Project Management Body of Knowledge* (4th ed.). Newtown Square, PA: Project Management Institute.

13. Bourque, P., and Dupuis, R. (eds.) (2005). *A Guide to the Software Engineering Body of Knowledge.* Washington, DC. IEEE Computer Society.

CHAPTER 2

Integrating Project, Information Technology, and Change Management

In this chapter, we will:

- *Describe and define management methodologies*
- *Describe each project, IT, and change management knowledge area*
- *Associate each knowledge area with its applicable process groups*

Introduction

HIT projects are highly complex, expensive, and challenging to undertake and complete successfully. Myriad factors contribute to both success and failure, and it is increasingly clear that formal approaches to managing HIT projects strongly correlate with success. The larger the project, the more likely that using a formal project management methodology will significantly increase an organization's likelihood of project success—completing the project in scope, on time, on budget, and with achievement of the desired strategic and tactical capabilities. It is therefore key to have a rational approach to understanding what a project management methodology is, how to use it best, and how to avoid its misuse.

The *Merriam-Webster Dictionary* defines *methodology* as "a body of methods, rules, and postulates employed by a discipline."[1] Important in this definition is that a methodology is a synthesis of both structured and unstructured components. The structured components include such things as methods and rules—these are the concrete and measurable items that define a methodology. At the same time, there are unstructured or conceptual aspects of a methodology; for example, postulates, philosophies, theories, or ideas. It is important to consider both of these perspectives because projects are at risk of failure if we adopt only the concrete and measurable parts and ignore the unstructured attributes of project management. Project management is as much an art as it is a science.

In many ways, project management is very similar to the concept of evidence-based medicine (EBM). According to Dr. David L. Sackett in the *British Medical Journal*[2]:

Evidence-based medicine is the conscientious, explicit, and judicious use of current best evidence in making decisions about the care of individual patients. The practice of evidence-based medicine means integrating individual clinical expertise with the best available external clinical evidence from systematic research. By individual clinical expertise, we mean the proficiency and judgment that individual clinicians acquire through clinical experience and clinical practice. Increased expertise is reflected in many ways, but especially in more effective and efficient diagnosis, and in the more thoughtful identification and compassionate use of individual patients' predicaments, rights, and preferences in making clinical decisions about their care. By best available external clinical evidence, we mean clinically relevant research, often from the basic sciences of medicine, but especially from patient centered clinical research into the accuracy and precision of diagnostic tests (including the clinical examination), the power of prognostic markers, and the efficacy and safety of therapeutic, rehabilitative, and preventive regimens. External clinical evidence both invalidates previously accepted diagnostic tests and treatments and replaces them with new ones that are more powerful, more accurate, more efficacious, and safer.

This definition indicates that optimal medical decision-making between providers and patients depends on using the best and most current scientific evidence (the concrete and measurable) hand-in-hand with individual preferences, cultural norms, and even intuition (the unstructured and philosophic). In both EBM and project management, the true skill comes in knowing how much of each to use in a particular situation.

The challenge in creating a book such as this one on project management is that it is far easier to write the structured than it is the unstructured aspects. Hence, many project management texts develop methodological models that define various project processes and their outputs. The processes are a sequenced set of specific activities the Project Manager or Project Team undertakes. The outputs are the documents they create and use in the execution of these processes. Project management from this perspective becomes akin to following a recipe—start with step A and move linearly through to step Z with the assumption that the project should succeed. For simple projects, this approach *may* be sufficient, but for complex projects it is very unlikely they will evolve in this way. With complex projects, there are many situations where the structured model simply is insufficient—in which knowing exactly what to do cannot be found in the recipe. Therefore, we believe that highly skilled Project Managers must learn not only the tools and techniques embedded in project management methodologies, they must develop a deeper conceptual understanding of the methodology including both its strengths and limitations.

The choice of any specific project management methodology is less important than the effective use of the methodology, or knowing *what works when*. Our goal is to define, as simply as possible, the core activities and concepts that a Project Manager and a Project Team complete to achieve specific objectives. We derive this core set from three distinct, yet overlapping, disciplines that are crucial to successful planning, deployment, and operation of HIT. As noted in Chapter 1, while organization success with HIT using any one such discipline is possible, drawing from all three disciplines is likely to increase the probability of project success.

We summarize the three disciplines below. The discipline of project management forms the core of our integrated methodology model, and from there we overlay aspects of the disciplines of IT and change management.

Project Management

The project management discipline is the foundation for the integrated methodology presented in this book. The *PMBOK® Guide* (Fourth Edition) provides a useful framework for describing key project management components. At its core, the *PMBOK® Guide* includes four important and interrelated concepts—processes, process groups, outputs, and analysis methods. We will deal first with processes.

Processes

In the simplest terms, a *process* is an activity conducted to produce an output. For example, in managing the project schedule, the Project Manager completes these activities:

- Define tasks
- Sequence tasks
- Estimate task resources
- Estimate task duration
- Prepare schedule
- Control schedule

Each of these activities is a process that describes a finite and relatively well-circumscribed piece of work to produce an output, for example, tasks, task sequences, and task resources. A very important conceptual point here is that you must think of processes within the project as occurring both sequentially and concurrently.

Process Groups

A *process group* is a collection of the processes that generally occur in distinct stages of the project over time. The *PMBOK® Guide* defines five process groups, each occurring in a consecutive (although overlapping) fashion:

1. *Initiating*—This initial set of processes in a project focuses on defining what the project or phase is about so the organization can make the decision to proceed.
2. *Planning*—The next set of processes revolves around planning the project in detail.
3. *Executing*—Once the Project Manager sufficiently completes the planning, the project moves to completing tasks with the resources necessary to achieve project objectives.
4. *Controlling*—When the executing process group begins, parts of the controlling process group also start. In short, the controlling process group involves reviewing the tasks and outcomes of the project execution and ensuring they conform to the objectives defined in the project plan. As such, there are, conceptually speaking, two main types of processes in the controlling process group. First, if the Project Team executes a particular set of tasks or completes an output according to plan, then the Project Manager simply documents this conformance. The second occurs when the Project Manager discovers a variance between what the plan calls for and what actually occurred. When this happens, the Project Manager has effectively two choices—either modify the plan to fit

| Initiating | Planning | Executing | Controlling | Closing |

TABLE 2.1   Process Groups

the results of the execution or re-execute the tasks and activities until the result conforms to the plan.

5. *Closing*—The last process group considers activities related to completion of interim project activities, as well as final completion of all project activities. The overall focus is on gaining acceptance of project results and transferring them successfully to operations to sustain and enhance benefits.

It is once again important to understand that while these five process groups appear, on the surface, to represent consecutive steps, in practice there is considerable overlap. Project planning continues after starting project execution because not all planning activity begins and ends simultaneously and then follows with execution. Projects include numerous activities that are not like a race where everyone starts at the same time. For example, in an EHR project there is user requirements management planning—determining how to best define what the EHR will do—and there is planning for EHR user training. The Project Team will execute the EHR requirements management plan before the user training plan.

Table 2.1 displays the five process groups.

Outputs

Now that we have the definitions for processes and process groups, we turn to the concept of outputs. Most processes the Project Manager undertakes or oversees result in an output. An *output* is a tangible result of a process. For example, the process *define task* noted above produces a document—the output—called the task list.

Confusion commonly arises around the term *output*. In an EHR project, for instance, there could be two types of things that we consider as outputs. The EHR itself is distinctly a tangible output. However, in the project management methodology, tangible outputs have a different meaning. In the project management model, the outputs are generally documents that support and inform the execution and control of the project. A task list is a document that maps out in detail all of the work a team must complete to build and implement the EHR—a document that can run a hundred pages (we cover this in more detail in Chapter 3). Given this differentiation, you could say an HIT project has two sets of outputs, as follows:

1. Documents that are outputs of project management.

2. Products of the project, such as an EHR.

The number of processes and outputs in major complex projects is daunting. In our book, we limit the processes and outputs to a manageable number, with the goal of using this subset of processes and outputs as examples of our methodology.

This entire book is output-oriented. It offers principles similar to value stream management, the process management theory behind the Toyota Production System. In essence, this means the project management processes an organization undertakes should produce an output that the customer needs. Focusing on just any output is wasteful. Here we focus on outputs associated with project, IT, and change management processes that add value to fulfilling project stakeholder needs. This increases effectiveness, that is, it provides value to an HDO's stakeholders, increases efficiency, and reduces cost.

Analysis Methods

Successfully managing a project requires completing the appropriate set of processes and outputs in each of the five process groups. The nature, size, and complexity of the project largely define ways to complete the set of processes and outputs. Take, for example, a typical process and output in the planning process group—creating the project budget. Preparing a project budget (an output—the project budget document) requires that the Project Manager work through one or more cost estimates.

There are several ways to prepare cost estimates in an EHR project. We could rely on the expertise of HDO personnel who previously implemented an EHR to estimate our project costs, i.e., expert judgment. We could estimate each individual part of the work until we assemble a total project cost estimate, i.e., a bottom-up cost analysis. The Project Manager is free to choose the method, so long as he completes the cost estimating process using the method he feels is most appropriate for the task. Every approach has strengths and weaknesses. The *PMBOK® Guide* defines these and other methods as *tools and techniques*. We refer to them as *analysis methods*.

Relationships

We noted above that process groups are at their core chronological. Closing a project simply cannot occur before initiating the project. However, the processes within this chronological structure are not always purely consecutive. Given this, it is useful to consider several types of relationships, including:

- *Consecutive*—A relationship where actions occur sequentially. For example, the Project Manager prepares a project budget during the planning process group followed by budget execution in the executing process group.

- *Concurrent*—A relationship where two or more actions occur simultaneously. For example, a Project Manager oversees project execution and performs quality assurance simultaneously to ensure adherence to predefined standards.

- *Iterative*—A relationship where an action occurs repetitively to break something down into parts to improve or obtain a more detailed understanding of it. For example, the Project Manager prepares a scope statement or a description of what the project includes and excludes in the planning process group. The Project Manager then prepares a work breakdown structure or list of project deliverables organized by category, for example, IT versus clinical training. The Project Manager may then update the scope statement reflecting refinements identified while preparing the work breakdown structure. This cyclical nature of project management processes is another key concept, which we will visit in more detail below.

The fundamental relationships between processes, process groups, and outputs are important to understand—even more so because keeping these relationships in mind simultaneously is challenging. The first of these is that all projects occur over time. Projects have an explicit beginning and end—this finite definition in time is what differentiates projects from regular and continuous work. Organizations initiate a project by developing a project plan. They then execute the project by following (as closely as possible) the plan, and once they complete all the project deliverables, they close the project. This temporal nature of a project means that some activities by definition occur before others and are consecutive. The nature of this consecutive flow is constant for all projects—small or large, simple or complex. Consider the example of a very simple project—baking a cake. The baker begins with a plan—*what sort of cake do I want to make?* Once decided, the baker consults a recipe, visits the grocery store, assembles the cake ingredients, mixes the ingredients, places the batter in a pan, and puts the pan in the oven. If all goes as planned, a delicious cake emerges. The consecutive arrangement of these steps is straightforward and relatively self-evident.

The second fundamental, and seemingly paradoxical, relationship is that most projects include activities that *also* occur concurrently. Simple projects may have only a few of these concurrent activities, but complex projects have dozens if not hundreds. Moreover, complex projects not only have multiple concurrent tasks, they also have multiple Project Team members executing these tasks. Returning to our baking example, consider baking 100 cakes for a large convention with 1,000 guests. This requires dozens of team members, each with different skill sets (shoppers, bakers, servers, and bussers) as well as a dedicated Project Manager who oversees the work of the team. In this case, the Project Manager—the executive chef—knows that this project is not quite so simple as beginning and end. In fact, the Project Manager must engage the Project Team to perform some tasks concurrently or the project timeframe will unnecessarily extend beyond the convention date. This adds more complexity, not only because the team performs consecutive and concurrent work simultaneously, but also because team members' tasks involve different expertise. For example, bakers are frosting and slicing cakes, servers are delivering portions to guests, and bussers are clearing tables to make way for dessert concurrently.

The third fundamental relationship is iteration. The baker may, for example, prepare the frosting by combining confectioner's sugar, butter, and cream in a mixing bowl and adding a little more sugar and cream alternately until the frosting is a good spreading consistency. This repetitive process refines the quality of the frosting iteratively. This additional relationship makes a project even more complex because, once again, there are teams performing consecutive, concurrent, and iterative work simultaneously, each involving different areas of expertise. Figure 2.1 displays this concept as relationships within process groups.

To further complicate matters, these relationships not only occur within a specific process group, they also occur *across* process groups. Figure 2.2 displays this concept as relationships between process groups.

If we go back to baking a cake, we could imagine an iterative relationship that cuts across process groups. For example, consider the simple baking project where we purchase the ingredients during the planning process, mix the ingredients during the executing process, and return to the planning process to purchase more butter to line the pan. In a complex project such as baking cakes for the convention, most of the bakers may continue consecutively mixing ingredients, while one of them shops for the emergency butter order.

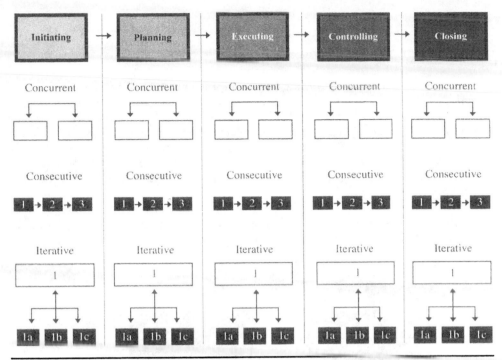

FIGURE 2.1 Relationships within process groups.

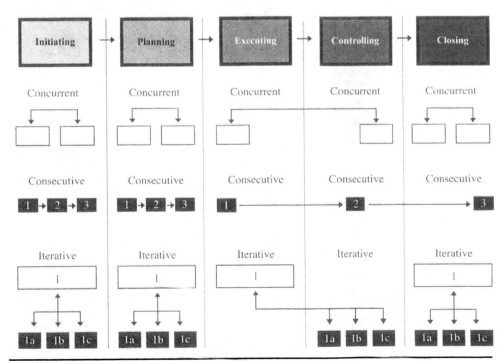

FIGURE 2.2 Relationships between process groups.

Cycles

Projects never go entirely according to plan—problems inevitably arise that require attention. Solving these problems requires a cycle of activities. To describe this process, W. Edwards Deming created the Plan, Do, Study, Act cycle.[3] A Plan, Do, Study, Act (PDSA) cycle is a continuous process improvement (CPI) model of repeatedly preparing a solution for change (Plan), testing the solution (Do), reviewing the results to identify improvements (Study), and refining and improving on the solution based on data gathered from the study (Act). Once you complete the initial PDSA cycle, the cycle starts anew.

Project management also requires similar cycles. In the project management methodology, the cycles are typically termed planning, executing, and controlling. Figure 2.3 compares the project management cycle and the PDSA cycle.

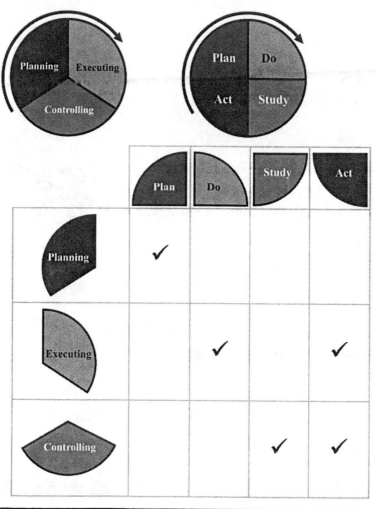

FIGURE 2.3   Comparison of *PMBOK® Guide* and PDSA cycles.

The difference between a typical CPI PDSA cycle and the iterative cycles in project management is that in a moderate to large project, there may be dozens of plan-execute-control cycles going on concurrently. Moreover, there may be nested plan-execute-control cycles. For example, consider an HIT project of implementing a nursing documentation system. At the micro level, a small group within the Project Team develops a range of templates that nurses use to complete their nursing notes in the EHR. Each of several nursing units may have variations in these templates—the Emergency Department (ED) will have one template, Pediatrics a different version, Cardiology still another. The Project Team will develop a documentation template, meet with nursing representatives from each department to review the template, and based on feedback from those users, modify the template and then recheck the template with these users. In this process of plan-execute-control, the team optimizes each template for each department's needs. At a higher, macro level, the Project Manager will report to a project executive the overall progress on the nursing documentation work. Ideally, senior leadership will elect to limit the amount of feedback/customization allowed for individual units for the sake of creating simple and consistent documentation across the hospital. This feedback requires revision of the plan executed by the Project Team at the micro level.

We apply the PDSA cycle to project, IT, and change management. We iteratively employ the following:

- Planning to prepare a solution based on expected results.
- Executing to build the solution.
- Controlling to check that the configured solution is compliant with expected results from planning. We include the controlling process repeatedly throughout this book to underscore the importance of iteratively checking for project compliance with expected results. As the saying goes, you cannot manage what you cannot measure.

Project Management Knowledge Areas

Project Managers execute process groups consecutively over time to complete projects successfully. Within each process group, the Project Manager undertakes a broad range of processes. Because the nature of complex projects is such that this range of activities is quite large, the *PMBOK® Guide* and similar models categorize these processes into logically related knowledge areas. A *knowledge area* is a field of expertise. For example, a Project Manager develops a project schedule, deploys a Project Team to complete project tasks, and controls the team's work to keep the project on schedule, amending the schedule as necessary. Similarly, the Project Manager estimates costs, determines the budget, and controls costs to complete a project within that budget. These tasks fall within the cost management knowledge area.

The *PMBOK® Guide* outlines nine defined knowledge areas. Each knowledge area includes a definition of the project expertise subset included in that area, a set of processes that the project undertakes, and a set of outputs created as a result of these processes. Below is a brief description of each of these, including their associated process groups:

- *Integration Management*—Initiating, planning, executing, controlling, and closing of all key project, IT, and change management plans, processes, and outputs required to achieve project success.

- *Scope Management*—Planning and controlling what a project includes and excludes.

- *Time Management*—Planning and controlling the schedule required to complete the project within an approved timeframe.

- *Cost Management*—Planning and controlling costs required to complete the project within an approved budget.

- *Quality Management*—Planning, executing, and controlling project processes and outputs according to approved standards.

- *Human Resource Management*—Planning, executing, and controlling the selection, assignment, and function of human resources to complete the project successfully.

- *Communications Management*—Planning, executing, and controlling project information exchange required to ensure project success.

- *Risk Management*—Planning and controlling how the project identifies and responds to potential threats to successful project completion.

- *Procurement Management*—Planning, executing, controlling, and closing acquisition of goods and services to support successful project completion.

Recognizing how process groups and knowledge areas interact is key to understanding how a project management methodology works. Process groups include a set of processes that occur chronologically over time. Granted, there are concurrent and iterative forms of processes, but process groups do have a sequence in the form of plan, do, study, act. Knowledge areas, on the other hand, include subsets of processes that the Project Manager oversees to address certain project aspects that do not necessarily occur sequentially. Table 2.2 displays the relationship between project management knowledge areas and the process groups with knowledge areas in bold, individual processes in normal text, and outputs in italics.

In this table, you will see various tasks and activities from each of the nine knowledge areas displayed across the five process groups.

For the reader of a project management text such as this one, the challenge may come in understanding that a book is by definition a linear approach to learning a discipline. In the case of project management, this linear constraint means the reader covers, for example, the project scope management knowledge area, then moves on to the project time management, and so on, finally completing the text by studying the project procurement knowledge area. The reader will soon realize that despite these knowledge areas occurring consecutively in the text, all nine knowledge areas occur consecutively, concurrently, and iteratively. As a metaphor, imagine a juggler. In this case, the juggler's objects include a rubber ball, bowling pin, and chain saw. In learning this feat, the juggler may consider each item in turn and learn its characteristics—its size, its weight, its speed of rotation, and how to grab and throw it. Yet when it comes to actually performing the act, the juggler must manage all three items simultaneously. And, if the juggler inadvertently throws an object too hard or too soft, or overthrows an object slightly in a left or right trajectory, the juggler must adjust the timing and position, which affects the catching and throwing of the other two objects. In this sense, while you need to study each knowledge area separately, when it comes to managing the project you will invariably draw from each knowledge area in no particular order—project changes from one knowledge area invariably affect processes and outputs in other knowledge areas.

Initiating	Planning	Executing	Controlling	Closing
Integration	**Integration**	**Integration**	**Integration**	**Integration**
Prepare the feasibility study and business case	Prepare project management plan	Manage project execution	Control project execution	Close phase or project
Feasibility study and business case	*Project management plan*	Performance report	*Organizational process asset update*	*Organizational process asset update*
Prepare project charter	**Scope**	*Change Request (CR)*	*Performance report*	*Deliverable*
Project charter	Define scope	*Deliverable*	*Change Request (CR)*	**Procurement**
	Scope statement	*Project document update*	*Project document update*	Perform final acceptance
	Prepare Work Breakdown Structure (WBS) and WBS dictionary	**Quality**	Perform integrated change control	*Organizational process asset update*
	Work Breakdown Structure (WBS)	Perform quality assurance	*Change Request (CR)*	*Deliverable Completion Certificate (DCC)*
	WBS dictionary	*Change Request (CR)*	**Scope**	
	Work package	*Project document update*	Verify scope	
	Time	**Human Resources (HR)**	*Deliverable Completion Certificate (DCC)*	
	Define tasks	Develop project team	*Change Request (CR)*	
	Task list	Project team performance assessment	*Project document update*	
	Sequence tasks	**Communications**	Control scope	
	Task sequence	Distribute information	*Organizational process asset update*	
	Estimate task resources	*Organizational process asset update*	*Performance report*	
	Task resource estimate	**Procurement**	*Change Request (CR)*	
	Estimate task duration	Select vendor	*Project document update*	
	Task duration estimate	*Selected vendor*	**Time**	
	Prepare schedule		Control schedule	
	Schedule		*Organizational process asset update*	
	Cost		*Performance report*	
	Estimate costs		*Change Request (CR)*	
	Cost estimate		*Project document update*	
	Prepare budget		**Cost**	
	Project budget		Control cost	
	Quality		*Organizational process asset update*	
	Prepare quality management plan		*Performance report*	
	Quality management plan		*Change Request (CR)*	
			Project document update	

TABLE 2.2 Project Management Knowledge Areas by Process Group

Initiating	Planning	Executing	Controlling	Closing
	Human Resources (HR)		**Quality**	
	Prepare human resources plan		Perform quality control	
	Human resources plan		*Organizational process asset update*	
	Acquire project team resources		*Change Request (CR)*	
	Resource assignment		*Project document update*	
	Communications		**Human Resources (HR)**	
	Identify key project participants		Manage project team	
	Project roster		*Organizational process asset update*	
	Plan communications		*Performance report*	
	Communications plan		*Change Request (CR)*	
	Risk		*Project document update*	
	Prepare risk management plan		**Communications**	
	Risk management plan		Report performance	
	Identify risks		*Organizational process asset update*	
	Risk register		*Performance report*	
	Perform quantitative risk analysis		*Change Request (CR)*	
	Risk register update		*Project document update*	
	Perform qualitative risk analysis		**Risk**	
	Risk register update		Monitor and control risk	
	Plan risk response		*Organizational process asset update*	
	Risk response plan		*Performance report*	
	Procurement		*Change Request (CR)*	
	Plan procurement		*Project document update*	
	Procurement plan		**Procurement**	
	Prepare solicitation		Administer procurement	
	Solicitation		*Organizational process asset update*	
			Performance report	
			Change Request (CR)	
			Project document update	

Table 2.2 Project Management Knowledge Areas by Process Group (*Continued*)

Information Technology Management Knowledge Areas

In the sections above, we defined five project management process groups and nine project management knowledge areas as well as described the somewhat complex and often confusing ways in which they interact and overlap. We also described some of the processes that take place and the outputs they produce in the various process groups. However, managing a project is certainly more than generating a large volume of documents such as the scope statement, schedule, or budget. The main output of an HIT project is the tools or software application—such as an EHR. This is the product of the project. Similar to the way the Project Manager uses the project management methodology to perform the project, he uses an IT management methodology to produce the product of that project.

Perhaps one of the most well-known IT management methodologies is from the IEEE, called the SWEBOK. SWEBOK bears striking similarity to the *PMBOK® Guide* in terms of structure. For example, we derived ten IT management areas involved in designing, developing, and implementing a system from the SWEBOK 2004 Edition. Below is a brief description of these knowledge areas, which we cover in depth in Chapter 4:

- *User Requirements Management*—Initiating, planning, executing, and controlling the identification and organization of stakeholders' needs to evaluate options and acquire a solution that achieves the project objectives. All system projects must address the future needs of users. Project team members are representative stakeholders that clarify these needs by working extensively with additional stakeholders.

- *Infrastructure Management*—Initiating, planning, executing, and controlling requirements for the location and configuration of the physical components of a new system. Examples include the location and configuration of the system's physical components such as networks devices, PCs, mobile computing devices, and servers.

- *Conversion Management*—Planning, executing, and controlling transformation and movement of data from existing manual and automated systems to a new system. In many cases, HDOs need to convert data from their legacy information systems for use in their new system.

- *Software Configuration Management*—Planning, executing, and controlling setup and selection of application options and features to meet user, technical, and security requirements. Each user group in a hospital is likely to have varying needs for EHR software configuration—the needs of a physician in the ED are different from the needs of a physician in the Psychiatry Department.

- *Workflow Management*—Planning, executing, and controlling the sequence of automated and manual steps that support delivery of an organization's products and services.

- *Security Management*—Planning, executing, controlling, and closing system access. Throughout HIT project planning and execution, teams must configure, test, and implement a range of infrastructure and system safeguards in order to secure system access.

- *Interface Management*—Planning, executing, and controlling the definition, development, testing, and implementation of information exchanges between one or more systems. HDOs do not have a single monolithic information system that handles every aspect of their work. A new EHR installation must communicate with, for example, a legacy pharmacy system, which involves an interface.

- *Test Management*—Planning, executing, and controlling how an organization verifies that a new system meets its specifications. A critical component of configuring a functional, secure, and safe EHR system is testing—how an organization verifies that a new system meets its needs.

- *Cutover Management*—Planning, executing, and controlling the switch from existing manual and/or automated systems to a new system. Each successful EHR project has a *go-live* point—switching from existing manual and/or automated systems to a new system.

- *Support Management*—Planning, executing, controlling, and closing technical maintenance of the system after cutover.

SWEBOK uses an organizing structure like the *PMBOK® Guide*. Once you compare the knowledge areas we derived from SWEBOK to the *PMBOK® Guide* knowledge areas, it is evident how to map SWEBOK knowledge areas to the *PMBOK® Guide* process groups. Table 2.3 displays how we included IT management knowledge areas in the five project management process groups with knowledge areas in bold, individual processes in normal text, and outputs in italics.

Change Management Knowledge Areas

Unlike project and IT management, change management has no widely accepted models or frameworks. There are no formal standards accredited by a standards organization, (e.g., the American National Standards Institute), conferred by an industry group or commercially accepted; or conformed to as a de facto or customary methodology. While we are all increasing our understanding of the various change management methods, in the absence of a standard, we must propose our own change management framework and integrate it with project and IT management.

What Is Change Management?

As defined above, IT management includes the processes undertaken and completed in developing and deploying *the product*—an EHR, a telemedicine application, or a patient web portal, for example. Project management similarly includes the processes and outputs undertaken and generated as an organization oversees building a final outcome or product. Examples of project management outputs are a scope document, work breakdown structure, budget, and similar documents. Change management focuses not on the project nor on the product, but rather on the people—the clinicians and patients and other workers in a healthcare organization who will use the HIT. One might ask if change management simply means training the users to use the new EHR. While training is an essential part of change management, much more is required. People need to know more than just how to use the system—they also need to know why the HDO is implementing the system, how it will change their lives, and the effect it will have on the lives of their

Table 2.3 IT Management Knowledge Areas by Process Group

Initiating	Planning	Executing	Controlling	Closing
User requirements	**User requirements**	**User requirements**	**User requirements**	**Security**
Prepare high-level user requirements	Prepare user requirements management plan	Prepare detailed user requirements	Control user requirements	Conduct ongoing security compliance
High-level user requirements	User requirements management plan	Detailed user requirements	Organizational process asset update	Security audit results
Infrastructure	**Infrastructure**	**Infrastructure**	Performance report	**Support**
Prepare high-level technology requirements	Prepare infrastructure management plan	Define detailed technology requirements	Change Request (CR)	Initiate ongoing support
High-level technology requirements	Infrastructure management plan	Detailed technology requirements	Project document update	Support tickets
Define existing technology architecture	Prepare facility modification plan	Prepare and order equipment	**Infrastructure**	
Existing technology architecture description	Facility modification plan	Equipment order confirmation	Control infrastructure	
	Prepare system installation plan	Complete facility modifications	Organizational process asset update	
	System installation plan	Site readiness confirmation	Performance report	
	Security	Install system	Change Request (CR)	
	Prepare security plan	Hardware readiness confirmation	Project document update	
	Security plan	Application readiness confirmation	**Security**	
	Conversion	**Security**	Control security	
	Prepare conversion plan	Define security requirements	Organizational process asset update	
	Conversion plan	Security requirements	Performance report	
	Interface	Define security roles	Change Request (CR)	
	Prepare interface plan	Security roles	Project document update	
	Interface plan	Configure security	**Conversion**	
	Software configuration	Test cases	Control conversion	
	Prepare software configuration plan	**Conversion**	Organizational process asset update	
	Software configuration plan	Prepare data conversion map	Performance report	
	Workflow	Data conversion map	Change Request (CR)	
	Prepare workflow management plan	Conduct data cleansing	Project document update	
	Workflow management plan	Data cleansing confirmation	**Interface**	
		Develop and test conversion solution	Control interfaces	
		Conversion solution confirmation	Organizational process asset update	
		Convert data	Performance report	
		Conversion confirmation	Change Request (CR)	
			Project document update	

Initiating	Planning	Executing	Controlling	Closing
	Test Prepare test plan *Test plan* **Cutover** Prepare cutover plan *Cutover plan* **Support** Prepare support plan *Support plan*	**Interface** Prepare interface data map *Interface data map* Develop and test interfaces *Interface software confirmation* Enable interfaces *Interface confirmation* **Software configuration** Define configuration requirements *Configuration requirements* Configure system *Test cases* **Workflow** Define workflow requirements *Workflow requirements* Perform workflow changes *Workflow changes* **Test** Define test cases *Test cases* Prepare test data *Test data* Train testers *Training completion confirmation* Conduct tests *Test results* Correct defects Conduct regression testing *Regression test cases* *Test results* **Cutover** Train cutover support team *Training completion confirmation* Conduct system cutover *Successful cutover confirmation* **Support** Prepare support requirements *System support requirements* Support roles and responsibilities matrix Provide support training *Training completion confirmation*	**Software configuration** Control configuration *Organizational process asset update* *Performance report* *Change Request (CR)* *Project document update* **Workflow** Control workflow *Organizational process asset update* *Performance report* *Change Request (CR)* *Project document update* **Test** Control testing *Organizational process asset update* *Performance report* *Change Request (CR)* *Project document update* **Cutover** Control cutover *Organizational process asset update* *Performance report* *Change Request (CR)* *Project document update* **Support** Control support *Organizational process asset update* *Performance report* *Change Request (CR)* *Project document update*	

TABLE 2.3 IT Management Knowledge Areas by Process Group (*Continued*)

patients. They need to overcome their fears—fear of technology replacing them and fear of looking foolish. They need to see a benefit to themselves and to the organization. In general, all people, including those who work in healthcare delivery, are resistant to moving from the old way of doing things—using a paper record, for example—to a new way of doing things—using an EHR. The reasons for this resistance are many, and we cover many of them in Chapter 5. For the present, we assert that this resistance is a major obstacle to successful completion of an HIT project and that project leaders and managers must develop a comprehensive set of activities to help people through change.

What Is a Meaningful Change Management Formula?

Like project and IT management, change management includes several processes and outputs that we classify into distinct knowledge areas. As with any methodology, you can label these areas differently, so long as you address the same key issues. For our purposes, we define change management to include the following knowledge areas:

- *Realization Management*—Initiating, planning, controlling, and closing what a stakeholder does to achieve the project objectives.

- *Sponsorship Management*—Initiating, planning, and controlling the selection, assessment, and mentoring of a project's most senior leader.

- *Transformation Management*—Planning, executing, and controlling the adoption of innovation by individuals or groups of stakeholders. The number of stakeholder groups might range from one to dozens. Managing innovation adoption by these stakeholder groups is critical given that HIT projects cause dramatic change and are very complex.

- *Training Management*—Planning, executing, and controlling project tasks for educating users to take advantage of workflow and system benefits. In addition to project leadership, there is also the full complement of users to educate regarding an impending HIT implementation. Given the range of functions in an EHR today, this may be a very large number of individuals within an HDO. These people must receive training so they can explore and educate themselves on how to use this new system optimally.

- *Optimization Management*—Planning, controlling, and closing continued improvement of the innovation. The process of reaching a high level of effective system use is usually an iterative one—there is a cycle of modifying workflow to use the new system, modifying the system configuration to better support the workflow, and so on. Optimization occurs after the project ends and the HIT system comes under the control of the organization's operations group.

Table 2.4 displays the relationship between change management knowledge areas and the process groups with knowledge areas in bold, individual processes in normal text, and outputs in italics. Figure 2.4 displays our change management formula that includes the five knowledge areas that must work together to increase project success.

Projects that fail to use *all* of these knowledge areas will have less successful change management when compared to those that do. We must use all five knowledge areas, without exception. We apply this same principle in project and IT management. For

Initiating	Planning	Executing	Controlling	Closing
Realization	**Realization**	**Transformation**	**Realization**	**Realization**
Define objectives	Define measurable outcomes	Conduct transformation	Control realization	Report outcome achievement
Objectives	*Measurable outcomes*	*Transformation tasks*	*Organizational process asset update*	*Dashboard report*
Sponsorship	Prepare outcome delivery schedule	*Transformation task completion*	*Measurable outcome achievement*	**Optimization**
Select the executive sponsor	*Outcome delivery schedule*	**Training**	*Performance report*	Perform optimization
Executive sponsor	Assign responsibility for objectives	Prepare training	*Change Request (CR)*	*Optimization completion confirmation for project*
	Objective responsibility list	*Training documentation*	*Project document update*	
	Sponsorship	Conduct training	*Achievement of an objective*	
	Assess executive sponsor	*Training completion confirmation*	**Sponsorship**	
	Executive sponsorship assessment results		Control sponsorship	
	Transformation		*Organizational process asset update*	
	Prepare change management team		*Performance report*	
	Change management team		*Change Request (CR)*	
	Prepare stakeholder map		*Project document update*	
	Stakeholder map		**Transformation**	
	Training		Control transformation	
	Conduct training needs assessment		*Organizational process asset update*	
	Training needs		*Performance report*	
	Prepare training plan		*Change Request (CR)*	
	Training plan		*Project document update*	
	Optimization		**Training**	
	Prepare optimization management plan		Control training	
	Optimization management plan		*Organizational process asset update*	
			Performance report	
			Change Request (CR)	
			Project document update	
			Optimization	
			Control optimization	
			Organizational process asset update	
			Performance report	
			Change Request (CR)	
			Project document update	

TABLE 2.4 Change Management Knowledge Areas by Process Group

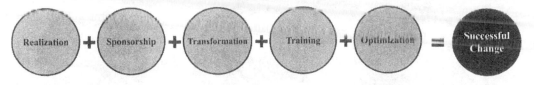

FIGURE 2.4   Change management formula.

example, project management is likely to fail if it does not include time management. IT management has a greater chance of failure when it does not include user requirements management. Projects that do not use all five change management knowledge areas encounter the following:

- *Confusion*—Trying to realize project objectives without measurable outcomes causes confusion because stakeholders do not understand what the project is supposed to achieve.
- *Frustration*—Conducting a project without sponsorship frustrates stakeholders because they are unsure how to proceed given sponsorship's lack of commitment.
- *Resistance*—Working on a project without actively supporting transformation causes resistance because stakeholders do not understand how to work effectively to resolve project challenges.
- *Anxiety*—Deploying a system without first training the stakeholder on how to use it causes anxiety because the project did not prepare them for something new.
- *Stagnation*—Implementing a system without modifying existing workflow, system configuration, training, and support fails to fully optimize it, which limits organizational growth potential and causes stagnation.

Figure 2.5 summarizes unsuccessful change associated with not including all five change management knowledge areas in a project.

Conclusion

The *PMBOK® Guide* includes a useful process group framework, including:

- Initiating
- Planning
- Executing
- Controlling
- Closing

Each *PMBOK®* Guide process group includes management knowledge areas, or expertise areas (e.g., the initiating process group includes integration management). Our integrated methodology continues to use these process groups, for example, IT management

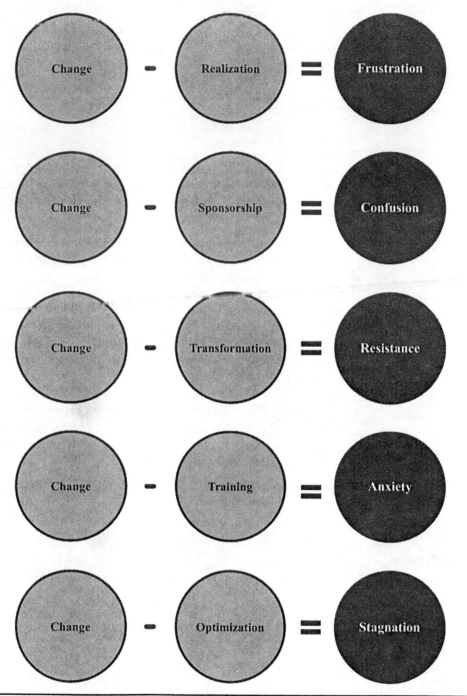

FIGURE 2.5   Unsuccessful change.

includes user requirements and infrastructure management in the planning process group. Each *PMBOK® Guide* process group includes management knowledge areas, or expertise areas (e.g., the initiating process group includes integration and scope management).

Unlike project and IT management disciplines, there are no widely accepted and sanctioned change management standards. Instead we must rely on best practices to define a structured change management method. Our structured change management approach includes the following knowledge areas:

- Realization management
- Sponsorship management
- Transformation management
- Training management
- Optimization management

Like project and IT management, change management organizes knowledge areas by process group. For example, the initiating process group includes realization management and sponsorship management.

In the next chapter, we describe project management process group knowledge areas in detail. This includes a description of the outputs each knowledge area process produces and applicable analysis methods.

Endnotes

1. Methodology (2010). Merriam-Webster Online Dictionary. Retrieved June 22, 2010, from www.merriam-webster.com/dictionary/methodology.
2. Sackett, D. L., Rosenberg, W. M., Gray, J. A., Haynes, R. B., and Richardson, W. S. (1996). Evidence-based medicine: what it is and what it isn't. *BMJ, 312,* 71–72.
3. Deming, W. E. (1982). *Out of the Crisis.* Boston: MIT Press.

CHAPTER 3

Project Management

In this chapter, we will:

- *Describe each project management knowledge area in detail*
- *Associate each project management knowledge area with processes and their outputs*
- *Define specific analysis methods associated with project management knowledge area processes and outputs*

In this chapter, we delve into the first of the three related disciplines, project management. As mentioned in Chapter 2, the framework of project management includes nine knowledge areas. We organized this chapter by these knowledge areas, beginning with integration management. In each knowledge area, we define the following:

- Processes the Project Manager organizes and oversees
- Outputs that arise from these processes
- How each of these processes and outputs occurs over time through the five process groups

INTEGRATION MANAGEMENT

Integration management is the initiating, planning, executing, controlling, and closing of all key project, IT, and change management plans, processes, and outputs required to achieve project success. Typically it includes only the scope, time, cost, quality, human resources, communications, risk, and procurement management knowledge areas. In our methodology, integration management also includes the IT and change management knowledge areas as displayed in Figure 3-1.

Integration management is one of the most important knowledge areas for the Project Manager to understand and use. Integration management, in essence, is the sum total of activities the Project Manager must oversee to complete the project successfully.

Table 3-1 displays integration management processes and their outputs (in italics) by process group.

During integration management, the Project Manager creates the feasibility study and project charter, and prepares the project management plan. While executing and

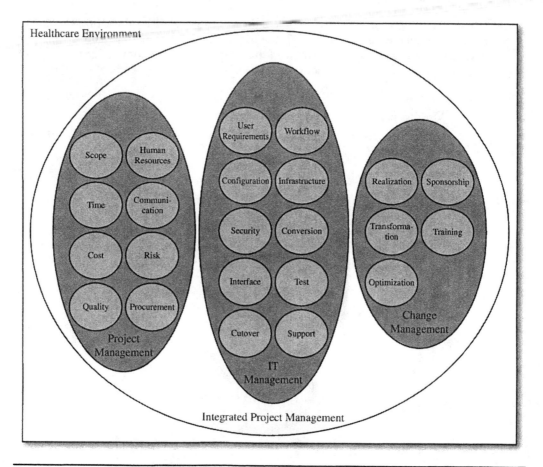

Figure 3-1   Integrated HIT management.

Initiating	Planning	Executing	Controlling	Closing
Prepare the feasibility study and business case *Feasibility study and business case* Prepare project charter *Project charter*	Prepare project management plan *Project management plan*	Manage project execution *Performance report* *Change request (CR)* *Deliverable* *Project document update*	Control project execution *Organizational process asset update* *Performance report* *Change request (CR)* *Project document update* Perform integrated change control *Change request (CR)*	Close phase or project *Organizational process asset update* *Deliverable*

TABLE 3-1   Integration Management Knowledge Area by Process Group

controlling this plan, the Project Manager delivers all project outputs and makes necessary changes. In closing the project, the final activity is the creation of the project closeout report.

Prepare the Feasibility Analysis and Business Case

We must first review some of the history of HIT and HIT strategy before examining integration. As we have noted before, information technology is not new to healthcare. We've had computer applications supporting the business of healthcare for over a half century—billing, ADT (admission, discharge, transfer), and the like. For the most part these administrative applications are mature technologies. For example, electronic billing in healthcare is effectively the standard. However, information technology in support of clinical work, with the electronic health record as the core model, is a much more recent development. Clinical computing tools have only recently reached the level of maturity where widespread deployment and effective use are possible. So despite the fact that information technology visionaries have been writing about the dramatic benefits that an electronic health record could bring to patient care, it is only in the very recent past that we have the applications—and the organizational willingness—to move whole-heartedly in this direction.

Having sufficiently mature HIT in electronic health records is, however, only half of the battle. Equally important is a distinct and clear organizational strategy as to *why* an HDO chooses to implement an electronic health record. There are many possible strategic reasons to invest in such technology, but experience has shown that the single clear strategy most likely to succeed is a strategy based on, not surprisingly, what healthcare has always been about—taking care of patients, safely, effectively, and efficiently.

In my organization, a number of us were convinced from the late 1980s that advancements in computer technology and medical computing applications had great potential to improve healthcare quality and safety and that it was time to begin advocating more strongly for HIT adoption. We spent all of the 1990s talking about this with our colleagues, trying to build a guiding coalition to champion this cause. In the latter half of the 1990s, there had been enough development in the field and enough support in the organization for leadership to think seriously about how and when to move forward specifically with EHR selection and implementation. We also reached a point within my own internal medicine clinic practice where there were enough individuals with a vision of what was possible and a sense as medical educators that we had a responsibility to teach the next generation of physicians using documentation and clinical decision support tools of the twenty-first century rather than those from the nineteenth and twentieth century. We started to see clinical documentation, clinical decision support, and knowledge resources all coming together on the same platform to help inform care at the bedside, in the office, and between visits. The question was not whether, but when, which required monitoring the literature and industry for evidence of sufficient success and vendor maturity to support our goals, building a business case, and determining the organizational culture changes that would be needed to make sure that once installed, the EHR would be regularly and appropriately used to support care quality, to educate health professionals, and to practice financial health.

Accomplishing the needed organizational culture change required assembling a group of people who could help both create a vision for the use of HIT and EHR systems to transform care and then helping the organization see, accept, and strive to achieve our shared goals. This proved to be too difficult to achieve in the late 1990s without data from a small, local demonstration project in our faculty group practice showing that EHR system adoption could be successfully achieved with adequate user acceptance and an acceptable cost–benefit result. As a result, physician champions from two of our primary care clinics got together in 2000 to invest some of their own resources to select and implement a scalable EHR solution to generate the needed data and serve as an example for the rest of the organization. We understood the enterprise as a whole was not yet ready to make a large investment in the technology or required organizational culture change, so we offered to pilot the experience in a couple of clinics that were ready to adopt an EHR system and include the entire organization in the selection process to promote buy-in in the event that the system was deployed later to other clinics. We decided to start with a relatively small EHR deployment that represented an affordable investment for the organization and us. We could manage the pilot project ourselves and serve as our EHR pioneers, if you will. If the EHR worked well and was regularly used, we could then make the argument for an enterprise-wide EHR rollout.

—Michael H. Zaroukian, MD, PhD, FACP, FHIMSS, CMIO, Michigan State University

Our vision of implementing an electronic health record started with a concept we entitled "Multivision." This was a series of conferences with our patients, providers, employees, and the key stakeholders and board members to talk about 'What does Multicare want to be, and how are we going to change the way we deliver care? What are some pain points? What would that vision look like? What systematic changes will need to take place in order for us to deliver the ideal patient experience? How can we be financially sustainable?' We called this series of conferences Multivision because we firmly believed it must be multiple voices with a single vision. As a result of that process, we put in place our current mission and vision for the organization, as well as a key road map for the next ten years. The road map included organic growth in developing centers of excellence in our care-line services, supported by an electronic health record that is an integrated solution rather than best of breed. Lastly we launched the "Multicare Difference" program in which we focused on customer service, cost effectiveness, clinical outcomes, and patient safety. These are a series of activities from the Multivision conference. The electronic health record system is a foundational part of the execution of that plan.

—Florence Chang, MBA, CIO, Multicare

The initiating process group is the first set of activities in any project. It determines which projects the organization should consider generally given its strategic direction and goals. To better evaluate potential projects, project initiators prepare a feasibility analysis and business case. A *project initiator* is a member of a small informal planning group responsible for starting a project. A *feasibility analysis and business case* is a document based on research and quantification created to guide management decision on whether or not to proceed with a project based on an assessment of its viability, costs, and benefits. *PMBOK* does not include the feasibility and business case because it precedes starting a project. While we understand and agree that this is true, we include it because it is a crucial resource and process for the entire project, including the project charter. It is also a project management stage that demonstrates the *kill point* concept. The main goal of creating the feasibility analysis and business case is to enable executive leadership to make a *go/no go decision*. As you might guess, the amount of time and resources you put into development of the feasibility study and business case is variable and always a trade-off. Ideally, the time should be sufficient to guide good decision-making, but limited so that decision-makers can decide and take advantage of associated opportunities.

Table 3-2 includes an EHR feasibility analysis and business case outline.

---

1. Background and Objectives
    1.1   Existing Clinical Environment
    1.2   Existing Financial Environment
    1.3   Existing Administrative Environment
    1.4   Existing Technology Environment
    1.5   Problems and Solutions
    1.6   Project Objectives
2. Options
    2.1   Retain Status Quo
    2.2   Acquire Commercial Off-The-Shelf (COTS) Solution
    2.3   Develop Custom Solution
3. Options Analysis
    3.1   Comparison of Options by Support for High-Level User Requirements
    3.2   Comparison of Options by Support for Project Objectives
    3.3   Comparison of Options by Support for Estimated Cost/Benefit
    3.4   Analysis of Options by Estimated Investment Performance
    3.5   Comparison of Options by Potential Risk
    3.6   Recommended Option
4. Recommended Option Impact
    4.1   Impact on Existing Clinical Environment
    4.2   Impact on Existing Financial Environment
    4.3   Impact on Existing Administrative Environment
    4.4   Impact on IT
5. Recommended Acquisition and Implementation Plan
    5.1   Acquisition Plan
    5.2   Implementation Plan
    5.3   Project Management
    5.4   Project Organization
    5.5   Project Roles and Responsibilities
    5.6   Project Management Processes

TABLE 3-2   Feasibility Analysis and Business Case Outline

In this outline of a feasibility analysis and business case, you can see several components. The document begins with a description of the organization's current environment and the potential impact on the proposed project. For example, it is worth noting whether an organization had previously attempted and failed to implement an EHR, currently faces significant financial constraints, or eventually plans to construct a new, multi-million dollar facility that requires significant management attention.

Any such description highlights an organization's Strengths and Weaknesses as well as Opportunities and Threats (SWOT)—a strategic planning method used to define and compare projects. Other typical drivers in terms of risks and opportunities in the market today include increasing requirements from payers and regulators for reporting quality and safety data as well as federal movement toward reimbursement based on meaningful use of HIT.

The analysis also includes a list of preliminary project objectives, generally driven by the organization's mission and vision included in a strategic plan. We should note these are preliminary project objectives, written at a high level and designed to briefly summarize the "Why we would do this?" question. Also included are high-level user requirements.

At one point we brought together a number of providers and staff from various departments such as family medicine and internal medicine, service providers like radiology and pharmacy, and other stakeholders with either an interest in or a responsibility to provide information that would feed into the EHR. We put together a feasibility estimate to try to determine if there was a financial as well as a quality business case for EHR deployment. We put together a statement of our shared goals and expected benefits. It started at a high level and got increasingly granular as we started looking at the various high-priority problems that having an EHR in place would potentially solve for specific stakeholder groups (e.g., instant chart access during nursing triage phone calls). We looked at our existing IT infrastructure to get a sense of the technology requirements and gaps we would need to close to implement a new system based on the technology available at the time.
—Michael H. Zaroukian, MD, PhD, FACP, FHIMSS, CMIO, Michigan State University

The feasibility analysis and business case process in HIT is often unique in the healthcare industry. For decades, HDOs developed robust and highly quantitative analysis about types of projects they typically plan to undertake—for example, building a new wing to the hospital or adding a new clinical service line. These sorts of projects lend themselves to a detailed financial analysis. On the other hand, many would argue that estimating costs—and especially financial returns—for HIT is notoriously challenging. Moreover, some projects drive HDOs by mission and vision alone.

Once the HDO defines its existing environment and clarifies its objectives, the document then lists at least two potential options for delivering the HIT successfully. Typically, today's HDOs focus on acquisition—purchasing a vendor product or a commercial off-the-shelf (COTS) system.

HDOs rarely *build* an EHR; most acquire COTS clinical systems. However, there are still options available within the COTS strategy. These include:

- *Best-of-Breed*—A best-of-breed (BOB) solution uses the most preferred software applications from a variety of different vendors. For example, an HDO could purchase an ambulatory EHR from one vendor and an inpatient EHR from another.

- *Integrated Software*—An integrated software solution is a suite or set of software modules from a single vendor that supports numerous functions. For example, an HDO could purchase an EHR from a single vendor for both inpatient and ambulatory settings.

Once the HDO defines its options, the feasibility analysis includes an evaluation of each option based on support for the following:

- Project objectives
- User requirements
- Cost/benefit
- Investment performance
- Risk

Finally, the analysis includes a summary of the impact of the selected option on the current environment and the preliminary plans required to acquire and implement this recommended option.

While HIT should improve patient safety and quality of care, a typical feasibility analysis and business case assesses the investment performance of viable options. A number of investment performance formulas are available to scrutinize each option as described below.

Return on Investment

A return on investment (ROI) is a formula that calculates the ratio of financial gain or loss on an investment relative to the amount of money invested.

$$\text{ROI} = \frac{(\text{Gain from investments} - \text{Cost of investment})}{\text{Cost of investment}}$$

This is a helpful financial tool because the best option has the highest ROI.

Let's suppose the total estimated cost of an EHR project is $1 million over five years. During that same period we believe we will gain $1.2 million dollars in improving clinical processes, eliminating paper records, increasing productivity and associated billing, and so on. We then calculate the net gain from this investment by taking the $1.2 million gain minus the $1 million investment cost or $200,000. Finally, we calculate the ROI by dividing this $200 thousand net gain by the $1 million investment cost for a ROI of 20% over five years. This investment is the best option if all other options have a lower ROI.

Payback Period

A payback period is a formula that identifies the time required to recover the costs of a proposed option. Calculation of the payback period enables you to define the breakeven point. A breakeven point is the point in time when the total costs of the project to date and the total dollar return or revenue are equal, or where there is no net loss or gain.

$$\text{Payback period} = \frac{\text{Required investment}}{\text{Net annual cash inflow}}$$

The option with the shortest payback period is the best.

Using the previous example, the total estimated cost of an EHR project is $1 million over five years. Assume this includes all of the one-time expenditures for hardware and software and the ongoing cost for technical support, training, process improvement, and so on. Let's suppose we arrange to pay for all of these expenditures annually, that is, $1 million divided by five years or $200 thousand per year. Assume we realize the $1.2 million gain evenly over five years in the same way we calculated the expenditures. Our monthly gain should be approximately $240 thousand or $1.2 million divided by five years. Now we calculate our net gain or the difference between our savings and expenditures, that is, $240 thousand minus $200 thousand equals $40 thousand net annual cash inflow. Finally, we calculate the payback period by taking the $1 million investment and dividing it by the net annual cash inflow of $40 thousand. Our payback period should be 25 months or just over two years. This investment is the best option if other options have a higher or longer payback period.

Net Present Value

The net present value (NPV) is a formula that evaluates an investment based on the difference between the present value of cash flows in the future and the investment amount today, shown as

$$NPV = Present\ value - Initial\ investment$$

A proposed project is viable if the NPV is positive. The best option is the project with the highest NPV.

Using the same example from above, consider that the HDO proposes to spend $1 million today on an EHR project. In years one through five, benefits exceed costs by $10, $25, $75, $100, and $150 thousand respectively or a positive cash flow in each year.

We then identify the time value of money or current interest rate as, for example 10%. The *time value of money* is the monetary worth of capital over a specified time. Then we calculate the present value of each annual cash flow to find out what, for example, the $10 thousand in year one is worth today. Assuming we have a present value table, identify the interest factor and multiply it by the cash flow in each year. A *present value table* is a list of interest rates used to determine the present value of a dollar amount over time. Next we take the interest factor for 10% in year one on the present value table, which is 0.909. We then multiply this interest factor times $10 thousand for a present value of $9,090 and perform this same calculation for years two through five as described below:

- *Year Two*—1.735 interest factor × $25 thousand = $43,400
- *Year Three*—2.487 interest factor × $75 thousand = $186,525
- *Year Four*—3.170 interest factor × $100 thousand = $317,000
- *Year Five*—3.791 interest factor × $150 thousand = $568,650

Finally we calculate the total present value from the previous step, or

$$\$1,124,665 - \$1\ million\ initial\ investment = NPV\ of\ \$124,665.$$

This positive NPV means the project repays both the original investment and has a sufficient rate of return to make a net gain.

It is important to recognize that all of these financial formulas are estimates that may have variable precision. Moreover, it is controversial whether these models are particularly meaningful when it comes to HIT projects. Some would argue that the major benefits of an EHR are not quantifiable in purely economic terms. As well, there are market environments in which a financial analysis is, in a sense, a moot point. For example, if CMS reimbursement mechanisms mandate all HDOs implement an EHR, financial tools have limited value. This does not mean HDOs should ignore the financial implications when making an HIT decision—rather we must weigh the value of such analyses in terms of all aspects involved in this strategic decision.

> *No one likes to put forward a proposal that's going to be in the tens of millions of dollars to implement and not necessarily have an ROI. But I think the leadership of this organization is enlightened enough to know that there are some investments that you need to make that are going to be solely for the quality of care that we deliver, and they may not have a clear ROI initially. We evaluate all technology on the merits of how it might improve patient care, and we view our EMR technology in a similar light.*
>
> *One of the important aspects that we all understood and agreed with early on was the rationale for why we were doing this project. It was never meant to be a cost-savings or necessarily efficiency producing initiative. We were all cognizant that we might be able to get those benefits from the system, but the primary rationale for implementing the system was to improve our quality of care and patient safety by using automation, decision support, and electronic tools. It was an important fundamental tone to set for the project, and when we struggled, we always returned to this principle to help guide us.*
>
> —Dan Nigrin, MD, MS, CIO, Children's Hospital Boston

A solid business case should provide a convincing argument to senior decision-makers. Table 3-3 displays such an example of an EHR return on investment in terms of dollars rather than percent return.

As noted above, the sole purpose of the feasibility analysis and business case is to provide executive management with sufficient information to make a decision on whether an HIT project is a rational choice for their organization. All such projects, whether related to HIT or not, require comparison with other options because there are perhaps dozens of ways in which a hospital might choose to spend its resources—an EHR, a new wing, community primary care clinics, and the like. Each of these options would ideally have a well-developed feasibility analysis and business case to compare the costs and benefits of each against other projects. In this fashion, an HDO chooses to fund the projects that show the most promise.

Should the feasibility analysis and business case indicate the HIT project is in fact the best option, and executive management approves it, the next step in integration management is to prepare the project charter. The activities involved in this step are quite similar to those we've just completed—but limited to the selected option.

Five-Year Projected ROI Consolidated Categories	ROI in Millions
Clinical Process Improvements	$12.31
Medicare Incentives	2.79
Decreased IT Support	3.16
Reduced Medical Record/Transcriptions	3.25
Revenue Cycle Improvements	52.00
Total Five-Year ROI Projection	$73.51

TABLE 3-3 EHR Return on Investment

Prepare Project Charter

If the business case and feasibility study indicate the project is viable, the next step in the initiating process group is to create the project charter. A *project charter* is a document that authorizes a project and summarizes key project elements including a project scope statement, objectives, and key stakeholders with roles and responsibilities.

One can think of the project charter as a contract with the following goals:

- Define what the project includes and excludes
- Identify what the project must achieve
- Specify who is responsible
- Authorize proceeding

Members of a project steering committee, the governing body responsible for guiding the project to successful completion, sign the charter, demonstrating their commitment and authorizing the selected Project Manager to proceed. It may seem odd to consider a contract signed by members of the same organization. Experience demonstrates, especially with complex multi-year HIT projects, key stakeholder memories vary about project scope, objectives, and responsibilities. A formal project charter becomes a very useful tool that the Project Manager refers to when ideas and opinions about project objectives, scope, and roles and responsibilities differ. It is the project touchstone.

> We put together a project charter, which I feel is key. It really delineates scope, identifies if there is a data conversion, what interfaces are required. It's really the key elements that I look at for executive sponsors. It really is my way to say this is the scope, these are the risks for this project, this is how we're going to mitigate those risks. Getting agreement on an organizational chart, how are we going to manage it, who is the executive sponsor, who are the decision-makers, and then to really talk about timeline and budget. Those are the pieces that are important to that group. Then internal to the department, the pieces that are important are who needs to participate in this project, do I need host system operative participants, do I need the patients, do I need DBAs [database administrators], again, what interfaces, what conversion, and it identifies the standards that we're going to utilize throughout the project.
>
> —Beatha Johnson, Director, Clinical Information Systems, VMMC

The charter summarizes key elements of the financial feasibility analysis and business case to reinforce organizational approval of the project. This is an important concept—while the outputs described so far might appear distinct and separate, in reality they are tightly integrated. The content of the business case and the feasibility study not only integrates with the project charter, there is significant overlap between these documents. The key is to understand the purpose of each document. Table 3-4 includes an outline of a project charter.

In summary, a project charter should include:

- *Objectives*—A definition of what the organization anticipates gaining from this project
- *Scope*—A statement of project parameters

```
1. Objectives
   1.1. Purpose
   1.2. Project Objectives
2. Scope
   2.1. Areas Included within the Project
   2.2. Areas Excluded from the Project
3. Estimated Schedule
4. Estimated Budget
5. Project Organization
   5.1. Project Organization Chart
          5.1.1. Steering Committee
          5.1.2. Project Manager
   5.2. Roles and Responsibilities
6. Risks
7. Project Authorization Signature Form
```

TABLE 3-4   Project Charter Outline

- *Schedule*—An estimated timeframe to begin and finish the project
- *Costs*—A preliminary budget estimate
- *Organization*—An organization chart identifying the project executive sponsor, defined later in this chapter, and supporting participants, with a brief definition of their roles and responsibilities
- *Risks*—Factors that may adversely affect the project
- *Authorization*—A signatory commitment approving the project and directing the Project Manager to proceed

Prepare Project Management Plan

Once the steering committee signs the project charter, the project moves from initiating the project to the second process group of project planning. The primary activity the Project Manager undertakes at this time is preparation of the project management plan. A *project management plan* is a collection of plans for each of the other knowledge areas—scope, schedule, budget, and so on—used collectively to successfully execute, control, and close the project. The project management plan furnishes an opportunity for thinking through the project details before proceeding. The Project Manager then uses the project management plan much like the PDSA cycle. The Project Manager plans and then executes activities following these plans, studies the execution results at each step, and then resolves variances between the execution results and the plans.

Because all plans are based on assumptions and predictions, the results will vary from these plans as the project proceeds. For example, a project management plan includes the project schedule with a four-week estimate for vendors to propose their EHR. However, due to a number of unforeseen factors, the actual time is six weeks. The initial four-week schedule is a *baseline* estimate—a benchmark used to measure and control actual project performance. The Project Manager executes each baseline plan and compares actual performance to that plan to identify variances or deviations. Depending on the comparison results, the Project Manager:

- Documents compliance with the plan if the actual performance matches the plan.

- Makes corrections if there is a plan deviation. In the above example, vendors will submit their proposals two weeks later than planned so the Project Manager may add additional team members to hasten proposal evaluation to recover this lost time.

- Re-baselines the plan. A *re-baseline* is a revised plan or modified benchmark reflecting changes in project conditions. If there are irresolvable reasons the schedule cannot recover the two-week delay for vendor proposals, the Project Manager may revise the plan or baseline. Re-baselining a plan requires formal justification and authorization, and is not something the Project Manager does just to accommodate actual performance and baseline variances. In a complex project, changing the due date for proposals may have significant implications for many subsequent project tasks and the supporting work of Project Team members assigned to those remaining tasks.

HIT involves some of the most intense, complex, and challenging projects that an HDO can choose to undertake. Some observe that the organization, at the end of the project, may not simply be a more efficient, higher quality organization—it may have become an entirely new organization. As such, planning is critical.

> *The planning piece was done at a level that I don't think had ever been done before, except for maybe building our new medical center. I don't think I'd ever seen a project plan at that level of detail, and it served us very, very well.*
>
> *It's the discipline of sitting down with the vendor and our Project Team and going through step-by-step what's going to happen at each phase and forcing ourselves to think it through. One of the things that became clear to us when we were having trouble putting it down on paper, was . . . we didn't understand it well enough yet. So that meant we had to dig a little deeper. Not that we got it perfect. It did mean, however, that we actually thought through each module, who it was going to impact, what resources we were going to need to work with them, and how to manage not just getting the system in, but significant organizational change in the way they did their work at the hospital. We had to make sure that one, we made the proper decisions about how to set the system up, and two, we communicated that and made sure that people were properly trained going forward.*
>
> —Robert Greenless, PhD, CIO–RLANRC

Manage Project Execution

Once the Project Manager completes the project management plan, project execution begins. During project execution, one can envision coordinating all of the processes and outputs as the Project Manager undertakes integration management. The Project Manager coordinates execution of all tasks Project Team members perform to prepare the project final product. At a conceptual level, understanding the integrated nature of this coordination is important—the activities that take place in the other project, IT, and change management knowledge areas generally all follow this theme. They include performing tasks that produce the following project outputs:

- Deliverables (A *deliverable* is a tangible and verifiable project output that is the result of a task or tasks.)
- Performance reports regarding work progress
- Change requests to the project management plans and other baseline documents
- Project document updates related to issues that do not affect baseline plans

There are key project documents—the charter and the scope, schedule, cost, communication, and risk management plans. The first challenge is to do those project documents so that they [are] substantial, well thought out, and meaningful. The next challenge is to actually use them to manage the project.

—Robert Greenless, PhD, CIO–RLANRC

Control Project Execution

The Project Manager monitors project work and reviews completed outputs during the controlling process. This includes monitoring work on tasks and reviewing completed project outputs to ensure they comply with the project management plan and other baseline standards. This results in the following outputs:

- Organizational process asset updates
- Performance reports regarding project status
- CRs affecting baseline project management plan and other project documents
- Project document updates

An *organizational process asset* is an information source used to influence project success (e.g., polices, procedures, plans, standards, guidelines, templates, reports, and lessons learned).

The controlling processes focus on identifying variances from defined standards, employing change requests to correct these variances, or modifying the standards to reflect project modifications. While we define these control processes as part of integration management, we use them in all project, IT, and change management knowledge areas. To avoid repetition, throughout this book we will provide control process information pertinent to each subsequent knowledge area and related examples of control issues and their resolution.

Perform Integrated Change Control

The Project Manager performs integrated change control during the controlling process. *Integrated change control* is identifying, assessing, making, and monitoring modifications to baseline project processes and outputs, for example, to scope, time, budget, and quality. The output of this process is a change request. A *change request (CR)* is a formal application to modify baseline deliverables and processes. It includes the following:

- Change title
- CR number
- CR date
- Related task/deliverable (e.g., either an existing task/deliverable or a new task/deliverable)
- Scope impact
- Schedule impact
- Cost impact
- Approval status

Table 3-5 displays an example of a CR form.

Change Request (CR) Initiation			
Change Title:	Train-the-Trainer	**Submitted By:**	Vendor
Vendor Affected:	Vendor 01	**Contact Email:**	N/A
CR Number:	002	**Contact Phone:**	N/A
CR Date Submitted:	3/23/09	**Date Required:**	4/3/09
Related Task/ Deliverable Number:	5a—Train-the-Trainer	**Related CR(s):**	N/A
Additional Description:	For the week of 4/6/09, vendor will be on customer site to conduct additional train-the-trainer training for up to six customer-training personnel. These trainees will be responsible for daily participation in five, eight-hour days of training by the vendor training. This will focus on EHR application functionality as installed in the customer production environment. Vendor trainer will conduct an in-depth explanation of the underlying logic, workflow, functional sequence, and rationale for training to support customer's clinical needs.		
Attachment(s):	N/A		
Criticality (1-5):	2		
Possible Criticality Codes:	1. Issue is on hold. 2. Issue is not currently stopping continued project performance. 3. Issue will affect project performance without timely resolution. 4. Issue requires a temporary work-around solution or is affecting project performance. 5. Issue is critical and will prevent the project proceeding on schedule without immediate solution.		

TABLE 3-5 Change Request Form

Evaluation Participants			
Vendor Project Manager:	*Vendor Project Manager*	Evaluation Date:	3/24/09
HDO Project Manager:	*HDO Project Manager*	Evaluation Date:	3/24/09

Scope Evaluation		
Scope Increase/ Decrease	Description:	No scope change
Scope Notes		Increased hours to train trainers required to support instructional needs of users during go-live.

Schedule Evaluation				
Task #	Task	New Task	Change to Existing Task	Expected Project Delay
5a	Train-the-Trainer	No	160 hours	80 hours
Schedule Notes		No adverse schedule impact due to available slack.		

Cost Evaluation						
Task/ Del. #	New Task/ Del?	Description	Budget Hours	Est. Hours	Total Chg.	CR Fixed Price Amount
5a		Train-the-Trainer	160	200	40	$8,000
Total			160	200	40	$8,000
Cost Notes		No adverse cost impact due to available contingency.				

CR Authorization						
	Approved:	X	Rejected:		Deferred:	
Reason:	Train additional trainers included on training team					
Vendor Project Manager:	Vendor Project Manager					
Vendor Signature:	*Vendor Project Manager*	Approval Date:	3/24/09			
Authorized Customer Representative:	Customer Representative					
Customer Signature:	*Customer Representative*	Approval Date:	3/25/09			

TABLE 3-5 Change Request Form (*Continued*)

FIGURE 3-2   The quadruple constraint.

The complexity of this form demonstrates that a CR requires several review and approval steps because such changes can be very significant to a project.

Change, particularly to scope, time, cost, and quality, is a balancing act. These four knowledge areas have a special relationship that all Project Managers must consider. This special relationship is the quadruple constraint. A *quadruple constraint* is balancing project trade-offs between the four measurable dimensions of scope, time, cost, and quality. Figure 3-2 displays the quadruple constraint.

Project managers must consider trade-offs between the quadruple constraints that may require:

- Increasing the budget to satisfy scope and time constraints
- Reducing the scope to satisfy time and cost constraints
- Increasing the time to satisfy scope and cost constraints
- Increasing scope, time, and cost to satisfy quality constraints

Project managers review these opposing dimensions by asking key stakeholders which one they want to change to offset the impact of another. For example, if stakeholders want the project completed faster, the Project Manager must tell them that they may need to spend more or cut quality. This is a shared decision. It is not the sole decision of the Project Manager. This decision is so important that the Project Manager must document it in a CR and receive written approval before proceeding.

The Project Manager also prepares project document updates for changes that are not part of the integrated change control process. A *project document update* is a change to information that is not relevant to baseline documents and processes. For example, suppose the project schedule includes a task to load patients' medical records to a new EHR for appointments occurring during the 30-day period after cutover. The current project schedule includes a 90-day task to load this information but there are no checkpoints to monitor progress during this period. After a quality review, the Project Manager receives feedback to add checkpoints every two weeks to review the number of records converted and those remaining for conversion during that 90-day task. This is a document update. It does not, for example, change baseline schedule dates, such as the EHR cutover date, so it does not require a CR. It just supplements the baseline schedule with a useful tool for monitoring adherence to the conversion timetable.

Close Phase or Project

The final set of integration management tasks occurs during the closing process group. A *project closeout* is finishing tasks, accepting deliverables, transferring completed work to operations, and completing the project. There are two important concepts here—the first includes phase closeout. A *phase closeout* is completing a set of activities conducted within a project. For example, an HDO may hire a vendor to prepare web-based training for self-paced user instruction. The Project Manager closes out this phase of activity when the vendor completes all of their tasks or work according to their contract with the HDO.

Second is project closeout. A *project closeout* is the project completion as signed off by the steering committee. This relates directly to what we describe in Chapter 2. Projects are finite—they have a beginning and an end. For example, in the case of an EHR project, this occurs after completing all tasks—installing the EHR, configuring and testing it, training users, and transferring completed work to operations.

The closing process group also requires development of a *closeout report*. In every project the executive sponsor, the Project Manager, and Project Team members discover several things about the project (e.g., the lack of IT responsiveness for support throughout the project, the reasons why the HDO was very supportive of the changes brought about by the EHR, the strengths of the training team, and so on). Many of these discoveries guide the organization toward better support after go-live and more effective performance during the next HIT project. *Lessons learned* are an important part of the closing process. Invariably, the Project Team, the Project Manager, and the executive sponsor all discover many things along the journey—things that went well and things that went wrong. Capturing these lessons informs the next HIT project the HDO undertakes, even though the level of exhaustion by the Project Team may be very high at this point.

We had a prior failure where they tried to do everything from replace registration all the way through implementing a new electronic health record system in one shot. So we had that bit of experience to say, well, we know that doesn't work. We were more conservative just by nature based on that experience.
—Robert Greenless, PhD, CIO–RLANRC

Documenting these lessons learned is a way to formally capture the institutional knowledge and experience gained. In short, the project charter initiates a project and the project closeout ends it. The output of this process is a final deliverable, signaling the major milestone of ending the project. Table 3-6 includes a closeout report outline.

1. Project Summary
    1.1. Project History
    1.2. Project Purpose
    1.3. Project Objectives and Their Achievement Status
2. Lessons Learned
    2.1. What Worked Well
    2.2. What Could Improve
3. Project Metrics
    3.1. Assumptions
    3.2. Scope Performance Summary
    3.3. Schedule Performance Summary
    3.4. Project Cost Performance Summary

TABLE 3-6 Closeout Report Outline

SCOPE MANAGEMENT

In the last section we covered the integration management knowledge area. In the following sections we also examine individual knowledge areas. As you will see in each section, the overarching theme is defining a set of tasks the Project Manager oversees—each of which leads to a project output. Simultaneously, Project Team members undertake these tasks as they create the overall project product while the Project Manager oversees their work. The sequence of these tasks occurs across the five process groups.

What follows is the second of the remaining eight project management knowledge areas. We start with scope and follow a sequence that continues with time, cost, and then quality. The logic of this sequence assumes the following:

- Define what the project will do (scope)
- Estimate how long it will take to complete the project (schedule)
- Prepare how much it will cost to complete the project (cost)
- Determine how the project will satisfy its stakeholders (quality)

We complete this chapter with the remaining knowledge areas of HR, communications, risk, and procurement management.

Scope management is the planning and controlling of what a project includes and excludes. In essence, scope management involves adhering to defined project parameters. Table 3-7 displays scope management processes and their outputs (in italics) by process group.

Define Scope

The Project Manager defines project scope during the planning process. The output of this process is a scope statement. A *scope statement* is a description of what the project includes and excludes. Both of these are of equal importance because every project is at risk of scope creep. *Scope creep* is uncontrolled project additions that change what a

Initiating	Planning	Executing	Controlling	Closing
	Define scope		Verify scope	
	Scope statement		*Deliverable completion certificate (DCC)*	
	Prepare work breakdown structure (WBS) and WBS dictionary		*Change request (CR)*	
	Work breakdown structure (WBS)		*Project document update*	
	WBS dictionary		Control scope	
	Work package		*Organizational process asset update*	
			Performance report	
			Change request (CR)	
			Project document update	

TABLE 3-7   Scope Management Knowledge Area by Process Group

project includes and excludes, for example EHR capabilities that users, sponsors, or team members want to add. This does not mean that you cannot add functions to the EHR, but the decision to add capabilities requires planning regarding the impact on schedule, budget, quality, and the like. The Project Manager prepares the initial scope to fully understand its implications (e.g., time, cost, and quality), and must plan subsequent changes as the project progresses. This facilitates understanding the implications and proper execution and control once key stakeholders approve scope changes.

We mentioned during the initiating process group the key stakeholders prepare the feasibility analysis and business case. Part of this output of the initiating process is to define project objectives leading to the development of the preliminary project scope or parameters. For example, stakeholders may initially describe an EHR project by indicating it will:

- Include the entire enterprise
- Require completely paperless records
- Offer computerized access at the point of care for all providers
- Enable electronic processes for managing all clinical, financial, and administrative follow-up

Now in the planning process group, the Project Manager will use this preliminary information to refine the project objectives, such as:

- *Check for Medication Interactions*—Link all patient medications to an automatic crosscheck system to assess for drug–drug interactions.
- *Improve Patient Flow*—Improve patient flow at the point of care in clinics by tracking and documenting patients' progress through the outpatient center including arrival, registration, laboratory, radiology, exam room, and treatment area, as well as any other scheduled appointments for that day.
- *Increase Timely Availability of a More Complete Medical Record*—Improve the timeliness, completeness, and accuracy of medical records.
- *Link Complexity of Patient Visit with Suggested Billing Codes*—Provide a summary of key features in patient notes necessary to document complexity of visit and appropriate selection of billing code.
- *Merge Separate Laboratory, Radiology, and Pathology Database Access*—Allow clinician access to all relevant patient data in a single view.
- *Provide 24/7 Clinician Access to Information from All Secured Locations*—Provide appropriate clinical and administrative information, including specific patient data, to all authorized clinic personnel 24/7 from all secure locations (e.g., home, outpatient center, hospital).
- *Provide Clinical Information to Clinical and Business Management*—Improve operations by providing clinical and business management with historical reporting, and providing clinic information to management and clinicians to support best-practice recommendations. For example, physicians and managers at one outpatient center could change their respective behaviors based on treatment information from another center leading to superior outcomes. This could contribute to standards development, internal benchmarks, improved

reimbursement support, business development, encouragement for clinician creation of a learning community for continuous improvement, and so on.

- *Reduce Medical Errors and Improve Patient Safety*—Improve patient safety statistics. Goals could include increasing the number of correct lab tests, improving communication and interpretation of orders, and increasing drug administration accuracy.
- *Replace Physician Written Orders with Electronic Orders*—Improve patient safety, reduce turnaround time, and enable electronic order checking by eliminating written orders.

Based on these project objectives, the Project Manager then facilitates key stakeholders in defining the full scope of what the project will include, such as implement a vendor's COTS EHR, delivered via Software as a Service (SaaS) to support:

- Alerts
- Care planning
- Clinical practice guidelines
- Confidentiality and security
- Cost measuring
- Current health data, encounters, health risk appraisal
- Demographics
- Disease management/clinical registries
- Encounter—progress notes
- Ergonomic presentation
- Input mechanisms, such as electronic data capture
- Integration, for example Picture Archiving and Communications System (PACS), Radiology Information System (RIS), lab
- Medical history
- Medications
- Orders
- Output to data repository
- Prevention
- Problem lists
- Quality assurance
- Results reporting

As described above, the scope management process requires that the Project Manager work with key stakeholders to define what the project scope includes *and* excludes. For example, an EHR might initially exclude the following:

- Clinical decision support
- Physician portal
- Patient location tracking

- Patient portal
- Patient resource scheduling
- Replacement of an existing pharmacy system
- Replacement of an existing scheduling system
- Implementation of a Computerized Provider/Physician Order Entry (CPOE) system

Remember that excluding any particular functions does not mean the HDO cannot add them later after successful implementation (or for that matter, the HDO may exclude certain EHR functions originally included in the scope). Any and all such changes are possible, but each has implications for project schedule, budget, and quality. If at some point in the project, the HDO leadership decides to include replacement of the existing pharmacy system, they can build it into the project plan as long as they address the impact on related project time, cost, and quality.

Prepare Work Breakdown Structure and WBS Dictionary

Once we have a scope statement or the parameters of what the project will accomplish, the Project Manager then needs to break it down into tasks and deliverables. The Project Manager achieves this through preparation of a work breakdown structure. A *work breakdown structure (WBS)* is a hierarchical list of project deliverables organized by category (e.g., technology, clinical, training). Figure 3-3 displays an example of a WBS.

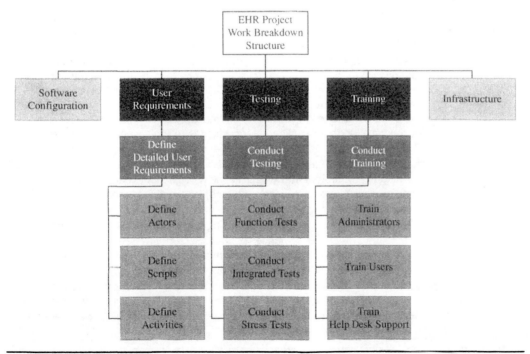

Figure 3-3   Example of a work breakdown structure.

In complex projects such as an EHR, the number of tasks included in a WBS can become surprisingly large. In such instances, it is also useful to create, in parallel, a document called a WBS dictionary. A *WBS dictionary* is a detailed description for each project component of work. This is a key document that:

- Helps define what the project produces
- Clarifies the project scope by defining what it includes (and sometimes what it excludes)
- Provides a useful reference or guide for all project work processes to stay within the scope while completing outputs

Table 3-8 displays an outline of a WBS dictionary.

---

1. **System Performance Testing**
   - 1.1. **Description/Objective**—Test of system performance in accordance with specifications and minimum performance standards.
   - 1.2. **Tasks**
     - 1.2.1. Prepare system environment for performance test
     - 1.2.2. Perform system testing
     - 1.2.3. Review test results
     - 1.2.4. Correct system performance defects
     - 1.2.5. Re-perform testing
     - 1.2.6. Accept results
   - 1.3. **Performance Period**—10/20/09–11/2/09
   - 1.4. **Due Date**—11/02/09
   - 1.5. **Roles and Responsibilities**
     - 1.5.1. **Vendor**—Responsible for assisting the customer in review of the specifications and mechanism for system performance testing. Vendor is responsible for assisting customer in ensuring that the *system load* used for testing represents how the application will function fully loaded in order to accurately determine the system limits. In addition, vendor is responsible for resolving adverse testing results, for example, assisting in their resolution, by modification to its application, or changes to the accepted hardware platform.
     - 1.5.2. **Customer Users**—Responsible for assisting in identifying the system load conditions that represent five-year capacity projections, including peak simultaneous users, by number and type, transactions, and archived and historical data volumes.
     - 1.5.3. **Customer IT**—Responsible for identifying and providing the tools required to perform system performance tests, creating the system load conditions as specified, conducting system performance testing, reporting results, and working with the vendor to determine defect resolution.
   - 1.6. **Completion Criteria**—System performance testing is complete when the results of this testing comply with pre-defined performance requirements for system load conditions that represent five-year capacity projections, including peak simultaneous users, by number and type, transactions, and archived and historical data volumes.

TABLE 3-8   Work Breakdown Structure Dictionary

The level of detail in a WBS dictionary can vary. For example, it can include the following:

- WBS number
- Task breakdown and descriptions
- Roles and responsibilities by organization
- Schedule
- Costs
- Process requirements
- Deliverable completion criteria

At this point during the scope preparation process, the Project Manager now has the basis for creating work packages. A *work package* is the lowest tasks and associated components for a deliverable. Figure 3-4 displays a work package.

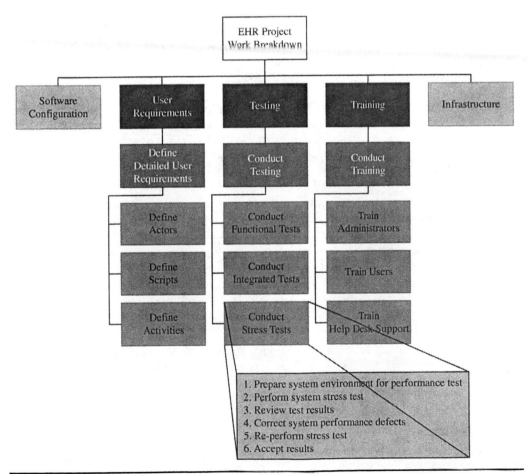

FIGURE 3-4   Illustration of a work package.

Work packages confirm the project scope baseline. A *project scope baseline* is the approved project scope and the collection of the scope statement, WBS, WBS dictionary, and work packages. It serves as the foundation for:

- Planning the project resource, schedule, and budget baselines
- Monitoring adherence to these baselines
- Controlling changes to these baselines

As noted above, the Project Manager creates the WBS and the work packages including listing individuals and teams assigned and held responsible for each and every deliverable in the project. Taking the time to include these individuals in this scope preparation process is important for reasons over and above aiding the Project Manager in coordinating the project. For example, it offers the following benefits:

- Engages team members early in the project
- Fosters their support because they have a stake in defining the deliverables they will produce
- Enables the team to produce the best project outputs

Creating these outputs (i.e., the WBS, WBS dictionary, and work packages), is not an easy task. As always, experience is critical. As well, there are multiple ways available to create these outputs. Potential analysis methods include:

- *Expert Judgment*—Create a definition based on the judgment of specialists or their resources that document their judgment (e.g., consultants, industry reports, prior experience, user requirements from another EHR project). If someone on the technology team has experience in training users in the effective use of a clinical documentation tool, using their expert judgment to estimate how long it will take, and how many trainers it will require to train clinician users offers a valid approach.
- *Bottom Up*—In this approach the project participants identify each individual part of the work until they assemble a complete picture, such as a WBS.
- *Top Down*—This is the opposite approach to bottom up and requires performing a functional decomposition. A *functional decomposition* is a process of breaking something down into individual components or functional parts. For example, consider defining how to prepare requirements for care planning. In a top down approach, a participant starts with high-level tasks required to define care planning, refining them into smaller sub-tasks. With continued refinement, the participants prepare a final set of *fully decomposed* tasks.
- *Reference Project*—In this method, the Project Manager uses an example of something previously prepared as a starting point. For example, the Project Manager might use a scope definition from an HDO that previously implemented a similar EHR system, updating it to reflect the current HDO's differences.

Verify Scope

In the controlling process, the Project Manager verifies scope. Scope verification ensures project deliverables comply with pre-defined standards or a baseline. A WBS dictionary defines tasks or the processes for creating a deliverable and expectations for the deliverable itself. A WBS dictionary is a powerful scope control tool. The tasks and the completion criteria above in Table 3-8 include scope verification processes and completion criteria.

If the vendor fulfills the requirements identified in a WBS dictionary, then the customer signs a deliverable completion certificate. A *deliverable completion certificate (DCC)* is a document that certifies completion of a project deliverable according to the WBS dictionary. Table 3-9 displays an example of a DCC. The scope verification process occurs by comparing a deliverable to its WBS dictionary entry and either accepting it or identifying updates based on the WBS dictionary. If the vendor fails to complete the work in compliance with the WBS dictionary, the customer issues a CR noting variances

---

Deliverable Completion Certificate
SYSTEM PERFORMANCE TESTING

Vendor hereby certifies to HDO that as of the date of this deliverable completion certificate, it satisfied all conditions in Agreement 452987, including satisfaction of the applicable deliverable (Del.) completion criteria subject to HDO's approval of the work performed, and that the Total Deliverable Payment amount set forth below is payable:

Task/ Del. No.	Del. Item Description	Maximum Amount (Fixed Price)	10% Holdback Amount	Del. Payment (Max. less Holdback)	**Invoice Amount**
2.c	System Performance Testing	$50,000	$5,000	$45,000	**$45,000**

The undersigned further represents and warrants that the Work performed in respect to such Deliverable is complete in accordance with the Scope of Work.

Attached hereto is a copy of all supporting documentation required pursuant to the Agreement and the applicable Deliverable completion criteria including any additional documentation reasonably requested by the HDO.

Vendor

By:
Contractor Executive Representative
Date:

Accepted by:

HDO

By:
    (print name)
    HDO Project Manager
Date:

TABLE 3-9 Deliverable Completion Certificate

between the deliverable and the WBS dictionary If there are only minor changes, the customer requests that the vendor perform identified document updates. The Project Manager submits all WBS dictionary compliant deliverables to the executive sponsor for provisional acceptance, subject to final acceptance by the steering committee.

Scope Control

The Project Manager controls scope during the controlling process. Scope control compares planned scope, or the baseline, to the actual scope, and resolves variances. Scope verification, in contrast, ensures individual deliverables comply with a pre-defined WBS dictionary. Scope control is not only the responsibility of the Project Manager, as described below.

> The scope was originally set out in very early discussions of the project, around what we thought we could manage in an initial implementation, and how much change we thought the hospital could support and absorb. There was some push to go further, to take it beyond the initial applications. Hospital leadership, the Project Team, and project leadership felt strongly that this was about all that the hospital could bear.
>
> We were not thinking in terms of measuring scope so much as just looking at how much of the hospital will need to change its behavior and, given their resources, how much could they absorb at one time. When we had four or five nurses on a particular area of the project, we thought we could be perhaps a little more aggressive because we had good, solid nursing support. In other areas, where the subject matter expertise was less deep, we might have chosen to be less aggressive.
>
> —Robert Greenless, PhD, CIO–RLANRC

The Project Manager monitors scope using the control process described in integration management. For example, sometimes you don't know enough about how a new system works to know what you can or can't leave out of your project. A provider we work with recently started an EHR project for their outpatient oncology center. Initially, the project plan included implementing EHR only, with new pharmacy and scheduling systems planned later. However, during the initial project stages it became clear that when configuring the EHR system (e.g., chemotherapy order sets), it made more sense to add the pharmacy system to the project. This represented a considerable scope change because the pharmacy system was at that point a separate project with its own team, requirements, scope, schedule, costs, and so on. Combining the two required a significant update to the EHR project, resulting in a CR for scope.

TIME MANAGEMENT

Time management is planning and controlling the schedule required to complete the project within an approved timeframe. Table 3-10 displays time management processes and their outputs (in italics) by process group.

Define Tasks

During the creation of the WBS, the Project Manager defines the range of tasks that the project will complete in the executing process group. Every task defined in the WBS will have a finite completion time associated with it. The output of this task definition process is a task list. A *task list* is an inventory of activities project resources must perform to produce all project deliverables. For example, the WBS dictionary in Table 3-8 included the following task list:

1. Prepare system environment for performance test
2. Perform system testing
3. Review test results
4. Correct system performance defects
5. Re-perform testing
6. Accept results

An EHR project often includes hundreds of tasks. The Project Manager organizes long task lists in groups of logical categories or phases. A *phase* is a specific group of tasks that occur during a distinct period. For example, an EHR project may include planning, acquisition, and implementation phases. The end of each phase may be a milestone. A *milestone* is an event or checkpoint to review and verify task, phase, and/or project status. For example, an HDO may use milestones after creation of the WBS, WBS dictionary, and work packages to review potential changes in the scope statement now that a baseline scope is in place.

Initiating	Planning	Executing	Controlling	Closing
	Define tasks *Task list* Sequence tasks *Task sequence* Estimate task resources *Task resource estimate* Estimate task duration *Task duration estimate* Prepare schedule *Schedule*		Control schedule *Organizational process asset update* *Performance report* *Change request (CR)* *Project document update*	

TABLE 3-10   Time Management Knowledge Area by Process Group

Sequence Tasks

A Project Manager sequences tasks during the planning process. The output of this process is a *task sequence,* which is a chronological relationship between one or more activities. The Project Manager needs to step back and organize task lists based on their dependent relationships. For example, an HDO tests its EHR system to ensure the configuration meets stakeholder needs. Testing includes a task list, such as prepare test plan, scripts, and data. The HDO also trains users on how to use the configured system, which includes a task list, such as prepare training plan, identify training audience, and determine audience-training levels. The Project Manager sequences the testing tasks to finish before training tasks begin. We refer to testing as the predecessor tasks that the project must complete before beginning the training or successor tasks.

Task predecessor and successor types include the following:

- *Finish-to-Start (FS)*—The successor task starts after the predecessor task finishes, that is, task 2 starts after finishing task 1. For example, the task to test standardized order sets begins only after finishing the task to configure the order sets. This is the most commonly used task sequence.

- *Start-to-Start (SS)*—Two tasks start concurrently, that is, tasks 1 and 2 start simultaneously. For example, the task of configuring the system also begins the task of documenting workflow requirements.

- *Finish-to-Finish (FF)*—Two tasks finish at the same time, that is tasks 1 and 2 finish simultaneously. For example, IT orders hardware for delivery upon finishing computer room construction. Hardware quickly becomes obsolete so IT wants to take delivery of, install, and use the hardware immediately instead of storing it while constructing the computer room. Likewise, IT does not want to have a new vacant portion of the computer room waiting for hardware arrival. Consequently, IT plans to take delivery of the hardware and finish computer construction concurrently.

- *Start-to-Finish (SF)*—A delay in the start of the predecessor task delays the finish of the task successor. For example, the predecessor task includes *provide hardware installers* and the successor task includes *install the hardware.* If the hardware arrives late, the installers will complete the hardware installation late. This is the most confusing and uncommon dependency.

Sequencing tasks according to a realistic timetable also requires introduction of lead time and lag time, described below:

- *Lead Time*—The *lead time* is the float or amount of delay one task has without causing dependent task delay. For example, IT completes the task of ordering EHR system servers knowing it takes six weeks before the servers arrive. Meanwhile, IT knows it takes only three weeks to complete the task of modifying the computer room to accommodate the new servers. IT could delay this overlapping task and start work on the computer room three weeks after placing the server order and still have the computer room ready. In other words, there is a three-week lead or float between ordering the servers and modifying the computer room.

- *Lag Time*—The *lag time* is the amount of delay between the end of one task and the start of the next dependent task. For example, an HDO cannot begin the task of evaluating proposals immediately after completing the task of preparing and releasing a solicitation to vendors. Vendors need six weeks to work on their proposals before submitting them to the HDO for evaluation. In this example, there is a six-week lag or delay between releasing the solicitation and evaluating proposals.

Estimate Task Resources

The Project Manager estimates task resources during the planning process. A *task resource estimate* is an approximation of the type and quantity of resources required to perform an activity, based on the requirements of that activity. Resources might include people, equipment, and supplies. For example, a physician is the most suitable resource to assign to the task of defining flow sheet requirements. The Project Manager needs to estimate how many physician hours are necessary given the complexity of this task.

Estimate Task Duration

The Project Manager estimates task duration during the planning process. A *task duration estimate* is an estimate of the work period required to complete an activity. Tasks longer than 80 hours require milestones to validate whether task progress or deliverable preparation is on schedule. This milestone serves as a checkpoint marking a specific stage.

Task duration and, at the larger level, project scheduling are activities that do require a significant degree of estimation, which in many cases are just that—estimates.

Once we had our secure patient messaging plan well in hand, we began the work. But very quickly we discovered significant problems with the project plan. Specifically the task list was changing quite rapidly. We found we had to assess progress almost daily as these tasks evolved. A common problem arose in the form of project time management. When a team member was asked 'How long will you need to complete this task?', the increasingly standard answer was 'Well, I don't know. I really don't know.' So, lo and behold, we kept missing our dates. We had to learn a new discipline about this. We came to the realization that it was irrational to try to set project schedules in the traditional way, because we'd never done this before. We actually don't know how long this will take. With no prior similar experience, schedule estimation was effectively wild guessing. Yet at the same time, we believed it would be equally irrational from a project management standpoint to not ask for an estimate. We need to ask for these but we need also to have flexibility as our experience grows. As long as we could ensure that no one was wandering off task, we felt we had the discipline and yet the understanding of the limits of the estimations.
—Ernie Hood, CIO, GHC

Creation of the project schedule is an example of a fundamental challenge in project management—that is, how to accurately estimate the length of time each task will take, and by extension how long the entire project will take to complete. There are several possible approaches to developing this analysis. In addition to the expert judgment, bottom up, top down, or reference projects described previously. There are other approaches as described below.

Parametric Estimating

This is a form of quantitative estimating that is useful for repetitive tasks. With parametric estimation, the Project Manager determines the time it takes to complete a single unit of work and multiplies that unit completion time by the total number of units. For example, if it takes a member of the Health Information Management (HIM) staff five minutes to enter the average existing patient record into the new EHR, and there are 4,000 patient records, it takes one person 20,000 minutes to complete this conversion task. The Project Manager uses this information to determine how many staff to assign to complete the amount of work required in the available time.

Scenario Estimating

For some task estimations one can estimate different scenarios or plans (e.g., likely, worst, and best case estimates to determine a range of task durations). We then take a combined view of these scenarios to calculate the task duration. For example, we need to estimate the time required to clean up *dirty* paper patient records before entry into the new EHR, but we may not know exactly how many there are. We start by estimating the likely, worst, and best case volume of dirty records and the time required to *purify* them. We then average the purification time, weighting the average based on the proportional number of dirty records in each scenario, to calculate the task duration.

Resource Leveling

Frequently the Project Manager must balance the schedule based on completing tasks within a specific timeframe and the availability of people to perform these tasks. Two sorts of problems can arise. In the first, we over-allocate an individual, giving him too much work so that timely task completion is impossible. In the second situation, we under-allocate people or fail to assign them fully to project tasks. Resource leveling can help resolve these problems. This involves identifying over- and under-allocated resources and changing the project schedule by, for example, taking advantage of task slack allowances. The result is fewer peaks and valleys, leading to smoother resource distribution. Resource leveling helps optimize tasks, resource assignments, and scheduling needs. Figure 3-5 displays an example of resource allocation in a histogram.

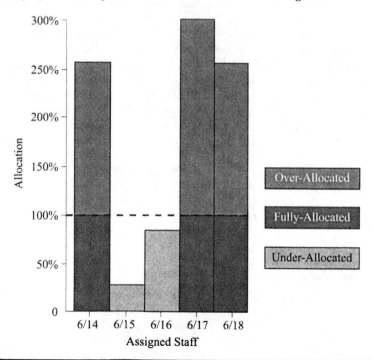

Figure 3-5   Example of resource allocation.

When you actually think through all that stuff, module by module, and then look at how it all has to come together, you have to think pretty carefully about next steps, making sure that things are coordinated, and that you've got an integrated test, before you can talk about training and go-live. Well, how do you make sure that all of the modules are ready at about the same time so you can move on to that stage? That very detailed thinking about what the steps were and who was going to do them was the answer. It's easy to get in trouble if you just think about what the steps are. That's fine, but if you don't plot out who's going to be involved at each stage, you can end up with a real gap there. Something is supposed to be happening, and all the resources are tied up on something else. It's not just sequencing tasks, but sequencing resources as well. And sequencing communication—"when do you tell them what"—so that the hospital's ready for this.

—Robert Greenless, PhD, CIO–RLANRC

Prepare Schedule

The Project Manager prepares a schedule as the last step in this planning process. A *schedule* is an organized task list based on their sequence, duration, and resource requirements, according to a timetable.

Creating a formal and detailed project schedule enables the Project Manager to also define a critical path. The *critical path* is the sequence of tasks that determines the minimum time needed for project completion. The project must complete this sequence of tasks on time if the project is to finish on schedule. Any critical path task delay will postpone the entire project unless there is an adjustment to the critical path to overcome the setback.

Calculating a critical path includes the following:

- Defining each predecessor task that a dependent successor task requires before starting
- Identifying the earliest that each predecessor task can start so it completes at the exact time the dependent successor task needs it
- Linking each of these predecessor and dependent successor tasks and noting the time it takes to complete each task
- Finding the longest path through the network of tasks and calculating the total time to complete this route

Figure 3-6 includes an illustration of how to calculate a critical path.

While there are software products such as Microsoft Project® that can calculate the critical path, it is important to understand how to calculate it manually because it includes so much valuable information. As outlined in Figure 3-6, critical path details include the following:

- *Critical Paths Determine the Project Schedule*—The critical path is the sequence of tasks that determine the minimum time needed for project completion. The project end date will not necessarily change if there is a delay in non-critical path tasks; however, a delay in a critical path task will cause project delay. For example, any delay in path A+B+C+D in Figure 3-6 will cause project delay because there is no available slack. There is no project delay if there is a two-day delay in path A+E+F+D. This non-critical path includes a five-day slack, which is enough to accommodate the two-day delay without causing project postponement.

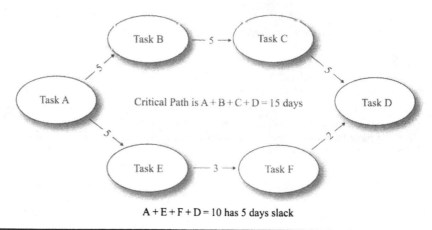

Figure 3-6   Calculating a critical path.

- *Critical Paths Change*—The tasks included in the critical path can change. For example, path A+E+F+D becomes the new critical path if there is a 20-day delay during completion of these tasks. Remember the critical path is the longest path. Initially path A+B+C+D was the longest route. Path A+E+F+D takes longer with this delay and is now the new critical path.

- *Multiple Critical Paths*—A project can include more than one critical path. For example, the paths A+B+C+D and A+E+F+D could equal the same amount of time. Multiple critical paths require project management attention to both pathways.

The Project Manager engages project staff by including those responsible for completing tasks in the definition, sequence, resource estimating, and duration and schedule development. Preparing a schedule often requires project scheduling software, such as Microsoft Project®. This and other similar tools are very complex and often difficult to use. Nonetheless, they are essential for large complex projects. It is most helpful if one Project Team member and a backup are very familiar with one of these tools. Figure 3-7 displays an example of a Gantt chart from scheduling software. A *Gantt chart* is a bar chart that displays, in this instance, planned project schedule, tasks, and resources.

Control Schedule

The Project Manager oversees the schedule during the controlling process. Schedule control compares planned project dates, or the baseline, to the actual schedule and resolves variances. Outputs produced to control the project schedule must be widely available and easily understood by project participants to encourage their schedule support and receive their input regarding schedule variances. Project participants may not fully understand reports from project management software, but the Project Manager may need this software to control the schedule. To resolve this, the Project Manager prepares reports with software such as Microsoft Project® and converts them to a Microsoft Word® table. This report should include planned start and end dates, actual start and end dates, and start and finish variance by task. Table 3-11 displays an example of this Word document.

Task Name	% Complete	Baseline Start	Baseline Finish	Actual Start	Actual Finish	Projected Start	Projected Finish	Start Variance	Finish Variance
- Phase 1 - Definition and Acquisition	62%	5/5/06	12/22/06	5/12/06	NA	5/12/06	12/29/06	5 days	0 days
- Task 1 - Prepare and Monitor Project Management Plan	13%	5/12/06	12/8/06	5/12/06	5/12/06	5/12/06	12/8/06	0 days	0 days
Task 1.1 - Prepare and Monitor Project Management Plan 1	100%	5/12/06	5/12/06	5/12/06	5/12/06	5/12/06	5/12/06	0 days	0 days
Task 1.2 - Prepare and Monitor Project Management Plan 2	0%	6/8/06	6/8/06	NA	NA	6/8/06	6/8/06	0 days	0 days
Task 1.3 - Prepare and Monitor Project Management Plan 3	0%	7/10/06	7/10/06	NA	NA	7/10/06	7/10/06	0 days	0 days
Task 1.4 - Prepare and Monitor Project Management Plan 4	0%	8/8/06	8/8/06	NA	NA	8/8/06	8/8/06	0 days	0 days
Task 1.5 - Prepare and Monitor Project Management Plan 5	0%	9/8/06	9/8/06	NA	NA	9/8/06	9/8/06	0 days	0 days
Task 1.6 - Prepare and Monitor Project Management Plan 6	0%	10/9/06	10/9/06	NA	NA	10/9/06	10/9/06	0 days	0 days
Task 1.7 - Prepare and Monitor Project Management Plan 7	0%	11/8/06	11/8/06	NA	NA	11/8/06	11/8/06	0 days	0 days
Task 1.8 - Prepare and Monitor Project Management Plan 8	0%	12/8/06	12/8/06	NA	NA	12/8/06	12/8/06	0 days	0 days
Task 2 - Conduct Research to Define Baseline EMR Scenarios/Scripts	62%	5/5/06	5/18/06	5/19/06	NA	5/19/06	6/1/06	10 days	10 days
Task 3 - Prepare Baseline Scenarios/Scripts	100%	5/19/06	7/10/06	5/19/06	7/10/06	5/19/06	7/10/06	0 days	0 days
Task 4 - Conduct Subject Matter Expert (SME) Reviews	85%	5/19/06	9/29/06	5/19/06	NA	5/19/06	9/29/06	0 days	0 days
Task 5 - Assemble RFP	0%	10/2/06	10/6/06	NA	NA	10/2/06	10/6/06	0 days	0 days
Task 6 - Define Evaluation Criteria	0%	10/2/06	10/6/06	NA	NA	10/2/06	10/6/06	0 days	0 days
Task 7 - Solicit RFP Responses	0%	10/16/06	11/3/06	NA	NA	10/16/06	11/3/06	0 days	0 days
Task 8 - Conduct Conference Room Pilot(s)	0%	11/6/06	11/10/06	NA	NA	11/6/06	11/10/06	0 days	0 days
Task 9 - Check References	0%	11/13/06	11/17/06	NA	NA	11/13/06	11/17/06	0 days	0 days
Task 10 - Conduct Site Visits	0%	11/20/06	11/22/06	NA	NA	11/20/06	11/22/06	0 days	0 days
Task 11 - Negotiate Contract	0%	11/27/06	12/22/06	NA	NA	11/27/06	12/22/06	0 days	0 days

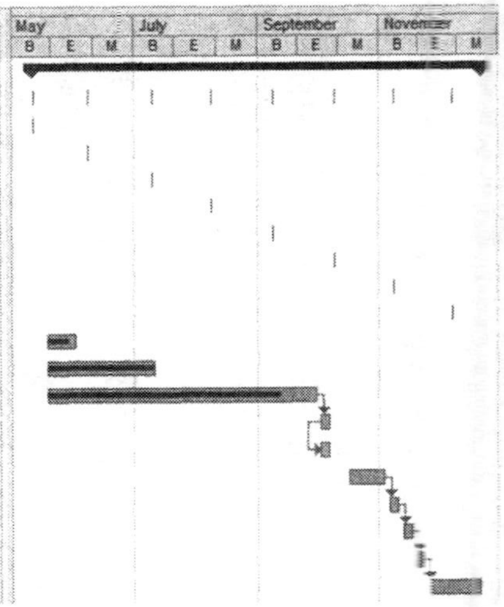

FIGURE 3-7 Project Gantt chart.

Task	% Complete	Baseline Start	Baseline Finish	Actual Start	Actual Finish	Projected Start	Projected Finish	Start Variance	Finish Variance
Phase I - Definition and Acquisition	62%	5/5/06	12/22/06	5/12/06	NA	5/12/06	12/22/06	5d	0d
Task 1 - Prepare and Monitor Project Management Plan	13%	5/12/06	12/08/06	5/12/06	NA	5/12/06	12/8/06	0d	0d
Task 1.1 - Prepare and Monitor Project Management Plan 1	100%	5/12/06	5/12/06	5/12/06	5/12/06	5/12/06	5/12/06	0d	0d
Task 1.2 - Prepare and Monitor Project Management Plan 2	0%	6/8/06	6/8/06	NA	NA	6/8/06	6/8/06	0d	0d
Task 1.3 - Prepare and Monitor Project Management Plan 3	0%	7/10/06	7/10/06	NA	NA	7/10/06	7/10/06	0d	0d
Task 1.4 - Prepare and Monitor Project Management Plan 4	0%	8/8/06	8/8/06	NA	NA	8/8/06	8/8/06	0d	0d
Task 1.5 - Prepare and Monitor Project Management Plan 5	0%	9/8/06	9/8/06	NA	NA	9/8/06	9/8/06	0d	0d
Task 1.6 - Prepare and Monitor Project Management Plan 6	0%	10/9/06	10/9/06	NA	NA	10/9/06	10/9/06	0d	0d
Task 1.7 - Prepare and Monitor Project Management Plan 7	0%	11/8/06	11/8/06	NA	NA	11/8/06	11/8/06	0d	0d
Task 1.8 - Prepare and Monitor Project Management Plan 8	0%	12/8/06	12/8/06	NA	NA	12/8/06	12/8/06	0d	0d
Task 2 - Conduct Research to Define Baseline EMR Scenarios/Scripts	62%	5/5/06	5/18/06	5/19/06	NA	5/19/06	6/1/06	10d	10d
Task 3 - Prepare Baseline Scenarios/Scripts	100%	5/19/06	7/10/06	5/19/06	7/10/06	5/19/06	7/10/06	0d	0d
Task 4 - Conduct Subject Matter Expert (SME) Reviews	85%	5/19/06	9/29/06	5/19/06	NA	5/19/06	9/29/06	0d	0d
Task 5 - Assemble RFP	0%	10/2/06	10/6/06	NA	NA	10/2/06	10/6/06	0d	0d
Task 6 - Define Evaluation Criteria	0%	10/2/06	10/6/06	NA	NA	10/2/06	10/6/06	0d	0d
Task 7 - Solicit RFP Responses	0%	10/16/06	11/3/06	NA	NA	10/16/06	11/3/06	0d	0d
Task 8 - Conduct Conference Room Pilot(s)	0%	11/6/06	11/10/06	NA	NA	11/6/06	11/10/06	0d	0d
Task 9 - Check References	0%	11/13/06	11/17/06	NA	NA	11/13/06	11/17/06	0d	0d
Task 10 - Conduct Site Visits	0%	11/20/06	11/22/06	NA	NA	11/20/06	11/22/06	0d	0d
Task 11 - Negotiate Contract	0%	11/27/06	12/22/06	NA	NA	11/27/06	12/22/06	0d	0d

Notes: d and w represent day and week, respectively.

TABLE 3-11 Project Management Control Schedule

The Project Manager monitors the project schedule using the control process described in integration management. For example, a long-standing client of ours recently indicated that they were worried their project was behind schedule and they wanted help to address this delay. We looked at their schedule, and noticed they had no critical path defined. This made it impossible for us to tell if the project was on schedule. Once the client defined the relationship between tasks and prepared the resulting critical path, they determined they had sufficient slack in the overdue tasks to accommodate the delay without affecting the project end date. The outcome was a document update incorporating the critical path into the project schedule to support ongoing schedule control.

Another example of controlling schedule is as follows:

One place where we didn't do so great is on estimating the size chunks, if you will, that the organization would be able to tolerate with respect to implementation time. For example what we initially thought was going to be a three-phase project ended up being closer to a four-phase, even five-phase project. We ended up having a Phase Ia, Phase IIa, IIb, Phase IIIa and maybe IIIb even. In addition, that was just because as we got into it, we recognized that we had misjudged the scope that people could tolerate with respect to change, and so we recalibrated along the way and broke things up into smaller components.

Part of the solution had to do with our Project Team, being inclusive of folks in the trenches and on the ground. Those are folks who, as we started to get into that large unbroken version of Phase II, for example, raised their hands and said, "you know what, I don't think we can do this much," and they gave their rationale as to why. In this particular case, we were going live with nursing documentation at the same time we were going live with CPOE—computerized provider order entry. When it came time to start implementing, the team was in the trenches and had a good objective sense of what would be tolerated and what wouldn't. Therefore, I think it's to the project's credit that we went back to recalibrate and rethink about how we would do things. It was clear to us that we needed to listen to our Project Team and to adjust the scope and schedule.

—Dan Nigrin, MD, MS, CIO, Children's Hospital Boston

COST MANAGEMENT

Cost management is planning and controlling costs required to complete the project within an approved budget. Table 3-12 displays the cost management processes and their outputs (in italics) by process group. In brief, the steps the Project Manager performs in the cost management process group include estimating project costs, preparing a budget, and then controlling actual costs during execution of the project budget.

Estimate Costs

The Project Manager estimates costs during the planning process. A *cost estimate* is an approximation of expenditures required to complete a project. A Project Manager prepares cost estimates based on the following sequential process:

- Define assumptions
- Receive approval of assumptions from key stakeholders
- Prepare estimates based on approved assumptions
- Revise estimates based on changes to assumptions

Table 3-13 includes an example of cost assumptions.

Remember that you cannot estimate costs effectively until you define what the project will do (scope) and how long the project will take (time). Consequently, a key information source required to prepare the cost estimate is the WBS dictionary and the fully resourced project schedule. In addition, cost estimating generally includes:

- Vendor estimates included in the feasibility study and business case and vendor contract cost information
- Market conditions (e.g., to estimate the current inflation rate)
- Historical information, such as:
  - Examples of vendor ongoing support costs
  - Estimates of several costs that are available from previous projects (e.g., HDO hardware, network, and conversion costs)
- Policies or standards used by the HDO (e.g., contingency/reserve, quality assurance, project management, and disaster recovery costs)

Initiating	Planning	Executing	Controlling	Closing
	Estimate costs *Cost estimate* Prepare budget *Project budget*		Control cost *Organizational process asset update* *Performance report* *Change request (CR)* *Project document update*	

TABLE 3-12   Cost Management Knowledge Area by Process Group

Assumptions
Administrative Fees—The estimates include overhead, for example, travel and per diem, and out-of-pocket expenses a provider of the recommended solution may include in work they perform on behalf of the HDO.
Contingency—The estimates include a contingency of an additional 20 percent of project costs to attempt to account for unknown or unforeseen factors.
Conversion—The estimates assume the HDO will convert existing records from their old to the new system.
Disaster Recovery—The estimates include additional costs for disaster recovery support for the new system.
Facilities—The estimates include expenditures for changes or additions to existing facilities at the HDO to support the new system.
Financing—The estimates do not reflect any financing alternatives the HDO may wish to select for this project.
Funding Source—The estimates do not address sources of funding whether existing or new.
Furnishings—The estimates include costs for changes or additions to furnishings to support PCs or changes in job functions (e.g., removal or construction of counter space, due to implementing the new system).
Hardware Platform—The HDO's IT objectives include a transition of all systems to Microsoft .Net architecture. The estimates assume the EHR requires new hardware supportable within the HDO's technological environment and consistent with the .Net strategy.
Inflation—The estimates assume current year dollars and reflect future adjustments for inflation.
Interfaces—The estimates includes costs for interfaces (e.g., between the new EHR and the existing patient accounting system).
Network Costs—The estimates include new expenditures for the local area network (LAN) and the wide area network (WAN) components that may be necessary to support full use of the proposed system within the HDO.
One-Time System Costs—The estimates include one-time hardware and software expenditures supplied by a COTS vendor of the recommended solution for an EHR.
Ongoing System Costs—The cost estimates include hardware maintenance and software support costs supplied by a COTS vendor of the recommended solution for an EHR.
Out-Of-Pocket (OOP) Expenses—This cost analysis includes an OOP estimate of 20% of total vendor fees for all on-site services.
PCs—The estimates include upgrades to existing PCs.
Power—The estimates address the ongoing cost for changes in electrical power consumption associated with the new system, if required.
Project Management—The estimates include the cost of internal HDO project management. The estimates assume HDO will provide its own project management other than project management provided by the vendor delivering the recommended solution.
Quality Management—The estimates include the cost for quality assurance and control.

TABLE 3-13   Cost Estimate Assumptions

Assumptions
Rounding Errors—The estimates may include slight rounding errors.
Supplies—The estimates include costs for supplies (e.g., forms, printer cartridges, paper stock).
Taxes—The estimates include costs for current and future taxes for services or tangible goods provided by third parties supporting the new system.
Time—The estimates use calendar instead of fiscal years.
Timing—The estimates assume it will take about 12 months to implement the new system. In addition, assuming there is a one-year warranty from the date of system acceptance, all ongoing system costs begin one year after acceptance.
Warranty Period—The cost estimates assume all warranties are for one year and all begin at once after acceptance of the new system.

TABLE 3-13   Cost Estimate Assumptions (*Continued*)

Many of the analysis methods identified above in the section on time estimation also serve the Project Manager well when preparing a cost estimate. These methods include using combinations of expert judgment, bottom up estimating, reference projects, parametric estimating, and scenario estimating.

An HIT project may include some unusual budget line items. For example, engaging line clinicians to participate not only in the training process but the planning process of the project typically takes these people away from their clinical duties. This may mean budgeting *backfill* clinical resources. *Backfill staff* are personnel provided to fill positions vacated by resources assigned to the project. It may also entail budgeting to pay key clinicians to participate in the project instead of providing patient care.

One important thing that we did right upfront was understand that if we're going to challenge nurses to be as productive during our go-lives as they are normally, we're going to need to overstaff at those times. We built backfill into the project budget for nursing time for several weeks during go-live because we fully expected to have to staff at higher levels. Likewise, we built into the project budget dollars that we would pay for physicians to be part of the Project Team where they were going to have dedicated time that they would contribute to being super-users for their particular clinical area. Consequently, we fully expected that there was going to be significant input that would take people away from their regular jobs, especially around go-live, but even during other project implementation periods. That was baked in from the start, and a critical aspect of both our overall success and not going over budget.

—Dan Nigrin, MD, MS, CIO, Children's Hospital Boston

An additional estimating method includes tools that rely on software metrics. A *software metric* is a measurement of software properties, such as Lines of Code (LOC), function points, or units of software functionality, or objects or entities of interest to a system. For example, an HDO must first acquire proprietary estimating software. Second, the HDO must estimate the size of the EHR software in terms of LOC, function points, or objects. Estimating the size of the HDO's EHR is crucial because this information tends to dictate the accuracy of the software estimate. If this information is wrong, the estimate could be incorrect. Estimating LOC for the EHR software is probably available only from the vendor that wrote the EHR software; calculating function points or objects requires specialized methods that are not necessarily available to the HDO. The Project Manager enters these metrics and many other factors into proprietary estimating software, assuming he has access to this information or is familiar with these specialized methods. Third, the software performs a quantitative analysis based on various rules and calculates estimates for project cost, schedule, defects, complexity, and other factors.

Prepare Budget

The Project Manager prepares the project budget in the planning process. A *project budget* is a prediction of maximum project costs and the baseline for managing these costs. The Project Manager prepares the project budget from updated information in the cost estimate and negotiated contract costs with the selected EHR vendor.

The budget is not just a single number, such as $5 million. Rather, the budget is a financial expression of the project. This includes, at minimum, scope, time, costs, and quality. Overseeing these plans from a budgetary perspective requires distributing costs over the project schedule by key cost categories. Figure 3-8 includes an EHR project budget based on a project schedule.

Control Costs

The Project Manager monitors project costs in the controlling process. The final budget serves as a baseline for managing costs similar to any other plan in the project management plan. The Project Manager monitors costs using the control process described in integration management. For example, a public sector provider asked us to perform quality management on an ongoing project implementing an EHR for a jail. The provider asked that we focus on cost management. We found that the Project Manager made hundreds of cost allocation changes without any change orders or document updates. This required us to perform an exhaustive financial audit of the entire project. Initially, indications were that the project was about $1 million over budget. There were even rumors that the Project Manager was involved in fraudulent activities; however, we found no evidence of fraud, just poor records management. In fact, our audit found that both the vendor and customer made numerous financial errors and the project was slightly *under* budget. This required a series of document updates reconstructing missing or inaccurate invoices, payments, and reconciliations, and a CR to establish ongoing project standards for cost management.

One particular control method is earned value management. *Earned value management (EVM)* is a method of measuring project cost and schedule performance. EVM assigns a dollar value to both planned and completed work. When a project completes work, it earns value. When a Project Manager compares the work earned to the work planned, for a specific period, there may be a variance between the two. If there is a positive variance, the work earned is more than the work planned and the project is ahead. Conversely, if there is a negative variance, the work earned is less than the work planned, the project is behind, and the Project Manager must correct this problem.

EVM is very useful; however, it depends on key assumptions, such as the following:

- A complete project task list, schedule, and budget
- A budget allocation for each scheduled task, that is, you know the cost and start and end date of each task

Cost Category	Five Year Total	Year 1	Year 2	Year 3	Year 4	Year 5
One-Time Costs						
HDO						
– Project and executive management	$ 750,000	$ 375,000	$ 375,000	$ -	$ -	$ -
– Software configuration	789,200	591,900	197,300	-	-	-
– Clinical team FTEs	1,600,000	528,000	1,056,000	-	-	-
– Backfill	469,000	154,770	309,540	-	-	-
– Infrastructure upgrades	850,000	637,500	212,500	-	-	-
HDO Total	$ 4,458,200	$ 2,287,170	$ 2,150,340	$ -	$ -	$ -
Vendor						
– Software configuration	$ 99,200	$ 74,400	$ 24,800	$ -	$ -	$ -
– Interfaces	182,000	12,000	170,000			
– Hardware	125,000	125,000				
– Training	81,090	12,164	68,927			
Vendor Total	$ 487,290	$ 223,564	$ 263,727	$ -	$ -	$ -
Other	$ 150,800	$ 100,800	$ 50,000	$ -	$ -	$ -
Contingency	1,019,258	522,307	492,813			
Total One-Time Costs	$ 6,115,548	$ 3,133,840	$ 2,956,880	$ -	$ -	$ -
Ongoing Annual Costs						
HDO						
– Clinical Support/Sys Admin FTEs	$ 3,000,000	$ 600,000	$ 600,000	$ 600,000	$ 600,000	$ 600,000
– JIT Training	250,000	50,000	50,000	50,000	50,000	50,000
HDO Total	$ 3,250,000	$ 650,000	$ 650,000	$ 650,000	$ 650,000	$ 650,000
Vendor						
– Software License/Subscription	$ 352,702	$ 70,540	$ 70,540	$ 70,540	$ 70,540	$ 70,540
– Software Support	352,702	70,540	70,540	70,540	70,540	70,540
– Hardware Support	300,000	60,000	60,000	60,000	60,000	60,000
Vendor Total	$ 1,005,404	$ 201,080	$ 201,080	$ 201,080	$ 201,080	$ 201,080
Total Ongoing Annual Costs	$ 4,255,404	$ 851,080	$ 851,080	$ 851,080	$ 851,080	$ 851,080
Total Cost Per Year	$	$ 3,984,920	$ 3,807,960	$ 851,080	$ 851,080	$ 851,080

Figure 3-8 EHR project budget summary.

In EVM, several formulas are used to measure project cost and schedule performance, which helps the Project Manager identify and resolve problems in a timely fashion. Figure 3-9 displays an earned value graph and its various components. EVM includes the following:

- *Planned Value*—The *Planned Value (PV)* is the budgeted cost of work scheduled. For example, we budgeted or planned to spend $500 thousand by the end of six months, so our planned value at week ten is $500 thousand.

- *Budget at Completion*—A *Budget at Completion (BAC)* is the total allocated budget. For example, if we expect the total budget will be $2 million for a two-year EHR project, the BAC equals $2 million.

- *Earned Value*—An *Earned Value (EV)* is the value of the project work performed to date. EV = PV × % Complete. For example, if 75% of planned work is complete, the EV is $375 thousand, that is, the PV of $500 thousand times 75%.

- *Actual Cost*—The *Actual Cost (AC)* is the amount the project spent on all performed work. For example, the AC is $625 thousand or all costs for project expenditures to date.

- *Cost Variance*—A *Cost Variance (CV)* measures the difference between earned value and actual costs. CV = EV – AC. Cost variance measures whether the actual cost is over (–) or under (+) planned cost. Using the example above, the EV of $375 thousand minus $625 thousand AC equals negative $250 thousand cost variance. Project work is costing $250 thousand more to perform than planned.

- *Schedule Variance*—A *Schedule Variance (SV)* is how much work we planned to complete compared to how much work we did complete. SV = EV – PV. The SV measures whether the actual schedule is behind (–) or ahead (+) of the planned schedule in dollars. Schedule variance is in dollars because it determines the financial value of the difference between actual schedule completion and planned completion. For example, if the EV is $375 thousand and we planned to spend $500 thousand, we have a negative $125 thousand SV. This indicates the dollar value of the work actually completed is less than the planned work.

- *Cost Performance Index*—A *cost performance index (CPI)* is a measure of how the project is performing against the budget. CPI = EV/AC. For example, the CPI is 60%, or the project is operating at 40% over budget, if you perform $375 thousand of project work and you actually spent $625 thousand. A CPI of one means the project is on budget, less than one means over budget, and greater than one means under budget.

- *Schedule Performance Index*—A *schedule performance index (SPI)* is a measure of how well the project is performing against the planned schedule. SPI = EV/PV. For example, the SPI is 75%, or the project is operating at 25% behind schedule, if the value of the work performed is $375 thousand and you planned to complete $500 thousand during that time. A SPI of one means the project is on schedule, less than one means behind schedule, and greater than one means ahead of schedule.

- *Estimate at Completion*—An *estimate at completion (EAC)* is the total expected cost of completing the project. EAC = BAC/CPI. Using the same example, we estimated the BAC would be $2 million. Given project performance we realize the budget at completion is no longer accurate and we need a new estimate or EAC. To calculate this EAC, we take the $2 million BAC and divide it by the CPI or 60%. The EAC is $3.33 million or we have a budget overrun of $1.33 million.

- *Estimated to Complete*—An *estimated to complete (ETC)* is the forecasted schedule or cost to complete remaining project work. ETC = Original time estimate/SPI. We plan to complete the project in 24 months. Given project performance we realize the schedule at completion is no longer accurate and we need a new estimate or schedule ETC. Using the same example, we are behind schedule by six months because the ETC is 32 months, that is, we estimated that the completion time in 24 months and divided it by the SPI of 75%.

  Cost ETC = EAC – AC. Given project performance we realize the estimated cost to complete the work is no longer accurate and we need a new estimate or cost ETC. Using the same example, we estimate the EAC was $3.33 million minus the AC or $625, which equals about $2.7 million to complete the project.

EVM has several limitations. For example:

- EVM fails to measure quality. EVM focuses on cost and schedule but not on quality. A Project Manager could, for example, deliver an EHR on schedule and within budget, but clinicians may still find the solution completely unacceptable.
- EVM is only as good as the estimates used in the calculations. If the estimates are either inaccurate or not timely, the output supplied is not useful for controlling the project.
- EVM requires accurate and timely cost and schedule data (e.g., tracking all project labor hours and associated costs, reporting this information in a timely manner, and calculating the project impact). Collecting and reporting this information requires a lot of sophisticated work that is not always available or easily supported by the project participants.

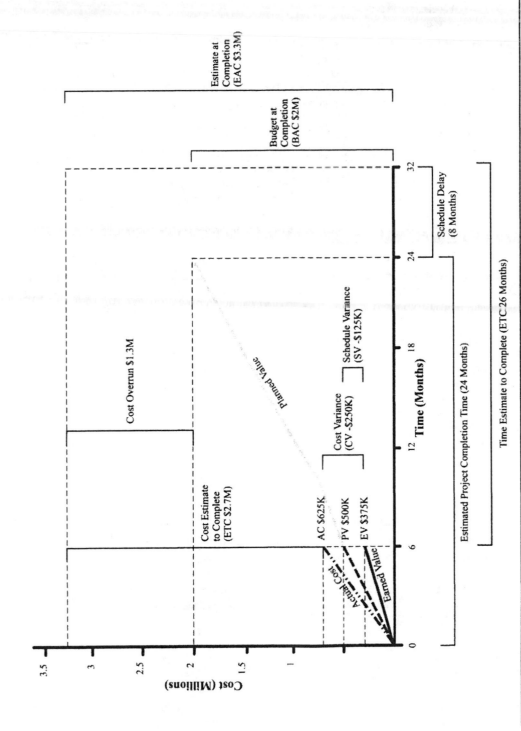

Figure 3-9 Earned value graph.

75

QUALITY MANAGEMENT

Quality management is planning, executing, and controlling project processes and outputs according to approved standards. Table 3-14 displays quality management processes and their outputs (in italics) by process group.

In project quality management the general steps the Project Manager oversees include creating the project quality management plan, performing quality assurance during project execution, and project quality control as the project completes each deliverable.

Plan Quality

The Project Manager prepares a quality management plan during the planning process. A *quality management plan* is a document that defines project standards and how the project will ensure compliance with them. Standards can take many forms. They may be the statements of functional requirements for the patient portal, flow sheet, order sets, and so on. These standards in the quality management plan define how the Project Manager and the senior leadership will measure whether the project is functioning and producing required products at the required level. As well, the quality plan also defines how the Project Team will work to comply with the standards and who is responsible for maintaining those standards. The standards are typically included in the project management plan, for example, the baseline scope, schedule, and the budget. Figure 3-10 displays a quality management process included in a quality management plan.

We had three quality management factors that helped us immensely. First, we had an independent third party perform quality assurance and control as oversight for our Board because we failed previously. This quality management team had the advantage of not being buried in the project. They could step back and look at the project from the outside and identify areas that may not have been fully thought out. That was extraordinarily valuable.

Second, our Project Director, who to this day says he is not an IT guy, asked difficult questions. If it didn't make sense to him as a financial-person involved in the process, he would ask, why are we doing this? Is this the right way? It didn't take us a long time to figure out that we needed to start anticipating these questions in our planning.

Third, we probably had the most actively involved steering committee that I've seen.

—Robert Greenless, PhD, CIO–RLANRC

Perform Quality Assurance

It is always a work in progress. We have not achieved perfection. There's always a little bit of tension between our Project Managers and the Project Management Office in terms of what the Project

Initiating	Planning	Executing	Controlling	Closing
	Prepare quality management plan *Quality management plan*	Perform quality assurance *Change request (CR)* *Project document update*	Perform quality control *Organizational process asset update* *Change request (CR)* *Project document update*	

TABLE 3-14   Quality Management Knowledge Area by Process Group

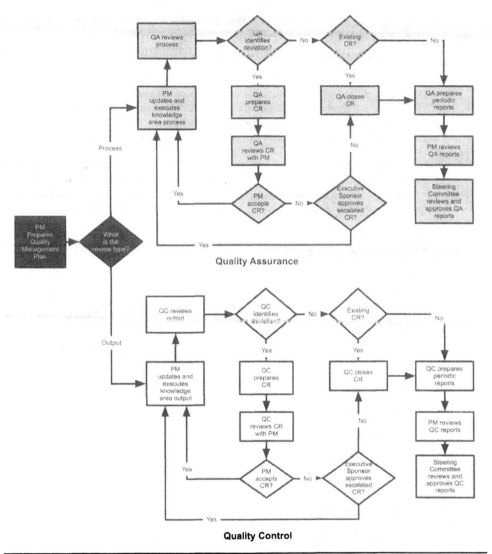

FIGURE 3-10   Quality management process.

Management Office is looking for and what the Project Manager thinks is an appropriate level of detail. I encourage them to continue that dialogue and stay engaged, but I understand the stresses on our Project Managers. I've been there and done that. But I also understand the value of having that voice in your ear saying, "you really haven't thought this through carefully enough." I'm OK with that little bit of tension there, actually.

What's working here is allowing this tension between the Project Managers and the Project Management Office and letting them work it out. If they can't resolve it, they come to my Associate CIO or to me and we talk it through. Both parties are bright, committed, hardworking people, and there's something of value in both of their points of view. It's a question about what's the balance, how do you want to play this, if we go to that level of detail, yes it's going to take a bit more time, or if we cut that corner here, are we increasing the risk over here in this other area? There's always *that dialogue, especially on big clinical projects, on the smaller ones not so much, it's less of an issue. We seem to have a balance that is working relatively well there.*

—Robert Greenless, PhD, CIO RLANRC

A Quality Manager performs quality assurance during the execution process. *Quality assurance (QA)* is regular, interim checks on tasks performed in the preparation of a project deliverable to ensure progress on the deliverable meets pre-defined project standards. The output of QA is a CR or project document update.

The QA process, as displayed in the top portion of Figure 3-10, includes the following:

- Conducting a review to identify quality issues, and documenting them and their impact. If no quality issues are found for some tasks during the review process, the Project Manager simply documents that the tasks conform to project standards. If there are quality issues, then the Project Manager prepares a CR.
- Reviewing each process CR with the Project Manager and updating it, as required
- Implementing CRs
- Reviewing outstanding process CRs
- Closing completed process CRs
- Addressing outstanding process CRs with the Project Manager and executive sponsor
- Escalating disputed process CRs to the executive sponsor, who makes the final decision on these disputed CRs
- Reporting all outstanding process CRs in a monthly quality assessment report

QA also requires an assessment of the QA process itself:

- Review the effectiveness of the CR process
- Identify trends that may disclose generic problems and potential preventive measures affecting reporting protocol compliance

Perform Quality Control

The Project Manager performs quality control during the controlling process. *Quality control (QC)* is the final check on a deliverable to ensure it meets pre-defined quality standards that were outlined in the WBS dictionary. The QC process is displayed in the bottom half of Figure 3-10.

The Project Manager monitors quality using the control process described in integration management. For example, a large hospital contacted us to review a very large HIT project that was not going well. Their Board was anxious to receive our feedback and gave us only 45 days to prepare and deliver our report. We initially conducted interviews to collect information on the system from project participants and found there were numerous scope, schedule, cost, communications, and other problems apparently rooted in unresolved software defects. We decided to conduct a code review and found that one of the core application programs contained *spaghetti code*, that is, program code that does not follow a logical flow. This can result from factors like inexperienced programmers, or highly complex programs modified continuously over a long time without completely rewriting them. We compared this code to company standards to illustrate the significance of the underlying problem. As a result, the hospital terminated the contract with the vendor and successfully implemented about 15 administrative, financial, and clinical applications across three inpatient facilities and all of their surrounding ambulatory clinics with a different vendor. While this is much more drastic than a typical CR, it demonstrates the significant role and value of quality management. In addition to the formal quality management process it is equally important to rely on informal feedback.

> *We have significant internal auditing functions within the hospital that oversee these types of projects. For example, we have very rigid change control processes, user provisioning and user security standards that we adhere to, and so this project was like any other project that we do. We adhere to those standards and conduct an objective audit as we go. I think, all that said, we also weigh the subjective feedback that we get from the clinicians in the trenches very heavily. When those clinical folks begin to tell us, "Yeah, this is working," we consider that probably the most important endorsement of the initiative. While the informal always happens, we consciously make sure our Project Team is extremely inclusive of clinical membership right from the get-go. From the very beginning of the project, we include lots of nurses, physicians paid to be part of the team, respiratory therapists, pharmacists, you name it. Therefore, a lot of that subjective feedback came directly from them, or from their peers to them, and then from them back into the project.*
> —Dan Nigrin, MD, MS, CIO, Children's Hospital Boston

QC employs many analysis methods to evaluate standards compliance. QC typically employs one or more of the following:

- *Cause and Effect Diagrams*—Identifies and organizes a problem by cause and effect. This is also known as the *Fishbone Diagram*. Alternatively, asking five whys often identifies the cause and effect or root cause of a problem. *Five whys* is a method of inquiry used to investigate cause and effect relationships and eventually identify the problem source.
- *Check Sheets*—Organizes a problem by tally sheets that classify data by trait, location, occurrence frequency, occurrence measurement by interval, or task checklists.
- *Flow Charts*—Identifies discrete steps according to a graphical display of processes and decisions to detect their impact and to develop process improvements.
- *Histograms*—Segments each variable and graphically illustrates the frequency of their occurrence with a vertical bar to help detect patterns and causes.
- *DMAIC*—Organizes process improvement according a Six Sigma® improvement process that includes:
  - Define the problem.
  - Measure or collect data.
  - Analyze or evaluate process details to explore improvement opportunities.
  - Improve or prepare a solution to the problem.
  - Control or monitor the solution and correct deviations to prevent future defects.

Six Sigma® refers to operating a manufacturing process with no more than 3.4 defects per million. Originally developed by Motorola, Six Sigma is an improvement method that seeks to identify and eliminate the causes of the defects.

HUMAN RESOURCE MANAGEMENT

With this section, we begin an exploration of the four knowledge areas of human resource, communication, risk, and procurement management. The first of these is Human Resource management. *Human Resource (HR) management* is the planning, executing, and controlling of the selection, assignment, and function of human resources—the people and teams that will work to complete the project successfully. Table 3-15 displays HR management processes and their outputs (in italics) by process group.

Prepare Human Resource Plan

The first step the Project Manager undertakes in this knowledge area is to prepare the human resource plan during the planning process. A *Human Resource (HR) plan* is a definition of how the Project Manager expects to acquire and assemble project staff. The Project Manager prepares the HR plan, revising, and updating it throughout the project to reflect changing requirements.

The starting point for the HR plan is the resource assignments identified in the project schedule. These assignments also represent project staffing requirements to complete each work package. The assignments provide the Project Manager with the information necessary to identify the:

- Quantity of project resources by expertise
- Availability of the resources internally or whether the project must contract externally
- Timing of resource work start and end dates on the project

Large and complex projects may benefit from using a resource loading histogram to help prepare the HR plan. As mentioned earlier in this chapter in the time management section, one risk, in terms of scheduling, is misaligning the schedule in terms of task completion within a given period of the project and the people, or teams available to the project during that same period. A *resource loading histogram* is a bar chart displaying the number of project resources according to the project schedule. The height of each bar indicates the number of resources required at a particular point in time. Figure 3-11 is an example of a resource loading histogram.

The Project Manager also assembles the project resource requirements into a project organization chart. This identifies reporting relationships to clarify resource requirements

Initiating	Planning	Executing	Controlling	Closing
	Prepare human resources plan	Develop project team	Manage project team	
	Human resources plan	*Project team performance assessment*	*Organizational process asset update*	
	Acquire project team resources		*Performance report*	
	Resource assignment		*Change request (CR)*	
			Project document update	

TABLE 3-15 HR Management Knowledge Area by Process Group

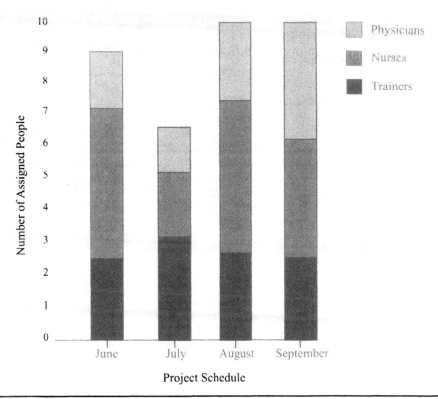

FIGURE 3-11   Resource loading histogram.

and their project roles and responsibilities, particularly in large projects involving many participants. Figure 3-12 displays a typical EHR project organization chart.

Below is a description of each principal role in the project organization. Experience has shown that for HIT projects, especially complicated ones such as the EHR, each of these entities in the organization chart is a critical and necessary component:

- *Executive Sponsor*—The *executive sponsor* is the individual with primary responsibility for achieving the project's objectives and motivating project participants through leadership. Examples of executive sponsor role requirements include:
  - *Integrity*—Adheres to commitment of what it takes to complete the project successfully
  - *Commitment*—Obligates the HDO to the project
  - *Mobilization*—Encourages HDO staff to achieve the project objectives
  - *Role Model*—Serves as an example of the future state by conducting frequent group and one-on-one meetings to demonstrate how stakeholders can achieve project success
  - *Resource*—Provides project resources (i.e., budget and personnel)
  - *Governance*—Makes decisions on key issues, scope, schedule, cost, conflicts, and so on

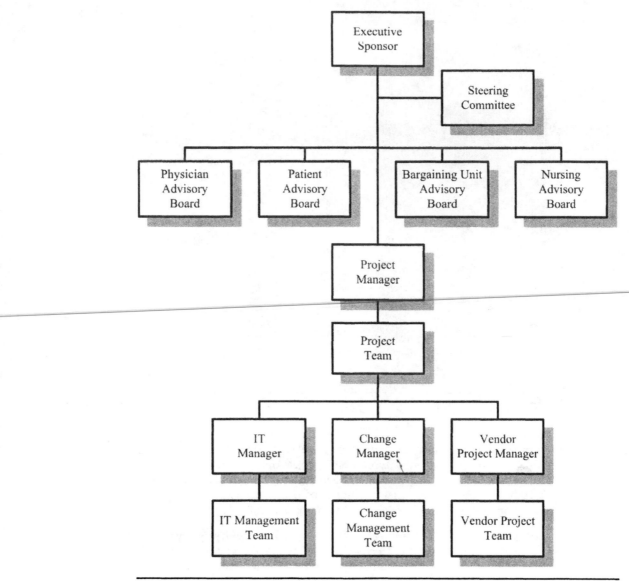

FIGURE 3-12   EHR project organization chart.

- *Steering Committee*—The *steering committee* is responsible for guiding or *steering* the project to successful completion. It is responsible for supporting, reviewing, and approving all project activities (e.g., resolving escalated issues, approving change requests, amending the contract, and accepting deliverables). In addition to the executive sponsor, an HDO EHR project steering committee membership often includes the Chief Medical Officer (CMO), Chief Nursing Officer (CNO), Chief Financial Officer, Chief Information Officer, and Chief Counsel.

- *Advisory Committees*—*Advisory Committees* are groups of key individuals appointed to make project recommendations on behalf of various stakeholder groups (e.g., physicians, nurses, patients, and bargaining units). These committees meet regularly with the executive sponsor to provide input on specific policy, procedural, and technical changes due to the EHR implementation.

- *Project Manager*—The *Project Manager* is the individual with primary responsibility for successful project completion. The steering committee may also appoint a deputy Project Manager to support the Project Manager and serve as a backup resource. The Project Manager is responsible for individual implementation teams, whose membership includes, at a minimum, project, IT, and change management resources.

- *Change Manager*—The *Change Manager* is the individual responsible for initiating, planning, executing, and controlling change management activities (e.g., realization, sponsorship, and transformation), as discussed in Chapter 5.

- *Vendor Project Manager*—The *Vendor Project Manager* is the vendor employee assigned to the HDO with primary responsibility for successful implementation of the vendor product, including, for example, orchestrating all vendor resources, their availability and timing, installing the system, and ensuring the vendor sustains system support after go-live according to the contract.

- *IT Manager*—The *IT Manager* is a senior HDO IT representative who has primary responsibility for successful delivery of technology, including infrastructure, security, and conversion.

Table 3-16 is an example of how the organization may allocate responsibilities by project roles for significant project activity groups to the individuals described in the list above.

Each project role has one individual with primary responsibility and one or more parties providing support. Organizations do not function well when two parties share the same responsibility. *Responsibility* is about having control over a particular role without having to seek authorization from another party. Sharing responsibility requires ongoing clarification about which party has authority over a role. This contradicts the definition of responsibility. Clarification also does not always happen, particularly in a fast-paced project environment, causing conflict between parties that share primary responsibility. Ultimately, this wastes precious time, fosters unnecessary conflict, and causes confusion among the Project Team membership.

Acquire Project Team Resources

After completing the HR plan, the Project Manager then acquires Project Team resources during the executing process. The output of this process is the Project Team resource assignments. A *resource assignment* is the designation of specific project tasks to a specific individual. This requires meeting with key project stakeholders, such as the CIO, the CMO, or the CNO, and identifying the candidates best suited for project assignments. Once identified, the Project Manager then negotiates with these people and with their supervisors. These negotiations require executive sponsor commitment. It is common that supervisors may be reluctant to free up the time of their best staff to work on the project and hence may be resistant to giving up hours to the Project Manager. This is where the support from the executive sponsor is invaluable.

Role	Responsibility*					
	Executive Sponsor	Steering Committee	HDO Project Manager	Vendor Project Manager	Change Manager	IT Manager
PROJECT MANAGEMENT						
Integration						
Feasibility study and business case	P					
Project charter	S	S	P			
Project management plan			P	S	S	S
Performance report			P	S	S	S
Change request (CR)	S	S	P	S	S	S
Organizational process asset update			P	S	S	S
Project document update			P	S	S	S
Deliverable		S	S	P	S	
Scope						
Scope statement	S	S	P			
Work Breakdown Structure (WBS)			P	S	S	S
WBS dictionary			P	S	S	S
Work packages			P	S	S	S
Time						
Task list			P	S	S	S
Task sequence			P	S	S	S
Task resource estimate	S	S	P	S	S	S
Task duration estimate			P	S	S	S
Schedule	S	S	P	S	S	S
Cost						
Cost estimate	S	S	P	S	S	S
Project budget	S	S	P	S	S	S

TABLE 3-16   EHR Project Roles and Responsibilities

Role	Responsibility*					
	Executive Sponsor	Steering Committee	HDO Project Manager	Vendor Project Manager	Change Manager	IT Manager
Quality						
Quality management plan		S	P	S	S	S
Human Resources (HR)						
Human resources plan	S	S	P	S	S	S
Resource assignments	S	S	P	S	S	S
Project team performance assessments		S	P	S	S	S
Communications						
Project roster		S	P	S	S	S
Communications plan	S	S	P	S	S	D
Risk						
Risk management plan	S	S	P	S	S	S
Risk register	S	S	P	S	S	S
Risk register update	S	S	P	S	S	S
Risk response plan	S	S	P	S	S	S
Procurement						
Procurement plan	S	S	P			
Solicitation	S	S	P			S
Selected vendor	S	S	P		S	S
Deliverable Completion Confirmation (DCC)	S	S	P	S		
IT MANAGEMENT						
User requirements						
User requirements management plan		S	P		S	
High-level user requirements		S	P			
Detailed user requirements			P			

TABLE 3-16   EHR Project Roles and Responsibilities (*Continued*)

Role	Responsibility*					
	Executive Sponsor	Steering Committee	HDO Project Manager	Vendor Project Manager	Change Manager	IT Manager
Infrastructure						
High-level technology requirements			S			P
Existing technology architecture diagram			S			P
Infrastructure management plan		S	S			P
Detailed technology requirements		S	S			P
Facility modification plan		S	S	S	S	P
System installation plan			S	S	S	P
Equipment order confirmation	S		S	S		P
Site readiness confirmation			S	P		S
Hardware readiness confirmation			S	P		S
Application readiness confirmation			S	P		S
Security						
Security plan	S	S	P	S	S	S
Security requirements			P	S		S
Security roles			P	S	S	S
Test cases			P			S
Security audit results	S	S		S		P

TABLE 3-16 EHR Project Roles and Responsibilities (*Continued*)

Role	Executive Sponsor	Steering Committee	HDO Project Manager	Vendor Project Manager	Change Manager	IT Manager
				Responsibility*		
Conversion						
Conversion plan			P	S		S
Data conversion map			S	S		P
Data cleansing confirmation			S	S		P
Conversion solution confirmation			S	S		P
Conversion confirmation	S		S	S		P
Interface						
Interface plan			P	S		S
Interface data map			S	S		P
Interface solution confirmation			S	S		P
Interface confirmation			S	S		P
Software configuration						
Software configuration plan		S	P	S	S	S
Configuration requirements			P	S	S	S
Test cases			P		S	S
Workflow						
Workflow management plan			P		S	S
Workflow requirements			P		S	S
Workflow changes			P		S	S
Test						
Test plan			P	S	S	S
Test cases			P		S	S
Test data			S	S		P

TABLE 3-16   EHR Project Roles and Responsibilities (*Continued*)

Role	Responsibility [*]					
	Executive Sponsor	**Steering Committee**	**HDO Project Manager**	**Vendor Project Manager**	**Change Manager**	**IT Manager**
Test						
Training completion confirmation			P			
Test results		S	P	S		S
Regression test cases			P	S		S
Cutover						
Cutover plan	S	S	P	S	S	S
Training completion confirmation			P		S	S
Successful cutover confirmation	S	S	P	S	S	S
Support						
Support plan		S	S	S	S	P
Support requirements			S	S		P
Support roles and responsibilities matrix			S	S		P
Training completion confirmation			S			P
Support tickets			S			P
CHANGE MANAGEMENT						
Realization						
Objectives	S	P	S		S	S
Measurable outcomes	S	P	S		S	S
Outcome delivery schedule		S	P	S	S	
Objectives responsibility list	S	P	S		S	
Achievement of an objective	S	P	S		S	S
Dashboard report	S	S	P		S	S

TABLE 3-16   EHR Project Roles and Responsibilities (*Continued*)

Role	Responsibility*					
	Executive Sponsor	Steering Committee	HDO Project Manager	Vendor Project Manager	Change Manager	IT Manager
Sponsorship						
Executive sponsor	S	P	S		S	S
Executive sponsorship assessment results	S	P	S		S	
Transformation						
Change management team	S	S	S		P	S
Stakeholder map	S	S	S		P	S
Transformation tasks	S		S		P	S
Transformation task completion			S		P	S
Training						
Training needs			S	S	P	S
Training plan			S	S	P	S
Training documentation			S	S	P	S
Training completion confirmation			S		P	S
Optimization						
Optimization management plan	S	S	S		P	S
Optimization completion confirmation	S	S	S		P	S

*Responsibility: P—Primary responsible party, S—Supports the primary party

TABLE 3-16   EHR Project Roles and Responsibilities (*Continued*)

We assembled the team in kind of a handpicked way. We knew that we had certain individuals that we thought would be great serving on the Project Team. However, we also had other individuals that self-selected. They said, you know what, I'm interested in IT and its relationship to health care and I want to contribute. It was a combination of leadership; handpicking folks that they trusted and knew would do a good job, but also with folks from within the trenches that self-selected.

—Dan Nigrin, MD, MS, CIO, Children's Hospital Boston

The Sponsor supports the Project Manager by:

- Committing to do this project with the best staff available to achieve associated objectives
- Announcing that the organization will backfill
- Compensating individuals at the same rate for their project time as their current assignment
- Supporting advancement of these assigned individuals based on their project participation even though they are not available to perform their normal job duties

In some instances, the Project Manager must also contract with outside resources either because the HDO does not have enough staff or the required expertise. This assumes the Project Manager will work with human resources, contracting, and so on, to acquire these resources.

We had an individual on our team, who was with IT, but he had 15 years of human resources experience. We made him our liaison to Rancho's Human Resources group. This may have been the best use of an individual on the project because he just kept us out of trouble completely. Our HR requests were taken care of, if we had a problem they were handled. HR became something that took very little of my time, because this individual was on top of it. That was a gift.

If we were going to do this, we needed to have this project staffed appropriately so that we could succeed. We got agreement. We had people who were dedicated to the project. They had no other duties except the project. They were from every area and they were at least two deep. We had clinical people assigned to the project, which was essential. A few of them, some of the nurses, the lab person, and physical therapist involved, had other duties, but they had to carve out a certain amount of hours per week to work on the project. However, we had the core Project Team that was dedicated. They had no other duties and they were separate from the IT organization at the hospital. I don't think there's any substitute for having enough people with the right skills dedicated to the effort.

The CEO, CIO, and Project Manager were long-term employees who knew what it would take to succeed. We also had a letter from the director stating that we had authorization to request any employee to fill project positions. We had a charter to go out and get the best and brightest.

—Robert Greenless, PhD, CIO–RLANRC

Develop Project Team

The Project Manager is responsible for developing acquired resources into a Project Team as well as assessing and improving the team performance during the executing process. Developing strong and effective teams is an art unto itself. Below are several key success factors the Project Manager should consider in this activity.

Building the Team

Many individuals assigned to a project or project resources may not have had previous experience working together. While not necessarily possible with virtual teams, we strongly favor preparing a project office to co-locate project participants. This helps to create a team-building environment that improves project communications and resolves project issues quickly.

In virtual teams, it is important to bring the team together for periodic meetings and engage them in face-to-face activities. In other instances, virtual team members temporarily swap work locations, which helps build appreciation for different work environments. For example, when implementing an EHR in multiple ambulatory settings, it helps to temporarily switch an outpatient pharmacist assigned to the project with a project pharmacist assigned to a different outpatient facility. This approach helps two individuals, while working virtually, gain an appreciation of each other and their respective work environments.

Minimizing Conflicts Between Permanent Job and Temporary Project Work Assignments

Project resources often find conflicts between their permanent job and temporary project assignments. This is particularly difficult for project resources that split their time between their permanent job and project assignments. These participants must balance their workload. While they must take initiative to communicate to the Project Manager about possible work conflicts, they are more familiar with their HDO supervisor regarding resolution of workload issues. Project resources also return to their permanent work after completing their temporary project assignments whether assigned full-time to the project, or splitting time between their permanent job and a temporary project assignment. This makes it difficult to refuse requests related to their permanent work. The Project Manager must monitor project resources and quickly resolve these conflicts. If the Project Manager has a committed executive sponsor, the Project Manager should feel comfortable working with a supervisor to resolve these workload issues and escalating these issues for prompt resolution if required.

Establishing Project Reporting Relationships

The project organization reporting relationships differ from those found in the HDO. While project reporting relationships may sometimes be consistent with the HDO, project participants may find they are reporting to a peer or a member of the project instead of their job supervisor. The Project Manager must recognize this represents a potential conflict and establish a clear understanding of project roles and responsibilities and reporting relationship described above. This coupled with engaging these individuals in task and deliverable definition helps these resources feel valued and motivated to prepare quality project deliverables instead of disputing project reporting relationships.

Training Project Resources

Many project resources participate because they are Subject Matter Experts. A *Subject Matter Expert (SME)* is an individual with specialized knowledge about how to perform certain tasks. A SME may, for example, be a Nurse Supervisor who created a patient assessment form. While key to an EHR project for nursing documentation, this SME may not have any experience defining user requirements. The Project Manager is responsible for introducing SMEs to the project and instructing them on how to contribute valued expertise.

> *We had one team lead that illustrates this point. She was a very strong knowledgeable player, very confident, smart, and had rock solid experience. She was unafraid to talk to anybody about anything. That served us well. She would talk to anybody from the Medical Director to a Medical Secretary to confirm her understanding of the process. She had that very broad knowledge of the whole process at Rancho. Together with her knowledge, she assembled a team under her that had a very detailed understanding of every specific piece in the process.*
>
> —Robert Greenless, PhD, CIO–RLANRC

Apart from and in addition to team development, the Project Manager is responsible for team performance assessments. A *Project Team performance assessment* is a gauge of team effectiveness. Assessment indicators may include:

- Turnover
- Timeliness of project tasks and deliverables
- Completion of project tasks and deliverables within scope, cost, and quality baseline standards

Manage Project Team

The Project Manager directs the Project Team during the controlling process. Project team management involves assigning project tasks, assessing ongoing and completed work against predefined baseline scope, schedule, cost and quality, and correcting variances.

The Project Manager monitors HR using the control process described in integration management contrary to the *PMBOK® Guide* (Fourth Edition). For example, a client asked us to help improve their project's success. One key problem we found was that they lacked a clear identification of project roles and responsibilities. Although the Project Manager made many very good decisions about task definition, resource assignments, and schedule requirements, the project was significantly behind schedule. We met with several project participants including the Project Manager. Many of them indicated that staff assignments and other decisions made by the Project Manager, who was on loan to the project, were routinely reviewed and overruled by his administrative supervisor, who had no project role. We met to review this role and responsibility conflict with the executive sponsor, who later directed the supervisor to stop second-guessing his subordinate's project work. This corrected the problem without a CR or a document update.

Managing team performance is an especially challenging project management issue, which requires special attention, because it involves conflict management. This involves applying a specific conflict-management style. A *conflict-management style* is a resolution method used to end differences between two or more people. There are many different conflict management styles. Jay Hall's *Conflict Management Survey: A Survey of One's Characteristic Reaction to and Handling of Conflict Between Himself and Others*,[1] includes the following:

- *Win/Lose*—Controlling or using power to win your position instead of resolving the conflict
- *Win/Yield (Lose)*—Neglecting your own position in the conflict to accommodate the other person's point of view

- *Win/Leave (Lose)*—Avoiding the conflict resolution
- *Win/Win*—Collaborating with the other person to find a solution that *fully* resolves the conflict to both parties' satisfaction
- *Mini Win/Mini Lose*—Compromising or seeking a middle ground, which *partially* satisfies both parties, but fails to *fully* resolve the conflict

The win/win conflict management style is clearly the best option and should be sought whenever possible. It requires collaborating to completely resolve the issue to the satisfaction of everyone involved. This required collaboration includes the following steps:

- Working together instead of competing, avoiding, compromising, or accommodating
- Investigating and identifying the underlying concern or root cause of the conflict from each party's perspective
- Learning about each party and the insights gained while investigating the underlying root cause
- Constructing a solution to the conflict that completely resolves all root cause conditions
- Monitoring the solution to confirm it is working and adjusting it on an ongoing basis to ensure that it does work

COMMUNICATION MANAGEMENT

Communications management is planning, executing, and controlling project information exchange required to ensure project success. Table 3-17 displays communications management processes and their outputs (in italics) by process group.

We could argue that communications management is one of the most crucial project management knowledge areas. It is so important that we treat it differently than *PMBOK*. We differentiate between communication activities specific to project management needs and communications required to change human behavior. We address the former in this section and the latter in Chapter 5. The general steps in project communications management include preparing a communications plan, identifying the key project participants who require information, distributing this information and reporting to stakeholder.

Identify Key Project Participants

The Project Manager identifies key project participants during the planning process. The output of this process is a project roster. A *project roster* is a directory of principal individuals involved in any aspect of the project. A roster can include key individuals—the Project Sponsor, steering committee members, and the Project Team members. The purpose for creating the project roster is twofold: First, to ensure you have not forgotten any key stakeholders, and second, to inform the next step in this knowledge area—developing the project communications plan.

Plan Communications

The Project Manager prepares a communications plan during the planning process. A *communications plan* is an organized identification of what information to collect throughout the project, who receives this information, the communications channel used with each participant or category of participant, and when to distribute it. A communications plan includes the following:

- *Communications Objective*—Results achieved by the communications that help increase stakeholder:
  - Awareness about completing project tasks and deliverables.
  - Confidence in project performance.
  - Feedback on project issues and risks.

Initiating	Planning	Executing	Controlling	Closing
	Identify key project participants *Project roster* Plan communications *Communications plan*	Distribute information *Organizational process asset update*	Report performance *Organizational process asset update* *Performance report* *Change request (CR)* *Project document update*	

TABLE 3-17   Communications Management Knowledge Area by Process Group

- *Audience*—The communications recipient (e.g., the steering committee, Project Team, IT Team, or other entities), identified in the project organization.

- *Key Message*—A communications topic or subject, such as a project status. The message detail differs by audience based on their position and concerns at specific times during the project. For example, the steering committee receives a monthly summary of the project status. In contrast, the Project Team receives a weekly detailed description of project status.

- *Approach*—Communication medium by audience, including:

  - *Face-to-Face*—Briefings, workshops, presentations, and meetings.

  - *Paper*—Reports and memoranda.

  - *Electronic*—Email, web sites, blogs, wikis, and virtual meetings.

- *Resources*—Tools (e.g., video projector, conference room, project blog) used to distribute and maintain information.

- *Feedback*—A mechanism to receive input from stakeholders about their concerns with the communications effectiveness.

- *Timing*—Schedule to distribute information. For example, Project Manager may provide the project schedule at the monthly steering committee meetings.

Distribute Information

The Project Manager distributes information on the project during the executing process. Within project communications management are two broad categories of communications discussed sequentially. The first is written communications, in essence the set of documents or online tools created to inform each project stakeholder about the project status. The second category includes verbal communication—typically required meetings conducted throughout the project.

Experienced Project Managers suggest it is impossible to over-communicate with HDO staff as the project unfolds, using as many channels as possible and as directly as possible.

> *I think walking the floor is very helpful; to get out there, be visible, see with my own eyes what's going on and where this project is going firsthand. This is part of communications with the stakeholders so that neither of you have any surprises. That served us extremely well.*
> —Robert Greenless, PhD, CIO–RLANRC

Methods of collecting, distributing, and maintaining information include the following:

- *Issues Tracking Database*—An *issue* is a project question that requires a project management response. An *issues tracking database* is a log of project questions and their answers. The Project Team identifies, prioritizes, assigns, schedules, tracks, escalates, and responds to issues and stores them in a readily accessible project database. Unresolved issues have an *open* status; resolved issues have a *closed* status. The Project Manager facilitates Project Team responses to issues during Project Team meetings, or escalates them to the executive sponsor for a response. When the Project Team cannot respond to an urgent issue, the Project

Manager attempts to respond to the issue directly, or escalates the issue to the executive sponsor if required

- *Project Library*—A project involves creating, maintaining, and distributing a variety of important documents. A *project library* is a location for storing, organizing, and controlling key documents produced or used by the project. Table 3-18 provides a list of example documents stored in a project library, their update frequency, input due date, distribution, and the party responsible for their preparation.

Communications management relies on a widely accessible collaboration mechanism to track issues and share reports/documents, such as SharePoint®, Google Docs™, a project web site, blog, wiki, and so on. The discussion above refers to a project library

Document	Update Frequency	Input Due Date	Distribution	Responsibility
Project Objectives*	As Needed		Project Steering Committee and Team	Project Executive Sponsor
Measurable Outcomes*	As Needed		Project Steering Committee and Team	Project Executive Sponsor
Project Charter	As Needed		Project Steering Committee and Team	Project Executive Sponsor
Project Management Plan	As Needed		Project Team	Project Manager
Deliverables		Per the Project Schedule	Project Steering Committee and Team	Project Executive Sponsor and Manager
CRs	Monthly or As Needed	Two days before meeting	Steering Committee and Project Team	Project Executive Sponsor and Manager
Contract Amendments	As Needed		Steering Committee	Project Executive Sponsor and Manager
Schedule	Weekly	Two days before meeting	Project Steering Committee and Team	Project Manager
Budget	Monthly	Two days before meeting	Project Steering Committee and Team	Project Manager
QA Report		Two days before meeting	Project Steering Committee and Team	Project Manager
Issues*	As Needed		Project Steering Committee and Team	Project Steering Committee and Team

TABLE 3-18   Project Library

Document	Update Frequency	Input Due Date	Distribution	Responsibility
Risks	Weekly	Two days before meeting	Project Steering Committee and Team	Project Manager
Project Team Performance reports	Weekly	Two days before meeting	Project Team	Project Manager
Steering Committee Performance reports	Monthly	Three days before meeting	Steering Committee	Project Manager
Closeout Report	At project completion		Project Steering Committee and Team	Project Manager
Requirements*	As Needed		Project Team	Project Manager
Stakeholder Map	As Needed		Project Steering Committee	Change Manager
Training Plan	As Needed		Project Team	Change Manager
Infrastructure Plan	As Needed		Project Team	IT Manager
Conversion Plan	As Needed		Project Team	Project Manager
Configuration Plan	As Needed		Project Team	Project Manager
Workflow Plan	As Needed		Project Team	Project Manager
Test Plan	As Needed		Project Team	Project Manager
Cutover Plan	As Needed		Project Team	Project Manager
Support Plan	As Needed		Project Steering Committee and Team	IT Manager

* Maintained in the project library as updated data accessible to the Project Team, rather than an uploaded reference document. The Project Manager distributes this information outside the team if needed.

TABLE 3-18   Project Library (*Continued*)

and issues tracking database instead of referencing a specific product or tool; however, all projects require this type of collaboration mechanism.

Report Performance

The Project Manager reports project performance during the controlling process. The output is a performance report. A *performance report* is a description of the results or the status of a situation at a certain point in time. As an example, the Project Manager presents performance reports in various meetings to explain project status and to enlist help to resolve adverse conditions like scope changes, schedule delays, cost overruns, risks, issues, and so on. Table 3-19 includes a list of meetings, their purpose, frequency, and participants.

Meeting	Purpose	Frequency	Participants
Steering Committee	Performance reporting	Monthly—Second Thursday of each month	Project Executive Sponsor and Manager
Executive Sponsor Meeting	Performance reporting and planning	Weekly—Every Friday	Executive Sponsor and HDO and Vendor Project Managers
Project Team Status Meetings	Performance reporting	Weekly—Every Friday	Project Team
Ad Hoc Team Meetings	To Be Determined (TBD)	TBD	TBD

TABLE 3-19   Project Status Meetings

The nature of these meetings and their participants are as follows:

- *Steering Committee Meetings*—Steering committee meetings occur monthly, with the exception of special meetings (e.g., approval of key deliverables, authorization to go-live). These meetings address:
  - Project performance comparing current and previous scope, schedule, and budget
  - Accomplishments during the current period
  - Planned accomplishments for the next period
  - Issues requiring management attention
  - Risks register review

  The membership participates in all meetings. Steering committee participants access the project library to review the performance report and prepare for their monthly meeting.

- *Executive Sponsor Meetings*—The executive sponsor and HDO Project Manager meet weekly to review project accomplishments, issues, and risks, and to discuss planned project activities. The project performance report is a more detailed weekly description of the monthly report provided to the steering committee. They meet for an hour and include the Vendor Project Manager for an additional hour at the end of the meeting.

  This meeting resolves open issues, identifies new issues, and sets expectations about what the project will accomplish during the next reporting period (e.g., continued Project Team configuration and workflow activities).

- *Project Team Status Meetings*—Project Team Status Meetings occur weekly. These meetings focus on the most detailed version of project activities identified in the project schedule, issues tracking database, and risk register. The membership participates in all meetings. Project Team participants access the project library to review the performance report and prepare for their weekly meeting. Team meetings typically involve reporting from each participant on the status of current tasks in the schedule and their associated issues and risks. For example, the Change Manager reports on the work the team is currently performing, such as preparation of a training plan, FAQs, and presentation to department heads. The meeting participants respond with questions and concerns regarding the team's report and how to resolve the issues.

- *Ad Hoc Committee Meetings*—Periodically, the Project Manager creates Ad Hoc Committees for a specific purpose and limited time. The Project Manager identifies participants, the meetings, and their schedules, and associated documents, as required.

The Project Manager monitors communications using the control process described in integration management. For example, we encounter many situations where we ask providers for their issues tracking log and they respond with, *which one do you want?* Many EHR and other HIT projects maintain multiple issue logs, which may include a technical log, non-technical log, vendor log, and customer log. We recommend maintaining a single log with various categories, such as by knowledge area. Multiple issue logs make it difficult to prioritize, assign, track, and resolve issues. For example, a vendor issue may have a customer implication that is lost in separate customer and vendor issue logs. A CR updating the communications plan greatly improves issue resolution throughout a project.

RISK MANAGEMENT

Risk management is planning and controlling how the project identifies and responds to potential threats to successful project completion. Every project faces a range of risks. HIT projects even more so given the complexity and the degree of organizational and personal change they entail. Risks come in myriad forms and potentially expand scope, extend the schedule, increase costs, and/or reduce quality. The major tasks the Project Manager oversees in risk management include developing the plan for managing risk (which requires identification of risks and possible responses to those risks) and then monitoring the effectiveness of these responses. Table 3-20 displays risk management processes and their outputs (in italics) by process group.

Prepare Risk Management Plan

The Project Manager prepares a risk management plan during the planning process. A *risk management plan* is a description of how the Project Team will identify, assess, and respond to potential problems threatening successful project completion. This plan includes the following:

- *Risk Management Method*—Defines the risk management approach used by the project. This includes whether the project will use quantitative, qualitative, or both methods to assess risks.

- *Risk Management Schedule*—While project resources may identify and document risks as part of their day-to-day activities, successful risk management requires setting aside a formal time to focus on project risks. With a regular schedule, Project Teams proactively define risks and increase the likelihood of a favorable risk response instead of a reactive *putting out fires* approach that is unplanned and likely to cause additional risks. This ensures that the Project Team:

Initiating	Planning	Executing	Controlling	Closing
	Prepare risk management plan *Risk management plan* Identify risks *Risk register* Perform quantitative risk analysis *Risk register update* Perform qualitative risk analysis *Risk register update* Plan risk response *Risk response plan*		Monitor and control risk *Organizational process asset update* *Performance report* *Change request (CR)* *Project document update*	

TABLE 3-20   Risk Management Knowledge Area by Process Group

- Identifies new risks
- Develops responses to new risks
- Monitors known risks
- Manages responses to known risks

We suggest devoting time during every weekly Project Team meeting as a workshop on risk management. This workshop provides time for reviewing the status of each identified risk and the effectiveness of the response.

- *Risk Categories*—Some key project areas are more likely to involve risks. For example, all projects have scope, schedule, and cost risks. From a technical standpoint, conversions and interfaces often have significant risks. EHR projects include workflow change, physician adoption, and training risks. Identifying these categories in the risk management plan provides a framework for risk identification and response.

Identify Risks

The Project Manager identifies risks and maintains them in a risk register during the planning process. It is important to note that this activity should begin early in project planning. A Project Manager might ask *How do you know the risk early in a project?* This is where experience in HIT project management is especially valuable as there are several well-known clinical system project risks. A classic example is significant and even dramatic clinician resistance to adopting HIT, such as physician documentation. Any HDO implementing an EHR should predict well in advance that some level of user resistance is likely and develop a response to this risk.

The *risk register* is a log of identified risks and their rank, their severity and probability of occurrence, impact, response, and party responsible for that response. Table 3-21 displays a portion of a project risk register.

An HDO must identify risks before it can document them in the risk register and respond to them. An HDO identifies risks using many of the previously identified analysis methods (e.g., five whys, flowcharts, DMIAC, expert opinion, and review of the literature). Project participants use these analysis methods to identify risks and their root cause(s). For example, one cause of unsuccessful physician adoption may be the lack of sufficient one-on-one physician coaches, instead of the training materials.

Once the Project Team completes the baseline risk register, the next steps include risk quantitative and qualitative analyses and updating the risk register to reflect the outcome of these two analyses.

Perform Quantitative Risk Analysis

The Project Manager performs quantitative risk analysis during the planning process. *Quantitative risk analysis* is an assessment of vulnerability based on probability, severity, impact, and rank using objective, statistical data. This method ideally uses precise analytical data gathering and interpretation on how to respond to a risk. The output of performing quantitative risk analysis is a risk register update. A *risk register update* is a change to a listed risk.

A sophisticated organization may maintain a database of project history, including statistics on project scope, schedule, budget and quality compliance by project type and

Risk/Rank	Probability*	Severity*	Impact	Response	Responsibility
Change in HDO administration may cause steering committee turnover.	2	2	Quality	Include multiple senior executives on the steering committee to diminish impact of turnover.	Executive Sponsor
Change in project requirements may occur due to timing of compliance with HDO re-organization.	2	2	Quality	Obtain new administration input on project plans.	Executive Sponsor
Change in administration may alter project steering committee membership familiarity with the project.	1	2	Quality	Re-introduce project charter and obtain steering committee commitment including member signatures.	Steering committee

*Risks ranked on a numeric scoring of probability plus severity, where Low = 1 point, Medium = 2 points, High = 3 points. For example, a risk with low probability and severity receives 2 points, whereas a risk with low severity and high probability receives 4 points.

TABLE 3-21   Project Risk Register

complexity. A Project Manager may use this database to statistically assess risks for a new project based on its similarity to these historical projects.

Perform Qualitative Risk Analysis

The Project Manager performs qualitative risk analysis during the planning process. *Qualitative risk analysis* is an assessment of vulnerability based on probability, severity, impact, and rank using subjective information. The Project Team and other resources subjectively decide how to respond to project threats. The output of performing qualitative risk analysis is a risk register update.

The Project Team completes the risk register, as highlighted in Table 3-21 above, with the following information:

- *Risk*—Description of the potential adverse event
- *Probability*—Subjective likelihood of risk occurrence on a scale of 1 to 3, where 1 is low, 2 is medium, and 3 is high probability. We recommend using a simple scale to avoid wasting time on unnecessary refinements.
- *Severity*—Criticality of the risk, again on a scale of 1 to 3
- *Impact*—Affected project area (e.g., scope, schedule, cost, and/or quality)

- *Response*—What the HDO plans to do to address the threat posing or causing the risk
- *Responsibility*—The individual assigned to respond to the risk

Finally, the HDO ranks each risk in the register by adding each risk probability to its severity. For example, a risk with medium probability and severity receives four points, whereas a risk with low severity and medium probability receives three points. The risk register organizes the risk list from high to low priority.

The primary purpose of qualitative and quantitative risk analysis is to predict, assess, and respond effectively to project vulnerability. The specific set of analytic methods the Project Manager selects depends on which are most compatible with the HDO and the project. If the HDO and project have the resources to assemble and efficiently conduct precise data analyses, then quantitative analysis may be appropriate. However, many organizations and projects do not have this sophistication. If the Project Manager can assess risks within limited time, budget, and data, using qualitative analysis is less costly and time-consuming than quantitative analysis. While both analysis methods are valid, the Project Manager should use the method that best fits the HDO's resource, expertise, and culture. There is a fallacy in believing that quantitative methods are by definition superior. This is especially disconcerting because we have seen Project Teams spend their precious time conducting sophisticated quantitative risk analyses instead of focusing on preventing project failure.

Plan Risk Response

After the Project Team completes a listing of risks for the project, the next step is to plan how the team will respond to each of these perceived risks. This requires preparation of the risk response plan for identified risks in the risk register. A *risk response plan* is the set of strategies the Project Manager, Project Team, and other project participants may choose to apply, depending on the significance of the risk. The following is an example of the types of identified risk management strategies an organization may use:

- *Accept*—Assume the risk. A project cannot preempt all risks. In some cases, the only option is risk acceptance. For low likelihood or low-impact risk, it may be perfectly reasonable to not attempt to proactively prevent the risk from occurring. The most important point, however, is to actively accept it and manage the project accordingly, instead of ignoring it, not understanding its root cause, and failing to address the project impact.
- *Avoid*—Eliminate the risk. This is effectively the opposite of accepting the risk and is often the rational choice for high-likelihood and high-significance risks. For example, a project conversion could take six months because it requires development of specialized software, testing the software, and conducting the conversion. We know from experience that one-time software development efforts are notoriously error prone and could cause significant conversion errors—meaning active risk avoidance requires a change in the project conversion approach. For example, the Project Manager could hire six people for three months to manually enter and verify the data to avoid the high risk of developing and implementing conversion software.

- *Mitigate*—Reduce the risk to an acceptable threshold. For example, each physician favors a particular learning style. Training physicians to use an EHR should embrace as many different learning styles as possible to facilitate clinician understanding of how to use the new system. Offering EHR training that best fits physicians' learning styles will increase training effectiveness, but it will not eliminate all physician education issues.
- *Transfer*—Shift the risk response and responsibility to a third party. For example, all contract insurance clauses transfer risk, (e.g., auto, professional, general liability). While the project is vulnerable, the insurance covers the cost of risk.

Monitor and Control Risk

With the risk management plan in place and the risk register complete, the Project Team monitors risks with regular frequency, looking for evidence about the effectiveness of each risk response. The output of this process includes the following:

- Organizational process asset updates
- Risk register update based on:
  - Identifying risks and maintaining risk awareness in weekly risk workshops
  - Eliminating risks that are no longer appropriate
  - Reviewing closed risks to determine if reoccurrence is possible
  - Determining whether each responsible party is effectively and in a timely manner executing each assigned risk response
  - Assessing the effectiveness of the responses and making adjustments if they are not effective (e.g., modifying or completely changing the response)
  - Re-ranking risk probability and severity as risks and the project change
  - Reassigning project resources based on risk re-ranking
- CRs when there are deviations from the risk management plan or project management plan
- Project document updates reflecting risk analysis and response modifications

. . . *one of the things I think we've done extremely well is risk mitigation planning. For the revenue cycle project, we knew that the major risk for us was to maintain our A/R days and not impact our A/R days as part of transition. So we put a mitigation plan in place to address that, and we had to work very closely with our billing team and so forth. And when we went live with CPOE and clinical documentation, we knew our biggest risk was the physicians, so how can we get physicians engaged for the potential naysayer out there? We did this mitigation plan on every single group. For the high-volume, high-dollar folks that we needed to pay attention, to get their buy-in from the very beginning. So risk mitigation is extremely critical, and that really comes with proper project management and processes.*

—Florence Chang, MBA, CIO, Multicare

PROCUREMENT MANAGEMENT

Procurement management is planning, executing, controlling, and closing acquisition of goods and services necessary to support the successful project completion. Table 3-22 displays procurement management knowledge area processes and outputs (in italics) by process group.

The procurement knowledge area follows the same general structure as those in all other acquisitions. Specifically, this includes developing a procurement plan, preparing a vendor solicitation, selecting the vendor, and then controlling the vendor activities. Procurement management also includes closing processes or completing vendor contract deliverables, which distinguishes it from many other knowledge areas.

Plan Procurement

The Project Manager prepares a procurement plan during the planning process. A *procurement plan* is a description of what the project needs to purchase, how to obtain these items or resources, and ways to control the selected vendor. Procurement is not limited to physical *things* such as computers or software. Procurement also includes human resources. For example, many HIT projects require many trainers that the HDO may not possess internally. The Project Manager needs to plan how and when to *procure* trainers. Because HDOs routinely contract for staff, we assume we do not have to focus on acquiring human resources. Instead, we focus on procurement of a clinical system, such as an EHR or CPOE.

In this HIT area, project management does address some unique issues. First, as discussed earlier in this chapter, HDOs complete the feasibility analysis and business case to support the decision of whether to build a new system in-house or to buy an integrated BOB or COTS system.

Second, because we previously addressed completing a feasibility analysis and business case, we do not address preparing and issuing a Request for Information (RFI) and evaluating vendor responses. An *RFI* is a planning solicitation to obtain information about options without contractually committing to select and acquire a product from a specific vendor. Like a feasibility analysis and business case, the intent of an RFI is confirming the validity of available choices and identifying a preferred option, not selecting a specific vendor representing that option.

Initiating	Planning	Executing	Controlling	Closing
	Plan procurement	Select vendor	Administer procurement	Perform final acceptance
	Procurement plan	*Selected vendor*	*Organizational process asset update*	*Organizational process asset update*
	Prepare solicitation		*Deliverable completion certificate (DCC)*	*Deliverable completion certificate (DCC)*
	Solicitation		*Performance report*	
			Change request (CR)	
			Project document update	

Table 3-22 Procurement Management Knowledge Area by Process Group

A *procurement plan* is a description of everything the organization needs to purchase over the course of the project, how to secure the items, and when the acquisitions occur. Typically, this includes the following procurement steps:

- HDO prepares a solicitation including user requirements and evaluation criteria
- Vendors respond to the solicitation
- Evaluators assess vendor responses based on the evaluation criteria and select two to three finalists
- Finalists demonstrate their EHR to HDO evaluators, who select two options
- Evaluators conduct site visits
- Evaluators conduct reference checks
- Evaluators recommend a vendor and a fallback option
- Negotiators, including vendor and HDO representatives, negotiate a contract

Two ways to sequence these procurements steps are conventional acquisition and rapid acquisition. Both are described below.

1. *Conventional Acquisition.* The traditional approach to acquisition involves preparing a solicitation that lists all user, technology, cost, and administrative requirements. The user requirements include line items (e.g., technical and cost requirements, scripts, or a combination of both). A script is a short vignette that defines what a system user does in a clinical setting. This script addresses any associated manual or non-system activities that the user must perform. The HDO prepares the solicitation. Vendors respond to it like a survey, indicating their level of support for all identified requirements. Evaluators then assess vendors to select the most viable option, including assessing responses to scripts, technical requirements, and costs. They then conduct demonstrations, site visits, and reference checks, and select the best solution.

2. *Rapid Acquisition.* An alternative to the traditional model is the rapid acquisition model. A rapid acquisition resolves a typical challenge with the traditional model. The rapid acquisition model streamlines the procurement process by first focusing the solicitation on scripted user requirement demonstrations instead of line-item requirements. Vendors initially respond by demonstrating their system's support for the scripts for the HDO's evaluators. The evaluators then select finalists, who subsequently respond to technology, cost, and administrative line-item requirements. This approach is effective because the scripted user requirements drive the procurement. To achieve its objectives, an HDO must implement an EHR that meets these needs. It does not select the cheapest solution and/or the system that supports its technical requirements, but fails to meet its EHR requirements. This approach is *rapid* because it saves time and money—only qualified vendors respond to technology, cost, and administrative line-item requirements and the HDO evaluates proposals from only those vendors. Figure 3-13 compares conventional and rapid procurements graphically.

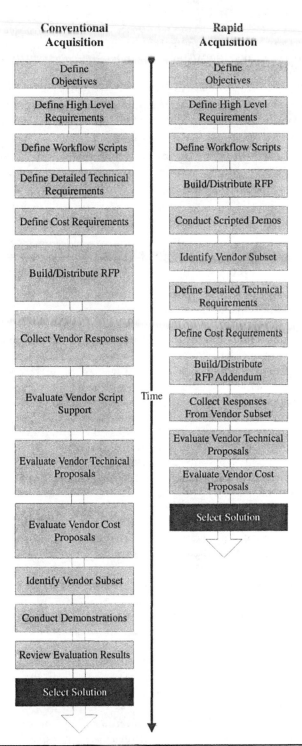

FIGURE 3-13   Conventional and rapid acquisition comparison.

Regardless of which procurement process the HDO chooses to use, the next step is to identify the roles and responsibilities of those participating in the procurement. Typically, these participants include the following:

- *Project Manager*—Coordinates the entire procurement process
- *Project Team*—Prepares user requirements, evaluation criteria, and participates in vendor response evaluations, demonstrations, reference checks, and site visits
- *IT Manager*—Prepares technical requirements, associated evaluation criteria, and the evaluation of vendor technical responses and demonstrations
- *Legal Counsel*—Prepares a contract included in the solicitation document, evaluates each qualified vendor's response to the contract, and negotiates an agreement with the selected vendor
- *Purchasing Department*—Provides the materials management policy requirements for the solicitation, and monitors the procurement process to ensure HDO and vendor compliance with the policy requirements
- *Vendors*—Prepare a solicitation response, and if selected, participate in demonstrations and contract negotiations

Of particular note is the contract. Vendors are in the business of selling their EHR and are very familiar with system procurement law. HDOs are not generally familiar with system procurement law and often agree to contract terms that prevent them from resolving implementation problems.

As an example, one HDO requested that the selected vendor custom develop a new system function, that is, a custom-developed flow sheet. The vendor provided this solution at a specified cost. The vendor subsequently wanted to sell this custom flow sheet to other customers. Who owns this customized solution, the vendor or the HDO? If the HDO owns the software, how do they ensure they receive vendor payments when another customer buys it from the vendor? Who is liable for patient injuries attributable to the flow sheet, the vendor or the HDO? It is possible to address these and many other system contract issues, but it takes an attorney experienced in this area of law to negotiate an agreement that safeguards the HDO.

This is now increasingly important given Software as a Service solutions are becoming popular and this arrangement has unique contract requirements. *Software as a Service (SaaS)* is the delivery of software over the Internet by vendors hosting the software themselves or through a third-party application service provider (ASP).

Because SaaS offers an attractive delivery approach, it is rapidly becoming available, and in some cases, EHR vendors offer only this option. The HDO's attorney should have SaaS agreement experience because SaaS contracts include some specific contract provisions as described in the SaaS sidebar in Chapter 4.

It is highly advisable to select legal counsel that has previous experience preparing *and* successfully administering the contract (ideally with the same vendor) through the entire process of successful implementation. It is not enough to have experience just preparing one of these contracts. The successful EHR implementation tests the value of the contract. For example, we encountered an EHR contract that included a budget prepared in Microsoft Word, while the Project Manager was using an Excel spreadsheet with supposedly the same budget. It finally became clear that there were deliverables missing from the contract budget worth a significant amount. The attorney prepared the contract budget with a word processor instead of a spreadsheet, which the Project Manager could later use as a basis for managing the vendor budget. This oversight did not occur to the attorney because he had no experience administering a system implementation contract. This illustrates what can occur between preparing and administrating a contract and the associated consequences.

Prepare Solicitation

Subsequent to assembling the procurement team, the Project Manager prepares the solicitation, typically a request for proposal (RFP), during the executing process group. An RFP is a formal invitation to vendors to prepare a competitive response to a request according to pre-defined evaluation criteria. This helps the HDO leverage its buying power because it is soliciting and evaluating competitive bids instead selecting a single non-competitively priced vendor solution.

RFPs include many, sometimes thousands, of items requiring a significant amount of time for vendors to respond to and for the Project Team to subsequently evaluate. At times, this is excessive and unnecessarily wastes time and money. Several specific analysis methods can help manage this challenge as described below.

Use Minimum Mandatory Requirements

A *mandatory qualification* is an imperative condition that a vendor must fulfill to qualify for the proposed project. For example, an RFP could include the following minimum qualification, *at least three different customers, which include HDOs similar in size to the soliciting HDO, must have the proposed vendor solution installed and in production use for three years*. An RFP should include no more than ten mandatory minimum qualifications that the HDO can use to immediately reduce the number of responding vendors and assist vendors in determining whether they should respond.

Prepare Requirements that Require a Discrete Response Wherever Possible

RFPs should include response types that require discrete answers to minimize evaluation time. RFP discrete response types include pass/fail, yes/no, and multiple choice. The RFP should allow responding vendors to provide comments for all items, including these response types; however, the HDO can reduce evaluation time by quickly scoring discrete item responses and reviewing those with comments instead of manually scoring long narrative responses. Using the pass/fail response type for all minimum qualifications also reduces the time the HDO spends identifying vendors that qualify for a subsequent thorough review. Table 3-23 displays examples of all response types.

Document Requirements Unambiguously and In Sufficient Detail

HDOs often spend a considerable amount of time crafting long and involved requirements that are unclear and have limited value. We recommend clearly phrasing each RFP item so the HDO can easily associate it with a specific project objective. Rephrase those items that do not clearly link to a project objective, and delete those items that the HDO cannot associate with an objective or add a new objective, if required. This helps ensure the HDO includes RFP items that are relevant to the project.

Use a Database Driven RFP

A database driven RFP supports collaboration. This approach enables multiple people in different locations to collaborate simultaneously preparing the RFP, the vendor

Response Type	Description	Response Score Examples
Pass/Fail	A binary response indicating whether a vendor supports Minimum Mandatory Requirements. The HDO does not consider vendors that fail to meet these requirements.	Yes (Pass) No (Fail)
Yes/No	A binary response indicating whether a vendor supports a specification.	Yes No
Multiple Choice	A selection list indicating varying levels of support.	**Supported More Than 6 Months**—The current system version, in use at one or more customer sites for more than six months, meets the specification. **Supported Less Than 6 Months**—The current system version, in use at one or more customer sites for less than six months, meets the specification. **Supported by Next Release**—The next release of the current system version will meet the specification. **Supported by Modification**—The modified current system version will meet the specification. **Not Supported**—The proposed system does not meet the specification.
Short Answer	A written statement and/or uploaded document describing support of a specification.	**Excellent**—Meets or exceeds specification or expectations. **Good**—Meets specifications or performs as expected. **Fair**—Achieves specifications with minor work-around or adjustment; meets specification, but not as expected or desired. **Poor**—Only achieves the specifications or presents significant performance/workflow issues. **Unacceptable**—Does not meet specifications or expectations.
Cost Worksheet	A detailed list of unit costs and quantities according to a specification and the distribution of all worksheet costs across a five-year period.	The proposal with the lowest cost receives the total possible points available for cost. If more than one proposal includes the lowest cost, each receives the total possible points available for cost.

TABLE 3-23 Discrete Response Types

response, and the evaluation of these responses in real time. This eliminates comparing and consolidating individual files and file types, e.g., documents and spreadsheet, and instead provides a structured collection of records stored in a computer system. Finally, it avoids common errors. A good example of this is the response due date. RFP documents often repeat the response due date, erroneously citing different dates. A database offers a preferred method by storing the due date in one place and referring to it multiple times throughout the RFP without error.

The HDO establishes evaluation criteria to compare and rank vendors based on how well they support the HDO's requirements. Examples of different evaluation options include the following:

- *Point Scoring*—Assign a point value and weight to each requirement before issuing the RFP. Assign a point value, for example, essential items receive five points and desirable items receive two points. Assign a weight to groups of similar items organized by topic, like scripted user requirements or technology line items. The weight is a multiplier applied to each itemized requirement value used to calculate a maximum possible score. The Project Team evaluates each proposal by scoring each item according to its available weighted value. The Project Team selects the vendor with the highest score.

- *Delphi Technique*—Each member of the Project Team reviews and evaluates each vendor's proposal and then exchanges their assessment with the other evaluators without the evaluator disclosing their identity to avoid a dominant individual influencing the team decision. The team repeats this cycle until the Project Manager determines that they reached consensus on a specific vendor.

- *Rank/Cost Tradeoff*—First, eliminate any dominant proposal, such as one that has a lower rank than another of equal or lower cost. Second, decide if the highest ranked proposal is worth the extra cost over the lower ranked proposals, and work your way down the list until you accept a specific proposal.

Proposal evaluation methodologies are generally quantitative. Like quantitative risk analysis, quantitative proposal evaluation methods can give a false sense of certainty about the final vendor selection. The Project Manager should recognize that the numbers used in these methods are often based on qualitative assumptions and as such have limitations.

After evaluation and vendor selection, do not throw away everything used to select the winning vendor. It is essential that you incorporate the provisions of the RFP, the responses and assurances of the vendor, both in the proposal and otherwise (e.g., verbal assurances), into the final contract.

Our EHR selection process was led by a combination of family medicine and internal medicine physician champions, along with other interested subject matter experts from other departments and service areas. Rather than limiting our views to our own departments, we each tried to act as representatives for the entire enterprise. We prepared RFIs and RFPs, developed user requirements, got responses, and carefully analyzed them. We included stakeholders representing a spectrum of departments, IT experience, IT skills, IT optimism, and other perspectives to try to make sure we were getting diverse and representative perspectives. Our only requirement was that people who participated in the decisions needed to be positively inclined to try to move forward despite the challenges and barriers, rather than detractors whose main goal was to avoid having to implement an EHR. We identified three vendor solutions that could potentially meet our needs, with two that came on site to give live system demonstrations, which we opened up to the entire organization, defining both the initial scope for the pilot project and then outlining a potential future phase in which we would rollout the system to the whole enterprise and of course, the ability to scale in size and work across a variety of specialties became important selection criteria.

—Michael H. Zaroukian, MD, PhD, FACP, FHIMSS, CMIO, Michigan State University

Select Vendor

An organization selects a vendor during the executing process. This process involves issuing a solicitation, receiving responses, evaluating responses based on the evaluation criteria, and choosing a vendor based on those criteria. The output of this process is the selected vendor. A *selected vendor* is the supplier chosen to deliver a service and/or product.

We did an RFP solicitation and evaluation based on those RFPs. We narrowed the field of potential vendors to three or so, which were brought onsite for demonstrations. We had very specific scenarios that we provided to the vendors, namely ones that stressed pediatric aspects of their systems and then we asked the vendors to demonstrate these scenarios. We opened up these demonstrations to a large subset of the organization to come in and kick the tires on each of the vendor products. We wanted to be very transparent. After those demonstrations, we solicited feedback from the participants and tallied their responses to come up with a final candidate.

—Dan Nigrin, MD, MS, CIO, Children's Hospital Boston

This process generally takes about 60 to 90 days. While this may appear to be a long time, it is very important to ensure that the vendors have sufficient time to respond and the HDO has time to evaluate and select a vendor. One way to reduce the time is to minimize or eliminate the bidders' conference. A *bidders' conference* is a pre-proposal meeting where vendors ask questions to clarify the intent of the RFP. Generally bidders' conferences are not particularly well attended or informative. Alternatively the HDO could request that interested vendors submit contact information indicating they plan to submit an RFP response. The HDO sets a deadline requiring that these vendors submit questions about the RFP. After the deadline, the HDO prepares and submits questions and a response to vendors that indicated they planned to respond to the RFP. This process eliminates the bidders' conference, controls the question and answer process, and documents everything to ensure all participants have the same information available to them.

The evaluation process begins once each vendor submits a response. The following is an example of the evaluation step included in this process:

- *Verify Minimum Mandatory Requirements*—In this step, the HDO eliminates those vendors that fail to meet the identified minimum mandatory requirements.

- *Select Finalists*—In this step, the HDO selects no more than the top three finalists from among those vendors meeting the minimum mandatory qualifications. This includes ranking vendors numerically by using the evaluation criteria described above to calculate their response scores (i.e., multiplying the value of each vendor response by its weight and priority). Evaluators award cost points to the lowest cost proposal. If two or more proposals are the lowest cost, both receive the total available cost points.

- *Conduct Demonstrations, Reference Checks and Site Visits*—In this step, the HDO scores and ranks its top two to three finalists, and selects the finalist with the highest score, based on the following separately scored activities:

  - *Demonstrations*—Finalists perform demonstrations based on selected scripted user specifications from the RFP. The HDO may interview the vendor during the demonstration on a variety of topics (e.g., additional product demonstration, response clarification, and follow-up questions). Evaluators score demonstrations using the scale as short answer response types, described previously.

  - *Reference Checks and Site Visit*—The HDO contacts references and conducts a site visit for two vendors selected from the demonstrations. The HDO uses pass/fail scoring. The HDO may consider other finalists, in rank order, if the first two finalists fail either reference checks or the site visit.

The selected finalist becomes the apparent successful winner subject to successful contract negotiations. A second-place vendor, if possible, offers a fallback option in the event of failed contract negotiations with the winner. Maintaining a fallback also provides the HDO with an advantage during contract negotiations with the finalist. The finalist will likely offer more favorable contract terms during negotiations if they know the HDO has a fallback vendor option.

Administer Procurement

The Project Manager monitors the procurement during the controlling process. This involves verifying that each contract deliverable complies with its WBS dictionary entry. The Project Manager monitors procurement management using the control process described in integration management. For example, we worked with a group of hospitals that failed to include an HIT contract in their EMR system solicitation. The project subsequently failed for a number of reasons, including the absence of an appropriate contract. We were then asked to participate in a new project. We worked with counsel to include a system acquisition contract in the solicitation. Although there were substantive vendor negotiations, they started with this baseline contract. This safeguarded the hospitals against starting with an agreement favorable to the vendor, and resulted in a negotiated contract satisfactory to both parties and a successfully completed project.

Perform Final Acceptance

The Project Manager performs implementation final acceptance during the closing process. This includes resolving open items and completing the vendor implementation.

In an EHR project, the contract does not end; instead, it shifts from implementation to ongoing vendor support. The output of this process is a DCC accepting the final project deliverable and organization process assets (e.g., updated contract administration policies, contracts with future vendors, and procurement practices). A DCC for the final deliverable confirms that the vendor completed the system implementation according to the contract. This typically results in a final implementation payment by the HDO.

The contract includes the WBS dictionary that defines acceptance criteria for each deliverable, including the final deliverable. The vendor submits the final deliverable for Project Manager acceptance. For example, the vendor submits a letter stating the vendor passed the final system acceptance period after go-live without additional software defects. The Project Manager verifies that the final deliverable complies with the WBS dictionary and issues a DCC accepting the final deliverable.

Conclusion

This chapter described each individual project management knowledge area. It provided details about the processes supporting these knowledge areas and the outputs of these processes. It also included examples of analysis methods used to prepare these outputs. Table 3-24 displays all project management knowledge area processes and their outputs by process group, with knowledge areas in bold, individual processes in normal text and outputs in italics.

> *One of the things I think we did very well is from the very, very beginning we identified this is not an IS project. I will repeat this over and over again. This is an organization project. If you want to have a successful implementation of electronic health records of this magnitude, you need to focus on the entire organization. You also need to have executive sponsorship from the top of the organization. For example, as a CIO I was partnered with our COO as well as our CEO as the executive sponsor of the project. I think that's important. Executive sponsorship as well as the focus on the organization, that's the number one. Number two is that we also put in place a project management office as a result of this initiative. You have got to have the project management discipline.*
>
> *So the appropriate governance, governance structure, the scope change request process, the issue management process, the risk management process . . .*
>
> *The third thing that we did well is that we also brought the right people into the project team. So, get the best and brightest from your clinical operation to be part of the team, and have them dedicate to the project, not the one-off, not ad hoc, so that their time is fully involved with the project from the beginning to the end. We could not have done without the subject matter experts that we brought on board to help with the system. Those sort of things worked extremely well for us.*
>
> —Florence Chang, MBA, CIO, Multicare

The next chapter includes a similar description except it focuses on IT management.

Initiating	Planning	Executing	Controlling	Closing
Integration Prepare the feasibility study and business case *Feasibility study and business case* Prepare project charter *Project charter*	**Integration** Prepare project management plan *Project management plan* **Scope** Define scope *Scope statement* Prepare work breakdown structure (WBS) and WBS dictionary *Work breakdown structure (WBS)* *WBS dictionary* *Work package* **Time** Define tasks *Task list* Sequence tasks *Task sequence* Estimate task resources *Task resource estimate* Estimate task duration *Task duration estimate* Prepare schedule *Schedule* **Cost** Estimate costs *Cost estimate* Prepare budget *Project budget* **Quality** Prepare quality management plan *Quality management plan*	**Integration** Manage project execution *Performance report* *Change request (CR)* *Deliverable* *Project document update* **Quality** Perform quality assurance *Change request (CR)* *Project document update* **Human Resources (HR)** Develop project team *Project team performance assessment* **Communications** Distribute information *Organizational process asset update* **Procurement** Select vendor *Selected vendor*	**Integration** Control project execution *Organizational process asset update* *Performance report* *Change request (CR)* Project document update Perform integrated change control *Change request (CR)* **Scope** Verify scope *Deliverable completion certificate (DCC)* *Change request (CR)* *Project document update* Control scope *Organizational process asset update* *Performance report* *Change request (CR)* *Project document update* **Time** Control schedule *Organizational process asset update* *Performance report* *Change request (CR)* *Project document update* **Cost** Control cost *Organizational process asset update* *Performance report*	**Integration** Close phase or project *Organizational process asset update* *Deliverable* **Procurement** Perform final acceptance *Organizational process asset update* *Deliverable completion certificate (DCC)*

TABLE 3-24 Project Management Knowledge Areas by Process Group

Initiating	Planning	Executing	Controlling	Closing
	Human Resources (HR) Prepare human resources plan Human resources plan Acquire project team resources Resource assignment **Communications** Identify key project participants Project roster Plan communications Communications plan **Risk** Prepare risk management plan Risk management plan Identify risks Risk register Perform quantitative risk analysis Risk register update Perform qualitative risk analysis Risk register update Plan risk response Risk response plan **Procurement** Plan procurement Procurement plan Prepare solicitation Solicitation		*Change request (CR)* *Project document update* **Quality** Perform quality control *Organizational process asset update* *Change request (CR)* *Project document update* **Human Resources (HR)** Manage project team *Organizational process asset update* *Performance report* *Change request (CR)* *Project document update* **Communications** Report performance *Organizational process asset update* *Performance report* *Change request (CR)* *Project document update* **Risk** Monitor and control risk *Organizational process asset update* *Performance report* *Change request (CR)* *Project document update* **Procurement** Administer procurement *Organizational process asset update* *Deliverable completion certificate (DCC)* *Performance report* *Change request (CR)* *Project document update*	

TABLE 3-24 Project Management Knowledge Areas by Process Group (*Continued*)

Endnote

1. Hall, J. (1969). *The Conflict Management Survey: An Assessment of the Individual's Reaction to and Characteristic Handling of Conflicts Between Himself and Others.* Conroe, TX: Teleometrics Ltd.

CHAPTER 4

IT Management
Knowledge Areas

In this chapter, we will:

- *Describe each IT management knowledge area in detail*
- *Associate each IT management knowledge area with processes and their outputs*
- *Define specific analysis methods associated with IT management knowledge area processes and outputs*

In the last chapter we covered in detail the project management process groups and knowledge areas. We defined the range of project resources and the activities and tasks they undertake. We defined the core activities a Project Manager undertakes in overseeing and controlling the Project Team's work. We also defined outputs that the Project Manager creates and updates to document and measure progress on the project according to pre-defined standards.

HIT projects have unique aspects that we address by integrating other methodologies. One of these is from IEEE, as documented in SWEBOK, a methodology designed to focus on IT—the product—rather than the project. In this chapter, we cover ten major components or IT knowledge areas. We also map these ten IT knowledge areas to the five project management process groups of initiating, planning, executing, controlling, and closing. Because the nature of IT management is in fact *building the product*, the great majority of these IT activities occur in the planning and executing process groups.

In short, it may help to consider project management as the process of *how to* manage a project whereas IT management is *what* tasks the Project Team performs to deliver a final product. The Project Manager leads and facilitates a range of Project Team participants. The IT participants perform the technology activities directly related to defining, acquiring, installing, and configuring the software and equipment that supports an EHR, for example. We derived these activities from SWEBOK (e.g., the Project Manager does not necessarily execute the processes within the IT knowledge areas, but does oversee and control the IT representatives on the Project Team as they work to produce a specified result). For example, the EHR, a complex amalgam of hardware and software, is without doubt a major project undertaking. A hospital or clinic that is installing an EHR may well engage a range of technical resources, such as clinical application analysts, network administrators, and security experts. We rely on the work of these people, and we organize and task them according to the management principles in SWEBOK. At the same time, the Project Manager uses the principles from the *PMBOK®*

User Requirements Management	Initiating, planning, executing, and controlling the identification and organization of stakeholders' needs to evaluate options and acquire a solution that achieves the project objectives.
Infrastructure Management	Initiating, planning, executing, and controlling requirements for the location and configuration of the physical components of a new system.
Conversion Management	Planning, executing, and controlling transformation and movement of data from existing manual and automated systems to a new system.
Software Configuration Management	Planning, executing, and controlling setup and selection of application options and features to meet user, technical, and security requirements.
Workflow Management	Planning, executing, and controlling the sequence of automated and manual steps that support delivery of an organization's products and services.
Security Management	Planning, executing, controlling, and closing system access
Interface Management	Planning, executing, and controlling the definition, development, testing, and implementation of information exchanges between one or more systems.
Testing Management	Planning, executing, and controlling how an organization verifies that a new system meets its specifications.
Cutover Management	Planning, executing, and controlling the switch from existing manual and/or automated systems to a new system.
Support Management	Planning, executing, and controlling technical maintenance of the system after cutover.

TABLE 4-1   Summary of IT Knowledge Areas

Guide—the knowledge areas, processes, and outputs—to oversee and coordinate the work and outputs of these various Project Team IT resources. As we will see in Chapter 5, the same considerations apply to Project Team change management resources. It is important to understand that project, IT, and change management have similarities and differences that a Project Manager must leverage successfully.

Table 4-1 identifies the ten IT knowledge areas that we derived from SWEBOK. As you will see, these knowledge areas fit within the five Project Management process groups of initiating, planning, executing, controlling, and closing.

USER REQUIREMENTS MANAGEMENT

User requirements management is initiating, planning, executing, and controlling the identification and organization of stakeholders' needs to evaluate options and acquire a solution that achieves the project objectives. Table 4-2 shows user requirements management processes and their outputs (in italics) by process group.

A user requirement describes *future*, not current needs for a system without regard to technology such as equipment. For example, an HDO's *current state* maintains paper medical records. The description of the *future state* is the replacement of these paper records with electronic equivalents. The HDO needs to define the future state that they want, not the current state that they have. The HDO must consider *future* user needs to identify and select a system that provides the highest possible level of clinical quality and patient safety.

A description of the user requirements must also describe *what* users need from a system instead of *how* the system supports their needs. For example, physicians have requirements to capture notes at the patient bedside. The *what* documents these needs. The *how* defines the technology required to deliver it, such as handheld computers, wall-mounted PCs, or cart-mounted computers. An HDO defines the *what* first to avoid any restrictions associated with the *how* (e.g., Microsoft Windows-based PCs versus Apple iPads). If an HDO selects the *how* first, they may unnecessarily restrict the range of available vendor options that support the *what*.

Prepare High-Level User Requirements

User requirements were at a high level. They were helpful back in 1995 through 2000 when we were looking for an electronic medical record, because at that time many of the vendors had some basic functionality developed and were in the process of developing more. It was helpful as an organization to identify what our future state was, what we really wanted to see in a vendor, and then to determine how much of what we wanted vendors had instead of vaporware.

—Florence Chang, MBA, CIO, Multicare

An HDO initially prepares high-level requirements to evaluate and rank identified alternatives when preparing the feasibility analysis and business case in integration management. A *high-level user requirement* is a general description of features and functions that a system must perform to meet user needs. This allows the HDO to effectively compare possible solutions to meet their needs when determining whether the project

Initiating	Planning	Executing	Controlling	Closing
Prepare high-level user requirements *High-level user requirements*	Prepare user requirements management plan *User requirements management plan*	Prepare detailed user requirements *Detailed user requirements*	Control user requirements *Organizational process asset update* *Performance report* *Change request (CR)* *Project document update*	

TABLE 4-2   User Requirements Management by Process Group

is worth pursuing. Once management approves the project, the HDO prepares a requirements management plan and proceeds by defining detailed user requirements.

At this stage of the project, these requirements are necessarily at a high level, but detailed enough to portray the HDO's scope to support effective and informed decision-making when selecting a preferred option. Remember, the purpose of the requirements definition efforts at this early stage of project initiation is simply to enable senior organizational leaders to make a *go/no go* decision. One approach to describing high-level user requirements is developing categories of clinical processes instead of detailed needs within these categories. For example, consider an outpatient chemotherapy clinic in which a clinician delivers various pharmaceutical agents to patients at each visit. Project initiators develop high-level requirements in terms of the following workflow (e.g., admitting patients and administering the chemotherapy). High-level categories may include:

- Record patient arrival
- Conduct new patient consult
- Conduct returning patient visit
- Create or change orders
- Prepare patient for infusion treatment
- Prepare patient for injection
- Administer blood products
- Administer drug

In addition to these categories, the HDO prepares high-level requirement line items describing specific features, functions, or other conditions that viable options must satisfy [e.g. supports integration with the existing ADT system module from GE, holds a Certification Commission for Healthcare Information Technology (CCHIT) EHR certificate, offers a fully integrated EHR solution].

Prepare User Requirements Management Plan

Once the HDO approves the project, the next IT management activity includes preparation of a user requirements management plan, an activity that occurs during the planning process. A *user requirements management plan* is a description of how an organization plans to successfully identify and manage stakeholder system needs. This IT management area focuses on learning what users need and documenting it so the Project Team can acquire, configure, implement, and optimize the selected EHR.

Preparing this plan includes a number of key activities described below.

Review Existing System

If an existing system is in use at the HDO, the Project Manager begins by reviewing existing documentation, participating in demonstrations of the existing system, and conducting interviews to gain an understanding of user expectations, issues, and roles. With no existing system, the Project Manager may use information from industry conferences, vendor product demonstrations, and healthcare publications as a starting point for interviews. In either case, interviews also help identify individuals to define the user requirements described in the next sections. This also helps the Project Manager gain a current understanding of the objectives and issues associated with the proposed system.

Assemble Requirements Definition Team

The Project Manager, with help from the steering committee, identifies seven to nine subject matter experts representing a cross-section of potential users (e.g., a nurse supervisor with experience in multiple departments throughout the HDO, a senior clinician with previous EHR experience, other individuals who understand the needs of clinical caregivers). It is the responsibility of this multi-disciplinary team to work effectively together to develop the plan.

Focus on the Future

Defining user requirements focuses on the future state. An HDO does not want a new EHR that reflects what they do now. Instead, they want a system that maximizes future needs and best practices not employed by the HDO currently. A key issue in preparing user requirements includes the Project Team's understanding of the future state. This is a particularly difficult in healthcare for two reasons:

1. Stakeholders are generally familiar only with the current state in their HDO.

2. The current state is often dysfunctional. For example, consider the HIT function of automated reporting of lab results to patients via a web portal into the hospital EHR. In the current workflow, the lab reports results to the physician (either on paper or electronically) and the physician may then call the patient or discuss the results on the next clinic visit. In this case, physician requirements may be an interface that alerts the physician of the results and provides the patient's phone number. In the future state, it is likely the patient could log onto the portal and view the lab results. Depending on the nature of the lab test, the clinical team may discover they need to create a new workflow to answer any patient questions about the significance of abnormal results, for example.

Education is the best way to inform users about the future state. There are several options and stakeholders should consider participating in more than one, such as:

- Attending demonstrations of various vendor systems (e.g., at a conference)

- Conducting demonstrations of the selected vendor's system, requesting that they describe best practices identified from similar customers

- Attending site visits where peers demonstrate their fully implemented system, share their experiences of capturing the future state, configuring the selected system, and implementing it and updating it to optimize use

Create a Requirements Baseline

Based on the above review, the project starts with baseline user requirements. An example of a user requirement for clinical alerts in the EHR might be *the system will present alerts at the appropriate time in the user's workflow, providing the ability to choose an alternate course of action or continue with current orders.*

The Project Manager and various Project Team members develop the requirements baseline in multiple ways using one or more of the following methods depending on prior experience and available expertise:

- *Expert Information*—Defining user requirements based on the judgment of specialists, such as consultants, vendors, or prior experience

- *Bottom Up*—Identifying each individual part of the work until you assemble a list of user requirements
- *Top Down*—Performing *functional decomposition* or breaking down the current workflow into its individual components or functional parts (e.g., care planning, ordering, medication reconciliation)
- *Reference Project*—Working with user requirements from an HDO that previously implemented a similar EHR system and updating it to reflect your HDO's differences

Relying on a combination of methods can prove useful, as described below:

You have to literally learn from others. We did a lot of site visits. I took my team to those sites already up with EPIC, that's the first thing. You learn from other teams, because transfer is transfer, patient services is patient services, everyone has to deal with records issues, you know, they were no different than us. So we went and did a lot of site visits, and borrowed as much workflow from others—how they had done it in their organization.

Second, is that EPIC also provided a lot of resources to help us, going through that entire design/build process. They also brought previous experience with other clients and helped us with that. Now, when we first went live, they didn't have their current model system. Now, they model systems that you can pretty much use 80% of what they have put in place already. You just modify or customize for your own organization. At the time, however, we went through a much more build from scratch process. So, that was the second way of learning from EPIC.

—Florence Chang, MBA, CIO, Multicare

Once the Project Manager creates the baseline document, the next step is refinement of the requirements through a process of iterative validation and broadening of the baseline. The team updates the requirements baseline in a series of facilitated group sessions described in the joint application design (JAD) sidebar.

Joint Application Design

Joint application design (JAD) is a series of collaborative workshops where SMEs and IT specialists analyze and design a computer system together, i.e., a *joint* effort. In 1977, IBM developed JAD to address a number of challenges with traditional system analysis and design methods. For example, without JAD, requirements definition typically occurs in a series of interviews that do not fully document user needs. These interviews continue over time. Since the users interviewed have other work to do, they are often not easy to reach for follow-up clarification. Eventually, the analyst documenting the interviews attempts to clarify the requirements on behalf of the users. For example, he might call the Lab Manager, but finds he is unavailable until tomorrow. The next day the analyst reaches the Lab Manager, but the Nurse Manager and other essential people required for follow-up are also unavailable. Because of this, the analyst attempts to prepare the requirements as best as he can without complete user input. The result is that the requirements definition is only partially reflective of the true end user needs. When the analyst then presents the completed requirements to the users they are reluctant to approve them because they did not fully participate in their definition.

JAD shortens the time to define user requirements, engages users early in the project, and improves the quality of the system they select. Because of direct stakeholder involvement, projects using JAD require fewer system and workflow changes after implementation.

Jane Wood and Denise Silver wrote their first edition of Joint Application Development in 1989.[1] We read and used it shortly after its publication. Over the years, we developed our own variation of JAD to define user requirements and applied JAD collaborative techniques to most project group interactions.

Successful implementation of these group interaction concepts requires clear description of the various roles of included group participants. Consider the following roles for your project group interactions:

- *Facilitator*—A *facilitator* is an impartial person with no self-interest other than achieving the project objectives effectively and efficiently. It is imperative that the Project Manager and other project group leaders learn how to facilitate their participants in successful collaboration.

- *Participant*—Select your group of participants carefully. It is critical to have the right people and the right number of people in the room. The best way to identify the right people is to ask. Ask the executive sponsor, members of the steering committee, and people you observe on the front line that are informal leaders to participate or recommend participants.

  There should be no more than four to nine (seven is a good average) permanent participants from all affected areas involved in the system. We derive this number from George Miller's law that our short-term memory can handle only about seven items.[2] We apply Miller's Law by maintaining we can handle only seven people providing input on a particular discussion topic. While you don't have to do the math each time you add a participant, just keep in mind that adding one more participant can have a huge impact on session effectiveness. The solution is to keep the permanent group small and augment it with temporary members on an as needed, short-term basis.

- *Scribe*—A *scribe* records decisions during sessions. The facilitator prompts the scribe to document these decisions only, instead of transcribing every spoken word into written form like a court reporter. The scribe uses a computer and projector with a screen in front of the participants to ensure he correctly records these decisions. The scribe distributes this information to the participants for review before the next meeting and confirms its accuracy and records any updates at the next meeting.

Group facilitation sessions also involve the following planning issues:

- *Research*—The facilitator interviews the participants in advance of the first meeting. It is important to understand what each participant does and cares about in terms of the session subject. Once the facilitator collects this information, he prepares a straw man or starting point intended to generate discussion at the next meeting about that particular session topic.

- *Logistics*—The legendary King Arthur was on to something when he created the Knights of the Round Table. The socio-physical arrangement of that table was critical to effective collaboration. While round tables are hard to find in most conference rooms, a square table or several tables arranged to form a square prevents an individual from sitting at the head and wielding the associated power. Sitting the facilitator and scribe at the front of the room also reduces the likelihood that any other participant will take charge.

The facilitator also prearranges for the room to include the necessary technology—a working computer, printer, Internet connection, projector and screen, whiteboard, erasable pens, eraser, flipchart, and markers to ensure he can focus on collaboration instead of trivial distractions.

Collaborative group sessions can occur via videoconference or in a face-to-face setting. Video conferences do, however, require special attention by the facilitator in terms of session preparation and research.

We successfully prepared user requirements and acquired EHR, pharmacy, and scheduling systems for a company that managed specialty outpatient clinics throughout the country. We combined face-to-face and virtual sessions. Initially, we conducted face-to-face sessions with local clinic team participants, facilitated numerous virtual sessions with remote clinic participants, had a midpoint face-to-face session with the local clinic participants and concluded with a final face-to-face session with the entire clinical team.

- *Meeting Norms*—A short list of norms that all participants agree to respect and follow is critical, including:

  o *Requiring Attendance*—Occasionally a participant will send a substitute in his place—usually a subordinate. This is not allowed except under special circumstances. Participants, such as the Project Team members, join these sessions for the duration of the project. Substitutes do not work because they force delays while they learn how to collaborate instead of contribute.

    Summarize the results of the meeting and provide it to everyone, including absentees, before the next session. Participants that repeatedly fail to attend or send a substitute require attention. The Project Manager needs to meet with them, find out why they are not attending, and resolve the problem.

    In those special circumstances, when a substitute replaces someone who is no longer available, the facilitator meets with and educates the new participant both in advance of the first attended meeting and after each meeting until the new member fully integrates into the group.

  o *Stopping Digressions*—The facilitator needs to keep the session on its agenda. Use participants' names when talking to them. This improves their attention. Use name *tent cards* during initial sessions to help participants remember the names of fellow members.

  o *Getting Unstuck*—This is tough work. When the group is stuck it is usually time to document an open issue and return to the agenda. It may also be the best time to take a formal break. Alternatively bring a treat like high-quality chocolate to distribute as an informal break and keep people attentive.

    When struggling on a key point, walk away by taking a break. You come back refreshed and often quickly know what to say.

  o *Conducting Purposeful Interruptions*—The facilitator should monitor discussion and know when to interrupt. Participants repeat themselves. This usually indicates it is time for the facilitator to summarize the decision, ask for group agreement, request that the scribe document it, and move on to the next agenda topic.

  o *Controlling*—The facilitator is the meeting referee. If he loses control of the *game*, the sessions are no longer a safe place to collaborate and achieve project objectives. Watch a child's team play a sport and observe the referee. If the referee loses control, someone else takes over (e.g., rough players, the rule-breakers, and parents on the sidelines). The game is no longer about playing the sport well. It may actually become unsafe.

During a break or even during the session the facilitator should speak to those who try to take control (a dominator) of the meeting. Ask the participant to offer his suggestions, but also allow others to do the same. The facilitator can alternatively retain control by immediately restating what a dominator says as a question to the rest of the group. This engages the group and shifts attention to productive discussion and away from the dominator.

Remember, your strongest ally is the group. Peer pressure is the most powerful tool you have as the facilitator. We frequently repeat the dominator's comment as a question to the rest of the group. The group takes over and the dominator complies because of the group not the facilitator. The group quells the dominator and the facilitator remains objective from the dominator's perspective. This also takes advantage of good suggestions often offered by dominators without letting them control the session.

- o *Awakening Shy Participants*—Each participant attends these sessions because he has something to contribute. If a participant is shy, the facilitator needs to ask him a direct question to ensure the group benefits from this participant's contribution.

- o *Ending Distractions*—Participants send email, text, engage in side conversations, sleep, and so on. These distractions adversely affect group effectiveness. Sometimes there are legitimate interruptions, for example, the transplant surgeon must leave the meeting because the long-awaited donor just arrived. However, these interruptions are very rare.

    Facilitating is a contact sport. Stand in front of the room and walk around while conducting the session. Walk directly next to the distracter and typically the offending behavior will stop. If not, be direct and ask the offending party to refrain from the disruption.

- **Preparing Agendas**—All meetings include an agenda that the facilitator distributes to participants before the meeting and uses to keep sessions on track.

- **Scheduling**—These meetings are intense. Productivity depends on keeping meetings short or at least with many breaks. While an all-day meeting is eight hours, actual meeting time is six hours if you account for four breaks and lunch. Schedule meetings for less time instead of more. The clock pressures everyone to stay on point and it is much more productive if you hold a series of meetings instead of a single marathon session.

    Respect your team by starting and ending on time. The first meeting must follow this regimen to immediately set an example. Arriving late or leaving early only says you think you are more important than your teammates. Remind participants arriving late or leaving early that mutual respect breeds collaboration. However, be sure to let everyone know that reasonable exceptions are acceptable, such as emergencies and requesting permission in advance to arrive late or leave early.

- **Tracking Open Issues**—The facilitator records open issues to avoid getting off track trying to resolve problems immediately. Record them on screen in front of the team so they can contribute to documenting the issue correctly. Participants often resolve these issues in subsequent sessions. The facilitator should report critical issues to the Project Manager or Executive Sponsor to ensure their immediate attention and resolution. The facilitator is also responsible for distributing any remaining open issues to appropriate parties, tracking their resolution, and reporting the results to session participants in a timely fashion.

Prepare Detailed User Requirements

The purpose of the high-level user requirements document is to inform the participants when initiating a project. In other words, it includes the processes and an output that are only sufficiently detailed so executive leadership can decide to continue or kill the project. It is part of the high-level *first take* on user requirements to best inform business case and the feasibility decision-making. If the executive team elects to go forward with the project, this high-level document serves as the basis for producing a more detailed requirements document or output. Should the project receive a green light, the next iterative step is to return to the high-level requirements document and flesh out a much more detailed level. This takes place during the executing process. A *detailed user requirement* is an in-depth description of the functions and data a system must support to meet user needs. The HDO uses these requirements to evaluate and acquire a solution to meet its needs. In facilitated sessions outlined in the user requirements management plan, the HDO expands the high-level requirements previously defined and maintained in a project database or library. Each user requirement process augments a high-level *script* to include both manual and automated system activities or events performed by or on behalf of one or more actors (e.g., nurse, physician, pharmacist), to accomplish a desired outcome or result. An *actor* is the entity—a person or a system—that executes the activity. The detailed user requirements document becomes quite extensive; for a large tertiary care hospital with dozens of service lines and multiple dozens of provider and patient roles, which sheer number of actors and events may require creating the requirements definitions using advanced methods.

> *Phase 1 was the revenue cycle and part of the clinical systems. For example, we included electronic MAR [Medication Administration Reconciliation]. The second phase was clinical documentation and CPOE with all three hospitals at the same time. So, you can imagine. It included the three hospitals, and one of them was Children's Hospital, so we had pediatric as well as adult. We had a lot of requirements documented in the new system so it was about several hundred pages of documentation.*
> —Florence Chang, MBA, CIO, Multicare

The resulting detailed user requirements include the following:

- Unified modeling language (UML) scripts described in the sidebar
- Line items describing specific features, functions, rules, or operational constraints required to support the HDO's user needs
- Line items describing the HDO's accessibility and usability requirements, such as:
  - *Error Minimization*—Reduces errors of commission (e.g., selecting the wrong patient) and of omission (e.g., overlooking or misinterpreting data due to poor information display)
  - *Simplicity*—Provides concise information display to accomplish specific tasks
  - *Naturalness*—Feels familiar to the user automatically
  - *Consistency*—Functions predictably internally (e.g., consistent use of concepts), and externally (e.g., how the application's user interactions compare to those of other applications)

- ○ *Minimized Cognitive Load*—Presents all information needed for each task
- ○ *Efficient Interaction*—Minimizes steps required to complete tasks and provides shortcuts
- ○ *Forgiveness and Feedback*—Promotes user discovery without negative results
- ○ *Language Effectiveness*—Employs language concisely in the context of user work
- ○ *Appropriate Density*—Balances providing all necessary information and limiting screen changes and clutter
- ○ *Color Use*—Applies color consistently and simply to convey meaning to users
- ○ *Readability*—Combines simplicity, density, and color to allow quick information scanning and comprehension
- ○ *Context Preservation*—Minimizes screen changes during task completion
- ○ *Efficiency*
    - □ Time to perform a scenario
    - □ Number of keystrokes and screens visited to complete a scenario
    - □ Frequency of *back* button use
- ○ *Effectiveness*
    - □ Error rate and severity
    - □ Path used for task completion
- ○ *Learnability*
    - □ Time to become an *expert* or perform a task compared to an expert
    - □ Number of icons remembered after task completion
    - □ Time spent referring to manuals
    - □ Time to execute a previously performed task
    - □ Frequency of Help function access[3]
- Supplemental documents providing detailed instruction on specific system requirements (e.g., HDO web presentation, security, and technology standards)
- Issues related to configuration and setup of the production, testing, and training environments, including:
    - ○ Static table values, such as order sets and departments, entered before system use
    - ○ Security and other access parameters required by HDO, governmental, or other regulatory or statutory body
    - ○ Information about existing systems that requires a conversion or an interface

Table 4-3 displays an example of detailed user requirement line items. Table 4-4 displays an example of a detailed user requirement script.

The HDO prepares user requirement scripts for soliciting, evaluating, selecting, configuring, and implementing a solution, generally through the process of completing an RFP, or request for proposal, which we covered in Chapter 3. The HDO subsequently starts with these scripts during preparation of configuration scripts.

#	Title	Description
3 6.	Clinical Decision Support	Requirements related to the mechanisms supporting clinical alerts, rules, and order checking
3.6.1.	Alerts in response to orders and abnormal assessment (Yes/No)	Generates reminders and alerts in response to orders and abnormal assessment data (e.g., alert for patient at high risk for skin breakdown)
3.6.2.	Alerts presented in workflow (Yes/No)	Presents alerts in the user's workflow, providing the ability to choose an alternate course of action or continue with current orders on the same screen
3.6.3.	Alerts work list for decision support (Yes/No)	Provides an alerts work list, making it easier to act on suggested actions and remove the alert when finished
3.6.4.	Arden Syntax support (Yes/No)	Supports Arden Syntax to facilitate sharing of rules across institutions and/or use of commercial libraries of rules
3.6.5.	Clinical reminder creation during order placement (Yes/No)	Generates clinical reminders or alerts during order entry as a by-product of the order being placed
3.6.6.	Dose range and limit order checking (Yes/No)	Supports automatic order checking that includes dose range and limit checking
3.6.7.	Drug interaction order checking (Yes/No)	Supports automatic order checking that includes drug interactions, such as drug–drug contraindication
3.6.8.	Drug-allergy order checking (Yes/No)	Supports automatic order checking that includes drug allergy
3.6.9.	Drug–disease order checking (Yes/No)	Supports automatic order checking that includes drug–disease
3.6.10.	Drug–food order checking (Yes/No)	Supports automatic order checking that includes drug–food

TABLE 4-3   Detailed User Requirement Line Items

Unified Modeling Language

In the mid-1960s systems analysis, design, and development methodologies started appearing. In the 1970s and 1980s well-recognized names, such as Edward Yourdon, Tom DeMarco, Jean-Dominique Warnier, and Ken Orr, pioneered additional software engineering methodologies. In the mid-1990s, Grady Booch, Jim Rumbaugh, and Ivar Jacobson consolidated different notations associated with the object-oriented analysis and design methodology by creating unified modeling language. *Object-oriented analysis and design (OOAD)* is a software engineering methodology for modeling interaction of objects or entities of interest to a system. *Unified modeling language (UML)* is a graphical notation used to visualize and specify how to construct software. UML communicates a system's requirements, design, and architectural blueprint (protocols and interfaces for interacting with other programs).[4]

#	Event/Actor(s)	Description	Outcome
	**Conduct new patient consult:** *Conduct physician initial consultation*		
1	Clinical assistant or registered nurse receives patient arrival notification. (User process)	Responds to notification regarding the arrival of a patient	*Flows to 2*
2	Clinical assistant or registered nurse completes pre-assessment questions. (User process)	Completes five pre-assessment questions and documents patient vital signs and complaints, if any	*Flows to 3*
3	Registered nurse requires intervention to address patient complaints? (Manual decision)	Requires intervention regarding patient overview or not	*Yes flows to 4, No flows to 5*
4	Registered nurse addresses patient complaints. (Manual process)	Consults with physician or nurse practitioner regarding complaints identified by patient	*Flows to 5*
5	Patient or registered nurse completes self-reporting history. (User process)	Documents patient history	*Flows to 6*
6	Physician meets with new patient. (User process)	Performs complete comprehensive patient assessment	*Flows to 7*
7	Physician or registered nurse completes or updates problem list. (User process)	Documents patient issues (e.g., allergies, medications)	*Flows to 8*
8	Proposed system charges patient. (System process out)	Charges patient	*Processes output for **Charge**, then flows to 9*
9	Physician prepares new orders? (User decision)	Determines whether or not orders must be written to facilitate continued treatment of a patient	*Yes exits to **Create or change orders**, No terminates*

TABLE 4-4   Detailed User Requirement Script

UML has many different diagrams divided into two general categories, including:

- *Structural Modeling Diagrams*—Communicate what the model includes and the relationships among the items.
- *Behavioral Modeling Diagrams*—Capture types of interactions and timing states within a model as it executes over time.

We use activity diagrams, a type of UML behavioral modeling diagram, to define user needs. An *activity diagram* is a UML graphical presentation for modeling process steps and actions. An activity diagram is a type of flowchart that includes designated shapes for activities, decisions, and start- and end-points. We use activity diagrams because they model:

- *User Requirements*—Displays the step sequences involving user interaction with a system. Using an activity diagram, an HDO can define EHR requirements to solicit vendor proposals, configure the vendor system, and test that system for compliance with the configuration.
- *Workflow*—Shows the interaction of automated and manual steps. Using an activity diagram, an HDO can define manual user activities associated with an EHR and document how to improve them. We define both the manual steps and system requirements simultaneously because they are so closely related.

We generally start with text instead of diagrams because graphical representation requires special software tools, is time-consuming to create and update, is difficult to fully display on a single page or screen, and is hard to use for search and replace operations. We verify the accuracy of our text description and then prepare the graphical version.

Table 4-5 displays a text version of an activity diagram that describes user requirements for stage and mix pharmacy orders. It includes, from left to right, an activity sequence number, the activity, and the next step. Each activity includes an actor. Activities also include a parenthetical reference to their type [i.e., manual process, system process, interface (in- or out-process), or decision]. Notice, step 1 in our example below includes a pharmacist or registered nurse, the actor, manually verifying an order, which flows to the second step.

An activity diagram is an abstract way of describing user tasks. You must ensure, however, that the diagram is both accurate and comprehensive. To do this, consider the impact of actors performing each decision in the activity diagram. An *actor* is the user or system that model information interchanges. An actor decision may result in performing a certain set of system tasks or a scenario. Another actor decision results in following a different scenario.

A *scenario* is a story of the system and actor interactions. A *primary success scenario* is the main story that an actor performs from end-to-end to achieve the desired outcome without taking any alternate steps along the way. An alternate scenario is a major plot variation in the story that documents common secondary activities or exceptions an actor performs before achieving the desired outcome.

Figure 4-1 displays an activity diagram of the text version described above but it displays only one of the available scenarios. In the text version, you can read the collection of possible scenarios that actors perform. Figure 4-1 documents the primary success scenario that achieves the goal of staging and mixing a pharmacy order correctly.

Figure 4-2 displays an alternate scenario. In this instance the pharmacist or pharmacy technician determines the set-up is incorrect and that they cannot proceed or succeed until one of them corrects it.

Figure 4-3 displays the primary success scenario as a swim lane diagram. A *swim lane diagram* is a grouping of activities by actor into parallel lanes, similar to the lanes in a swimming pool. Each swim lane visually defines which actor is working on what. It displays a single scenario and who is responsible for each part of it according to a specific sequence. This helps verify that your activities are accurate and assigned to the correct actor.

In summary, activity diagrams support the following:

- Identifying each individual sequential automated step an actor supports
- Identifying each individual sequential manual step an actor supports
- Combining automated and manual steps into scenarios illustrating how to best configure both the system and the supporting manual steps according to different circumstances

Stage and mix pharmacy order: *Set up drugs and supplies to prepare patient-specific drug*		
1	Pharmacist or registered nurse verifies order is correct? (Manual decision) Pharmacist and nurse compare aloud label versus order for order accuracy and to check patient identifiers (e.g., patient's exact name, birth date, medical record number, diluent, rate of infusion, drug dose, drug name, volume, solution, route, and solution color) for correctness or not.	*Yes flows to 2,* *No exits to Review pharmacy order*
2	Pharmacy technician assembles drug products and sets up preparation. (Manual process) Sets-up drug products for sterile mixing.	*Flows to 3*
3	Pharmacist or pharmacy technician determines set-up is correct? (Manual decision) Determines set-up correct or not.	*Yes flows to 5,* *No flows to 4*
4	Pharmacist or pharmacy technician corrects assembly. (Manual process) Fixes order set-up errors.	*Flows to 5*
5	Pharmacist or pharmacy technician withdraws doses and prepares final products. (Manual process) Measures and removes amounts from drug vials and prepares final products.	*Flows to 6*
6	Pharmacist logs preparation of hazardous drug. (User process) Tracks preparation of hazardous drugs.	*Flows to 7*
7	Pharmacist or pharmacy technician determines final product correct? (Manual decision) Determines drugs withdrawn and assembled correct or not.	*Yes flows to 8,* *No loops to 4*
8	Pharmacist or pharmacy technician makes drug available for pick-up. (Manual process) Places drug in pick-up area.	*Exits to re-verify pharmacy order*

TABLE 4-5   Text Version of an Activity Diagram

Activity diagrams are easy to understand and communicate system needs. When working with providers, we start our sessions with a metaphor. We assemble a group of participants or Project Team and tell them that they are playwrights writing a play where they are the actors in a series of short scripts about what they do at work. We explain that collectively these scripts tell the story of how a new system and manual steps will work together to meet their needs. The group understands immediately and starts to work right away.

With the results of sessions you conduct, you have the power to use activity diagrams for:

- *Requirements Definition*—To prepare a comprehensive set of user requirements to acquire a vendor system that support the user needs

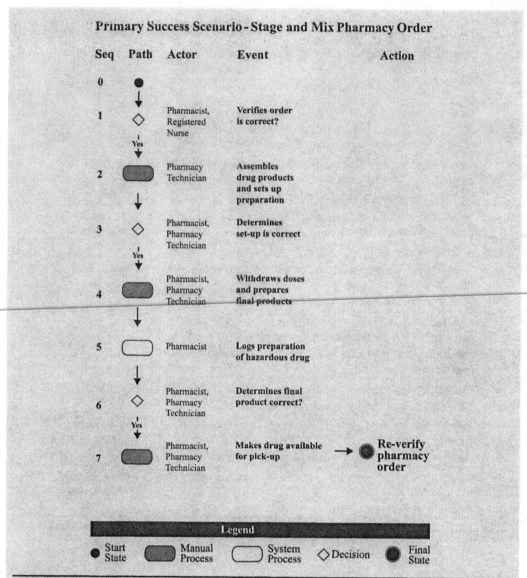

Primary Success Scenario - Stage and Mix Pharmacy Order

Seq	Path	Actor	Event	Action
0	●			
1	◇ Yes	Pharmacist, Registered Nurse	Verifies order is correct?	
2	▭	Pharmacy Technician	Assembles drug products and sets up preparation	
3	◇ Yes	Pharmacist, Pharmacy Technician	Determines set-up is correct	
4	▭	Pharmacist, Pharmacy Technician	Withdraws doses and prepares final products	
5	▭	Pharmacist	Logs preparation of hazardous drug	
6	◇ Yes	Pharmacist, Pharmacy Technician	Determines final product correct?	
7	▭	Pharmacist, Pharmacy Technician	Makes drug available for pick-up	→ ● Re-verify pharmacy order

Legend

● Start State   ▭ Manual Process   ▭ System Process   ◇ Decision   ● Final State

FIGURE 4-1   Primary success scenario.

- *Vendor Evaluation*—To demonstrate vendor proposed systems according to activity diagram scenarios
- *System Configuration*—To document how to configure the selected system according to activity diagram scenarios
- *Workflow Changes*—To document how to redesign automated and manual workflow according to the documented system configuration

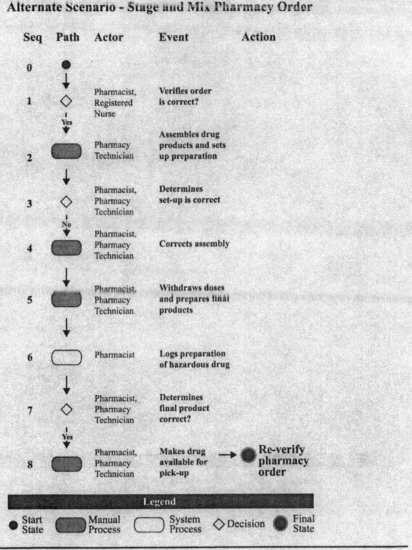

FIGURE 4-2 Alternative scenario.

- *Testing*—To verify that the fully configured system functions according to the system configuration documented in activity diagram scenarios
- *Training*—To use the final activity diagram scenarios that include the system configuration and workflow to identify training requirements and support preparation of training materials

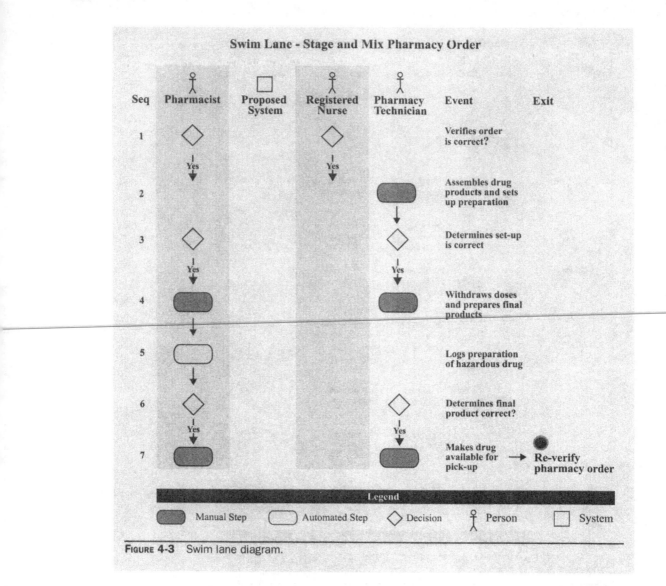

Figure 4-3   Swim lane diagram.

Control User Requirements

The Project Manager monitors user requirement preparations during the controlling process. The user requirements management plan serves as a baseline for managing user requirements similar to any other plan in the Project Management Plan. The Project Manager monitors user requirements management using the control process described in integration management. For example, the CIO of a provider independently selected a vendor to implement their EHR. The eventual result was an expensive failure because none of the clinicians had a stake in vendor selection. The provider's new CIO subsequently hired us to work with their clinicians to prepare requirements, and then acquire and implement their EHR. We completed the requirements using JAD, with a cross-section of representative clinicians, and facilitated their successful vendor selection and system implementation.

INFRASTRUCTURE MANAGEMENT

In the last section, we discussed the importance of interacting directly with HIT users to understand their needs. In this IT management area, we focus on an assessment of HIT project *details* through infrastructure management. *Infrastructure management* is initiating, planning, executing, and controlling requirements for the location and configuration or the physical components of a new system. *Infrastructure* is the system hardware and other physical components supporting it and the facilities housing that equipment.

> . . . we upgraded our network infrastructure to create a redundancy, and we changed our network infrastructure to accommodate wireless infrastructure for both clinics as well as hospitals. We put in place the EMPI [Enterprise Master Patient Index] and, . . . the whole disaster recovery, business continuity strategy and plan.
>
> Knowing that in the future, which was then in 2008, we would bring up the hospital clinical information system, we had strategically done all that work to get ourselves ready for the electronic health record implementation for the hospital. So when we went live, none of this became an issue and we did not have to worry about these devices. Most of the devices we used had to do with workstation on wheels that we had in some areas, especially in some patient service areas that were way too small. We had nurse services outside of patient rooms. We tested out some of the laptop devices, especially for respiratory therapists, because they were going back and forth between multiple rooms, and those worked well for them. Those probably, and desktops, those are the major devices we put in place for the clinicians.
>
> —Florence Chang, MBA, CIO, Multicare

Table 4-6 displays infrastructure management processes and their outputs (in italics) by process group.

Initiating	Planning	Executing	Controlling	Closing
Prepare high-level technology requirements	Prepare infrastructure management plan	Define detailed technology requirements	Control infrastructure	
High-level technology requirements	*Infrastructure management plan*	*Detailed technology requirements*	*Organizational process asset update*	
Define existing technology architecture	Prepare facility modification plan	Prepare and order equipment	*Performance report*	
Existing technology architecture description	*Facility modification plan*	*Equipment order confirmation*	*Change request (CR)*	
	Prepare system installation plan	Complete facility modifications	*Project document update*	
	System installation plan	*Site readiness confirmation*		
		Install system		
		Hardware readiness confirmation		
		Application readiness confirmation		

TABLE 4-6 Infrastructure Management Knowledge Area by Process Group

The general steps in infrastructure management include planning high-level and then detailed technology and architecture requirements, preparing the facility modification and installation plan, preparing the equipment orders, modifying facilities, and then installing the equipment.

Prepare High-Level Technology Requirements

An HDO prepares high-level technology requirements during the initiating process. A *high-level technology requirement* is a general description of technology constraints, and capacity and performance information required to support a proposed system. It identifies vendor costs based on number of users, patients, and other parameters a vendor's system must support to meet the HDO's needs. The HDO uses these technology requirements when evaluating available vendor options as part of a feasibility study or business case. Table 4-7 displays examples of high-level technology requirements.

These high-level technology requirements should define only the specific technology that is mandatory (e.g., the HDO's strategic plan dictates migration to a .NET environment, current messaging system requires interface with Microsoft Exchange). As with the high-level user requirements described in user requirements management, at this stage of the project, these technology requirements are at a high level because this sufficiently informs key executives with the necessary information required for a decision on whether to proceed.

The experience of VMMC provides a good example of the reasoning behind preparing high-level technology requirements.

We knew that no vendor could do everything. Therefore, our strategy was to have a primary vendor for clinical, a primary vendor for patient registration and patient accounting, and a primary vendor for financials. We also knew we were going to manage our own infrastructure. This decision will vary based on the technology strengths and culture of any given organization. Because we chose to manage our own infrastructure, there were capabilities within the department that drove some of our technology decisions. One of the vendors we looked at used a technology we had no expertise in. It was also a vendor that couldn't demonstrate the integration points we wanted. That made it an easy decision to eliminate the vendor. The vendor we did choose was integrated AND was able to support the technical capabilities we had a skill set in.

—Beatha Johnson, Director, Clinical Information Systems, VMMC

1	Do you provide your EHR as a SaaS or hosted environment?
2	Do you provide your EHR as client-hosted-licensed software?
3	Is your system developed for a Microsoft .NET environment?
4	Does your system use a Microsoft SQL Server database?

TABLE 4-7 High-Level Technology Requirements

Define Existing Technology Architecture

Virtually every HDO already has an installed base of technology hardware and software that a new system must accommodate. It is important to create a description of this existing technology architecture during the initiating process to ensure that the HDO can accommodate the new system. This includes preparing a description of existing technology architecture. An *existing technology architecture description* is an overview of the systems, software, and other technical components currently supporting users that are critical to understanding the current environment. The HDO prepares this overview to evaluate the impact of proposed solutions on their existing technology environment. This information helps the HDO to evaluate potential solutions during a feasibility study and business case. It also helps vendors determine if they can support the HDO's transition to a new system, and what, if any, portion of the current environment must change to support the new system.

Prepare Infrastructure Management Plan

Assuming the HIT project receives approval, the project shifts to the planning process, and the next IT management step is to prepare an infrastructure management plan. An *infrastructure management plan is a description* of how an organization will address the physical components of a system, including hardware components, system capacity and performance requirements, physical and environmental constraints, and changes to existing facilities. It generally addresses the following:

- Specific existing hardware, network, or other equipment components supporting the new system that the HDO uses *as is* or upgrades as appropriate
- New hardware, network, or other equipment components supporting the new system that the HDO purchases, configures, installs, and tests
- System capacity, performance, and availability requirements that supporting hardware must meet
- Physical and environmental hardware constraints (e.g., temperature control, hazard protection, power consumption, and space requirements)
- Changes to HDO facilities or physical plant supporting the identified hardware

Define Detailed Technology Requirements

We had a team that worked together with operations before and during the project duration. They actually walked through every single floor, unit, and department to identify device requirements, and the placement of those devices. Just like you built a new facility, you walk it with your blueprint. We took that blueprint and marked all the locations, the type and number of devices they needed. I think that the learning from that process is no different from when you build a house. It looks good on paper, but what you end up putting in place may require a lot of changes. I would say one of the major things we encountered is that at the very beginning, nobody, no one wanted to look at the workstation on wheels. They said we want a stationary desktop. We want a wall mount. We don't want a workstation on wheels, because we don't have room for this. We don't have room to move the cart back and forth. No one wanted that, and again this is a change management issue, because nobody ever thought about doing the bedside documentation. The mindset is very different. So that was the original requirement.

Once we started putting devices in place, in less than a week, the requirement changed completely. Folks wanted more workstations on wheels. They started realizing the benefits of bringing the cart to the patient bedside. It was so much easier than taking a piece of paper and going into the hall to complete the documentation. Here again, it's a learning process, because until you get the system in place, it's difficult to understand what kind of device you require. We took that learning from other sites to subsequent implementations. We took them to Tacoma General to look at how we set it up, in order for them to finalize their data device requirements.

—Florence Chang, MBA, CIO, Multicare

A detailed technology requirement is the extension of the high-level technology requirements created earlier. A *detailed technology requirement* is an in-depth description of the equipment, and environmental and regulatory criteria (e.g., sizing and performance criteria, power, temperature, and physical space considerations), and regulatory constraints the selected vendor must support.

The HDO begins defining its detailed technology requirements from existing HDO standards and other available documentation. However, technology considerations are the purview of specific individuals or IT members of the Project Team. Typically selected technology representatives (e.g., director of clinical applications, network manager, or other IT representatives) identify or update existing documentation regarding the technical environment. This process also identifies specific concerns or constraints that the supporting physical equipment must address, in the following areas:

- Required system capacity (e.g., simultaneous users, estimated transaction volumes, estimated record retention)
- Required system performance (e.g., application response times, user wait times)
- Required system availability (e.g., operating days and hours, minimum uptime percentage)

The HDO uses detailed technology requirements for soliciting, evaluating, and selecting a solution to implement. The HDO subsequently relies on these requirements during implementation to address facility modifications, equipment installation, and performance testing described in other sections.

One example of the concepts included in technology requirements is system performance. Table 4-8 displays an example of estimated user and transaction volumes, both measures of system performance requirements. Table 4-9 displays an example of system availability requirements. Table 4-10 provides an example of response time requirements.

Prepare Facility Modification Plan

It is almost certain that the new infrastructure required for an HIT project, such as the EHR, will include modifications to the physical plant of the HDO. For example, if the HDO is coming from a purely paper-based medical record, there may not be sufficient cabling, power, and space to support the dozens or hundreds of new workstations that the EHR may require. Therefore, the HDO must research the facility modification requirements in patient rooms and clinical work areas.

An HDO prepares a facility modification plan during the planning process. The *facility modification plan* is a description of how an organization identifies, schedules, and completes changes to its facilities to accommodate a new system. The HDO determines

User and Transaction Type	Estimated Volume
Estimated number of annual outpatient visits	436,288
Estimated number of Medicare outpatient visits	183,973
Estimated number of workstations	1,191
Estimated number of concurrent users	851
Estimated percent growth per year	5%
Estimated Named Users by Type:	
Administration	80
Billers	30
Clinical Assistant	130
Dietician/Psychosocial	30
Financial Counselor	10
HIM Clerk	50
HIM Coder	20
HIM Manager	10
Lab Manager	10
Laboratory Technician	30
Medical Secretary	50
Patient Service Representative	80
Phlebotomist	0
Physician	10
Receptionist	30
Registered Nurse	150

TABLE 4-8   Estimated User and Transaction Volumes

Operating Hours	Operating Days Per Week	System Availability Hours	System Availability Days Per Week
24 Hours	7 days/wk	24 Hours	7 days/wk Unless there is a scheduled outage
Minimum uptime requirement: 99.99%			

TABLE 4-9   System Availability Requirements

System Response	Description	Time	Unit
Record Retrieval Time	The interval from the execution of a command to retrieve a record until the last character of that record displays on screen and the system is available for use by the user at that equipment.	4	Second(s)
Record Search Time	The interval from the execution of a command to perform a record search until the last character of the search result displays on screen and the system is available for use by the user at that equipment.	4	Second(s)
Screen Edit Time	The interval from the execution of a command indicating completion of data entry on a particular screen until the system is available for use by the user at that equipment.	2	Second(s)
Field Edit Time	The interval from the execution of a command indicating completion of data entry on a particular field until the system is available for use by the user at that equipment.		Subsecond
New Screen Page Time	The interval from the execution of a command to access a new screen until the last character of the new screen displays and the system is available for use by the user at that equipment.	2	Second(s)
Processing Time	The interval from the execution of a command initiating a process until the equipment receives the last character pertaining to that process and the system is available for use by the user at that equipment.	2	Second(s)

TABLE 4-10   Response Time Requirements

the scope of facility modifications based on a review of their facilities and the selected vendor's response to the technical requirements, including such factors as temperature control, hazard protection, power consumption, equipment footprints, secured facility access, and so on.

Prepare System Installation Plan

While the customer was evaluating vendor functionality, our technology partners (i.e. host hardware, network, servers, devices) were evaluating the technology. They completed a technology assessment for the top three vendors by having the vendor complete a questionnaire followed by peer-to-peer conversations. When final deliberation occurred, their input was at the table. They were not the decision-makers, but the decision-makers were clear on the technology pros and cons associated with each vendor choice. Once the vendor decision was made, they participated in the contract review to ensure the required infrastructure was represented. Finally, they had a say as to when the project could get started as they were responsible for data center space, cooling, power, and so on. The above did not become a constraint for our project, as potential challenges were mitigated during the time

(years) we evaluated potential vendors. Today, we formally complete an annual capacity plan to ensure that hardware growth is accommodated and planned as part of each budget cycle.
—Beatha Johnson, Director, Clinical Information Systems, VMMC

An HDO prepares a system installation plan during the planning process. A *system installation plan* is the description of the hardware, application, and system software planned for installation and configuration to support a new system, and the timing and scope of installation.

If the system installation is a SaaS configuration, the vendor server hardware is at their facility as described in the SaaS sidebar. The vendor must prepare an equipment installation plan that supports system environment configuration, staging (testing and training), and production. A *system environment* is a collection of hardware and software to perform certain computing activities like development, testing, training, and production.

Table 4-11 displays an example of vendor system environments supporting a SaaS-delivered EHR.

Environment	Hardware
Production	Web Servers Redundant web farm of Dual Xeon servers, Windows 2003 Server operating system. Microsoft Windows 2003 Server ColdFusion MX7 Server IIS 6.0 on Windows 2003 Servers NET Framework 2.0 SSL Certificate Database Servers Microsoft Windows 2003 Server Microsoft SQL 2005 Standard Edition
Staging	Web Server Single instance of web and database mirroring production to be used for QA and load testing. Microsoft Windows 2003 Server ColdFusion MX7 Server IIS 6.0 on Windows 2003 Servers NET Framework 2.0 SSL Certificate Database Server Microsoft Windows 2003 Server Microsoft SQL 2005 Standard Edition
Configuration	Web Server Microsoft Windows 2003 Server ColdFusion MX7 Server IIS 6.0 on Windows 2003 Servers NET Framework 2 Database Server Microsoft Windows 2003 Server Microsoft SQL 2005 Standard Edition

TABLE 4-11   System Environments

Software as a Service

Software as a Service (SaaS) is the delivery of application software and data to customers as an on-demand service. SaaS vendors deliver software over the Internet by hosting the software themselves or through a third party application service provider (ASP). SaaS is the evolution of what used to be called service bureaus. A *service bureau* is an organization that provides a variety of IT services such as data storage and time-share applications. The customer connects to the service bureau and uses the provided computer resources. Banks used to rent their mainframe computer capacity to hospitals in order to provide a variety of computer services. Amazon and Google do this today via the Internet as SaaS.

The best HIT example of a service bureau offering (or similarly a SaaS) is the Shared Medical Systems (SMS) Corporation, which is now a part of Siemens Healthcare. SMS started by offering IT solutions to the hospital market, but hospitals did not have the expertise to install, operate, and maintain computer systems. SMS subsequently decided to offer terminals at customer hospitals. These hospitals connected to the SMS centralized mainframes on a time-share basis, without having to install, maintain, and operate premise-based systems, very much like SaaS.[5]

The case for SaaS requires consideration of many factors. For example, while HIT includes many significant costs, SaaS solutions offer lower capital costs (i.e., hardware platform), when compared to traditional hospital or premise-based solutions. Assuming the HDO realigns their IT resources, staff could spend less time on hardware installation and maintenance to focus on issues like software configuration and workflow redesign for better clinical care delivery.

These and many other factors make SaaS attractive. This requires adding some new items to system procurements, removing others that are no longer applicable, crafting a new type of vendor contract that relies on attorney expertise not necessarily available at your HDO, and monitoring IT service delivery in a way that may be new to your HIT professionals.

A SaaS project should address the following:[6]

- Architecture
  - Use of Rich Internet Application (RIA) technology—RIA features allow the SaaS application to execute functions locally on PCs rather than via an Internet-based web server. This increases the connection speed between your computer and the SaaS application.
  - An application configured by the vendor to comply with your organization's web accessibility and presentation standards.
  - Limitations on customization and configuration now that you share your application with other SaaS customers.
  - Contract definition of your data ownership.
  - Provision and testing of a suitable method for retrieving your data in a format you can use with other applications or tools, should you terminate your relationship with the SaaS vendor.
  - Automated load-testing tools as part of the vendor implementation.
- Performance Reliability
  - Bandwidth upgrade and monitoring requirements that your environment must now support given higher network transaction volume due to SaaS usage.

- Performance metric Service Level Agreements (SLAs) with monetary penalties (e.g., failover response time, transaction time, system uptime, and network connectivity 24/7, 365 days per year). This issue has significant operational impact because it assumes you have the time and expertise to monitor SLA compliance.
- Tools to measure application availability offered by the SaaS vendor (e.g., Internet access to ongoing and historical system uptime, outages, and degradations).
- Information about how the SaaS vendor manages planned growth in demand without adversely affecting your system use.
- Geographic proximity of the SaaS vendor data center (i.e., the closer the data center to you, the better the performance).
- The performance impact of software updates and whether you have the option to control the schedule of these updates.
- Data integration between your internal or other SaaS applications and your new SaaS addition.
- Off-line data access without using the SaaS application, if possible.
- Disaster recovery and high availability capabilities and facilities that ensure continuous uninterrupted software availability.
- Backup capabilities that ensure prompt and complete data recovery, including periodic testing of data recovery procedures.
- Continuity plans that now include your new SaaS vendor.
- Security
  - Vendor willingness to cooperate in your defense due to a data security breach.
  - Vendor compliance with your eDiscovery response time and data hold requirements.
  - Vendor-dedicated data security personnel.
  - Vendor acceptance of annual third-party white and black box security tests. White box testing considers the internal workings of a system. Black box testing addresses external issues, such as user access, functional restrictions based on user roles, or other configuration-established parameters controlling who can do what in the application.
  - Vendor maintenance of a well-documented security infrastructure.
  - Vendor audit log that you can access immediately after a breach (before the log is lost or overwritten).
  - Vendor maintenance of incident protection and detection software.
  - Vendor encrypted data storage and transmission that compensates for performance implications.
  - Vendor estimated response time from support personnel when contacted regarding security issues.
  - Vendor supplied incident response plans (e.g., listing of user activity, including deletions, backups, and exports).
  - Vendor login and password policy compliance with your organization's standards.

- ○ Data storage geographical considerations, such as requiring vendor notification when the vendor moves your data to another geographical location.
- ○ Prohibition against maintaining your data offshore.
- ○ Delegation of user provisioning administration to the customer.
- ○ Vendor maintenance of physical controls over ingress/egress of the software production/delivery facility.

Each environment represents a fully functioning EHR installation supporting specific user needs. Preparing to install a system includes the following tasks to verify the environments are appropriate before system configuration:

- HDO reviews and confirms its capacity and performance requirements for each environment based on the expected demand for testing, training, and production use, using the system capacity requirements
- Vendor reviews and accepts these capacity and performance criteria, and subsequently provides environments that meet these criteria
- HDO verifies that the installed environments meet the identified criteria (e.g., as defined in the capacity requirements)

The system installation plan also addresses required updates or replacements to HDO workstations or network infrastructure.

A SaaS-delivered EHR is a 100% web-based application, accessible via a standard web browser, such as Internet Explorer or Firefox. Through SaaS, there may or may not be specific requirements that the HDO must meet for the EHR to operate properly on their workstations. Third-party applications or plug-ins (including ActiveX controls) may be required to access the system. As part of the equipment installation plan, the HDO confirms its workstations are capable of running a current web browser (Internet Explorer, Firefox, and so on) and an Internet connection with appropriate third-party applications or plug-ins.

Figure 4-4 is an illustration of a sample network and web infrastructure.

Prepare and Order Equipment

An HDO prepares orders for the required hardware during the executing process. The HDO prepares an order, contacts the appropriate suppliers, identifies required lead times, specifies funding sources, and places the required orders. The output of this process is an equipment order confirmation. An *equipment order confirmation* is a written acknowledgement by a manufacturer that an organization is purchasing items, including their description, manufacture, model, type, and quantity.

The HDO orders equipment, such as user workstations, tablet or other handheld computers, and servers and network equipment. In a SaaS environment, ordering, installing, and configuring of hardware occurs at a vendor facility; however, the HDO still needs to order workstation and network equipment.

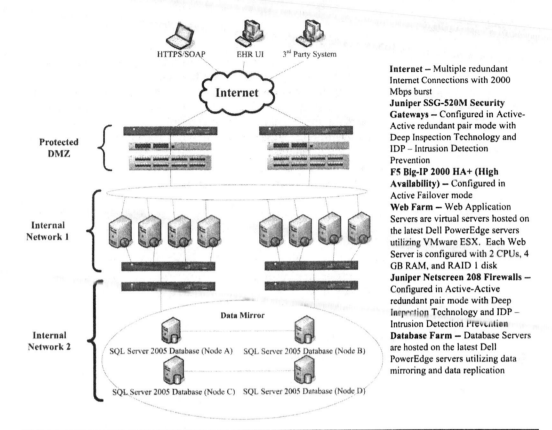

FIGURE 4-4 Sample infrastructure.

Complete Facility Modifications

An HDO completes required facility modifications during the execution process. This is the process of specifying, scheduling, contracting, executing, and monitoring construction at an organization's facilities according to a previously prepared facility modification plan.

Examples of facility modifications that HDOs encounter include installation of:

- Network cables
- Wireless networks
- Power-supply upgrades

The output of this process is a site readiness confirmation. A *site readiness confirmation* is a written acknowledgement, issued by the vendor after a review of the modified facilities, indicating the results of modification or renovation to an organization's facilities comply with vendor infrastructure requirements. For example, a vendor could inspect the HDO's site and send an email attesting to its readiness.

Install System

An HDO completes the installation of required hardware and any associated system software during the execution process. The vendor or HDO installs each piece of equipment according to the manufacturer's specifications based on the system installation plan. The output of this process is a hardware readiness confirmation. A *hardware readiness confirmation* is a written acknowledgement provided by the vendor (in a SaaS environment) or HDO (in a premise based environment) indicating installation compliance of all equipment and hardware according to manufacturer-specified standards and readiness for configuration.

An HDO also completes the installation of the required application software on the previously confirmed hardware during the execution process. The vendor or HDO installs each application software component according to the manufacturer's specifications based on the system installation plan. The output of this process is an application readiness confirmation. An *application readiness confirmation* is a written acknowledgement provided by the vendor indicating installation compliance of all application software components according to manufacturer specified standards and readiness for configuration.

For a SaaS-delivered application, the vendor notifies the HDO that the system environments specified in the infrastructure management plan are available for use. The vendor also provides network or Internet addresses, initial user IDs and passwords, and initial access instructions at this time.

Control Infrastructure

The Project Manager monitors infrastructure management during the controlling process. The infrastructure plan serves as a baseline for managing the infrastructure similar to any other plan in the project management plan. The Project Manager monitors infrastructure management using the control process described in integration management. For example, a provider that we work with manages specialty clinics for different hospital customers throughout the United States. As part of their EHR implementation project, we initially prepared infrastructure pricing assuming each clinic would operate a separate database on shared hardware. The provider first established this approach after the EHR project approval and vendor selection, and *then* decided it was imperative to keep each clinic physically separate and required individual servers running with stand-alone databases. This significant scope change required a technical assessment, cost analysis, and discussion with the vendor to address how they would accommodate this change. The resulting CR updated the scope, cost, and infrastructure management plans to reflect the increased cost.

CONVERSION MANAGEMENT

A data conversion is a project managed just like the application implementation is managed, just like the interfaces are managed. Depending on the size and scope of each component, we may have multiple individuals managing a single project: someone specifically managing the data conversion, someone specifically managing the interface work, and someone specifically managing the application build. Each of those areas can, dependent on scope, be intense efforts.

—Beatha Johnson, Director, Clinical Information Systems, VMMC

In the last section, we discussed the activities necessary to check and modify hardware and physical facilities necessary to support the requirements of the new system. In the same way, the HDO must also assess and modify its existing data (e.g., using existing information on patients in the new system). It is likely this data currently exists in multiple formats—from paper to electronic. *Conversion management* is planning, executing, and controlling transformation and movement of data from existing manual and automated systems to the new system. Table 4-12 displays conversion management processes and their outputs (in italics) by process group.

Prepare Conversion Plan

For every project, we document business requirements and develop a project charter. A component of those documents is identifying if there is a requirement for data conversion. We have only had to complete two data conversions. One was the initial project when we set up the clinical data repository in 2001. That project was predominantly interfaces and data conversion. The second data conversion was completed in March 2010 when we replaced a legacy chart tracking system with a module from our clinical vendor.

—Beatha Johnson, Director, Clinical Information Systems, VMMC

An HDO prepares a conversion plan during the planning process. A *conversion plan* is a description of how an organization plans to move and/or transform data from an existing manual or automated system to a new system.

Initiating	Planning	Executing	Controlling	Closing
	Prepare conversion plan *Conversion plan*	Prepare data conversion map *Data conversion map* Conduct data cleansing *Data cleansing confirmation* Develop and test conversion solution *Conversion solution confirmation* Convert data *Conversion confirmation*	Control conversion *Organizational process asset update* *Performance report* *Change request (CR)* *Project document update*	

TABLE 4-12   Conversion Management Knowledge Area by Process Group

Conversion of existing information into a new EHR is a critical and complex activity. An HDO may store current data in one or more different systems, each designed and built to support a specific aspect of patient care as well as the full range of financial and administrative functions such as billing and admitting, respectively. In addition, an HDO maintains extensive paper records on each patient. Maximizing the usefulness and effectiveness of an EHR requires consolidation, organization, and transformation of this disparate set of information for use in a single source.

The HDO prepares its conversion plan by completing the following activities:

- *Identify Conversion Scope*—Define the type and volume of records the HDO plans to transfer to the new system.

- *Identify Conversion Type*—Determine how conversion will occur for each information source identified. Available options include:

  o *Automated Conversion*—A computer application used to identify, compare, adjust, and transfer selected information between the existing and the new systems.

  o *Manual Conversion*—Selected records in the existing system or paper records manually entered into the new system.

  o *Hybrid Conversion*—A combination of automated and manual conversion. For example, the HDO initially transfers data from one or more sources using automated tools and manually updates this automatically converted data once it is in the new system (e.g., to reflect specific formatting and reorganization where the new system requires additional information not available from existing data).

- *Identify Conversion Timing*—Define staging of multiple conversions for system configuration, testing, training, and cutover.

- *Identify Straddle Records*—A *straddle record* is a record added to the old system after conversion but before cutover to the new system. For example, the HDO performs its final pre-production conversion on May 1; however, the cutover to the new system does not occur until May 5. Straddle records are all records added or updated in the old system during the five-day period that the HDO must add to the new system at cutover.

- *Map Data Exchanges*—Map data sources and destinations and define the data attributes to facilitate accurate data entry where data in the current system does not directly match data in the new system.

- *Identify Volume of Data for Conversion*—Estimate number of records included in conversion and the time required to complete it.

- *Define Requirements for Data Cleansing*—Identify volume of data inconsistencies and anomalies (e.g., duplicate patient records that may require correction as part of the conversion).

- *Identify Tools for Automated Conversion*—Identify existing or planned software applications, utilities, macros, or other tools for converting data from each available source.

Record Type	Volume
Patient Master (Medical record #, patient name, date of birth, sex, etc.)	765,406
Physician Master	34,028
Insurance Plans	4,992

TABLE 4-13 Conversion Scope

- *Assign Resources to Complete Manual and Automated Conversion*—Assign specific personnel (e.g., temporary staff or Project Team members) to complete data cleansing, manual entry, and verification of manual and automated conversions.

Table 4-13 provides an example of existing records available for conversion.

Prepare Data Conversion Map

We just went live moving from Meditech to EPIC, so we had a separate project to convert all the data. They had about 10 years of data converted to EPIC. So there was a separate conversion project going on in parallel with the rest of the project.

Our conversion took us about six to eight months. We spent the time doing the documentation, the review, and the mapping ahead of time, then doing the conversion process. Conversion itself, the act of conversion itself, usually doesn't take that much time. It is the whole mapping process at the front end, which is critical to the success of conversion.

—Florence Chang, MBA, CIO, Multicare

An HDO prepares a data conversion map during the execution process. A *data conversion map* is an identification of the characteristics of each piece of information planned for transfer to the new system from an existing source. Examples of these properties include:

- *Field Name*—A designation or title for a piece of information (e.g., expiration date)
- *Description*—The definition for a specific piece of information (e.g., birth date)
- *SQL Type*—A standard field type for a specific piece of information (e.g., binary, integer, text, timestamp)
- *Field Size*—A field length associated with some structured query language (SQL) types (e.g., datetime, which is an industry standard database format)
- *Nullity*—Whether a field can be left blank (e.g., middle initial)
- *Range*—The upper and lower limit of acceptable values (e.g., 1-50, A-G)
- *Picture*—The data entry format (e.g., MM/DD/YYYY)
- *Default*—A value used when leaving an entry field blank (e.g., none)
- *Expected Value*—An example of the kind of information entered in a field (e.g., John Q. Smith)

The HDO maps source and destination data by comparing the data properties in the source (i.e., the existing data) to the destination (i.e., the new system). This helps specify the parameters used by automated conversion tools to move the data to the new system. Table 4-13 displays an example of a data conversion map.

Data	System	Field Name	Description	SQL Type	Field Size	Nullity	Range	Picture	Default	Expected Value
Person ID	Legacy Records (source)	PID	A unique identifier indicating a specific individual receiving treatment	char	6	No	1-999999	aaaaaa		009493
	EHR (destination)	PatientID		int		No		nnnnnn	n+1	9493
First Name	Legacy Records (source)	namefirst	The given name of an individual	char	25	No				John
	EHR (destination)	FirstName		char	40	No				John
Middle Initial	Legacy Records (source)	MI	The single letter representing an individual's second or middle name	vchar	1	No				Q
	EHR (destination)	MiddleInitial		char	1	Yes				Q
Last Name	Legacy Records (source)	namelast	The surname or family name of an individual	vchar	25	No				Smith
	EHR (destination)	LastName		char	40	No				Smith

TABLE 4-14 Data Conversion Map

Data	System	Field Name	Description	SQL Type	Field Size	Nullity	Range	Picture	Default	Expected Value
Telephone	Legacy Records (source)	phone	The telephone number for an individual	vchar	10	Yes		nnnnnnnnnn		2135551212
	EHR (destination)	PrimaryPhone	The primary contact telephone number for an individual	vchar	13	Yes		(nnn) NNN-NNNN		(213) 555-1212
Email Address	Legacy Records (source)	N/A								
	EHR (destination)	ElectronicMail	The electronic mail address for an individual	vchar	50	Yes		aaaaaa @aaa.aaa		test@test. com
Comments	Legacy Records (source)	Notes	Additional information associated with an individual	vchar	500	Yes				
	EHR (destination)	AdditionalInfo		text		Yes				

Table 4-14 Data Conversion Map (*Continued*)

Conduct Data Cleansing

An HDO performs the data cleansing during the executing process. *Data cleansing* is the process of identifying and resolving corrupt or inaccurate information so that it will convert properly to a new system. This may include merging duplicate patient records, resolving conflicts or inconsistencies among different potential sources, or updating records so they conform to the format required by the new system.

The HDO prepares and executes queries of the date required for conversion to sample and identify the scope of data cleansing required and then estimates the time and resources required for data cleansing before conversion. The time required to complete the data cleansing varies. Sampling the source database provides information necessary for estimating the scope and time required for this task. For example, an HDO has 5,000 patient records requiring conversion from the source or incumbent system to the target or new EHR. Assume the HDO samples the source database and determines that 15% or 750 of the patient records are duplicates. The HDO then runs tests where Health Information Management (HIM) staff research and merge duplicate records in the source system. Suppose it takes HIM staff an average of 15 minutes to research and merge a duplicate record. They have already identified 750 duplicate records. For one person to cleanse the data, it will take 11,250 minutes (15 minutes times 750) or 187 hours, requiring more than 23 eight-hour days for completion. The HDO could include several people in this task to reduce the calendar time to complete it.

The output of this process is a data cleansing confirmation. A *data cleansing confirmation* is a written verification that completed data cleansing meets requirements for conversion and subsequent system use.

A recent example of the process used to identify data cleansing needs is as follows:

I would say the biggest challenge we had was duplicate medical records. So far the most challenging one, because that required individual review of the records, making sure they were indeed duplicate records, and then we dealt with merging. So if anything, that was our biggest challenge from a data integrity perspective.

The typical process is to take a subset of data, across the whole spectrum of your database, and do an initial run. Use that as your base to estimate the amount of cleansing that you need to do for the system. With that snapshot, you'll have a very good picture of the amount of time you need to cleanse things.

—Florence Chang, MBA, CIO, Multicare

Develop and Test Conversion Solution

An HDO develops and tests the conversion solution during the execution process. If the HDO decides to conduct automated or hybrid conversion of the existing data, it accomplishes this by testing the selected option to ensure it works properly within the project schedule. The output of this process is a tested conversion solution confirmation. A *conversion solution confirmation* is a written acknowledgement that the manual, automated, or combined method used to move data from an existing source to the new system works properly within the project schedule.

Often vendors may have existing conversion tools or services for transferring data from existing systems to their EHR. If not, the vendor, HDO, or a third party develops the required conversion tools. These tools may include a combination of the following:

- Custom-built or standard routines that populate the new system database from one or more different exported source file types [e.g., SQL server database extract, Excel spreadsheet, comma separated value (CSV) text file]
- Custom-built applications that populate the new system data with specific data (e.g., patient master records, using one or more industry-standard formats, such as HL7)
- Custom-built or standard interfaces included in the new system to populate its database on an as-needed basis as part of ongoing data sharing with one or more third-party systems (e.g., patient accounting, pharmacy, patient scheduling)

The HDO tests the conversion tool by using it with sample data and comparing it to expected outcomes. It then documents successful conversion by preparing a conversion solution confirmation.

This activity may occur several times. For example, the HDO converts a limited amount of data for system configuration, more data for testing, additional for training, and all of the data for cutover. Each conversion occurrence may require configuration changes to conversion tools to address the specific data converted at that time. The HDO must test this new configuration each time before converting any data.

Convert Data

An HDO conducts data conversion during the executing process. The output of this process is a conversion confirmation. A *conversion confirmation* is a written acknowledgement of the accuracy and completeness of converted data. This process uses the conversion methods and tools identified in the conversion plan to transfer existing information to the new system.

Control Conversion

The Project Manager monitors conversion during the controlling process. The conversion plan serves as a baseline for managing conversion similar to any other plan in the project management plan. The Project Manager monitors conversion management using the control process described in integration management. For example, one hospital we worked with identified conversion errors after cutover. We typically test the quality of the conversion periodically throughout the entire conversion process. This helps us correct problems early in the conversion process instead of waiting for conversion completion and trying to correct a large number of accumulated problems. For this hospital we researched the post-cutover errors and determined that while the conversion functioned properly, there were previously unidentified format errors in the source data. This had no direct project impact *per se*, and required only limited post-cutover data cleansing by operations.

SOFTWARE CONFIGURATION

With user requirements fully assessed and facility modification and data conversion well underway, we can turn to software configuration. *Software configuration* is planning, executing, and controlling the setup selection of vendor application options and features to meet user, technical, and security requirements. Table 4-15 displays software configuration management processes and their outputs (in italics) by process group.

Software configuration generally takes one of two forms:

- *Configuration*—Changing setting in an application's operational parameters, populating selection lists, turning on or off optional functionality, modifying or adding customizable fields, and selecting from available reports or other client-specific settings that affect the application's workflow, data, or reports. This makes an HDO's application experience unique and tailored (within a given range of options) to its specific requirements without requiring modification to the underlying code.

- *Modification*—Making alterations or additions to the underlying source code or supporting database of a software application so that it functions to the precise specifications of the HDO. This is generally very limited and focuses on unique needs of an HDO or special circumstances (e.g., to change a function so it increases patient safety).

Our book focuses on configuration and not on software modification.

There are two primary options to software configuration. In the first option, the HDO prepares highly configured software satisfying perceived user needs. However, this configuration may come at a cost. It assumes users can predict the future state without previously using the system. The HDO must spend time carefully configuring the system before cutover or users will require substantial reconfiguration after cutover. We will discuss how to minimize this problem later in this section.

The second option involves making very few changes to the configuration as described below:

> *If we were going to implement an EHR, we had to decide whether we felt we knew enough about what the screens should look like or how the EHR should adapt to fit our workflow. This helped us justify a*

Initiating	Planning	Executing	Controlling	Closing
	Prepare software configuration plan *Software configuration plan*	Define configuration requirements *Configuration requirements* Configure system *Test cases*	Control configuration *Organizational process asset update* *Performance report* *Change request (CR)* *Project document update*	

TABLE 4-15   Software Configuration Management Knowledge Area by Process Group

focus on making it look just the way we want it to. We questioned whether we would be better off picking from the available tools and focusing on getting really good at using them before deciding how much energy to focus on customizing the system. We asked ourselves whether we felt we could trust the fact that other practices had successfully implemented this software before and it might be best to just use it "out of the box" for 6 to 12 months and then change things we felt needed to be changed from the vantage point of experienced users. We recognized even in selecting which out-of-the-box tools to use and considering changing them that it would be virtually impossible to customize any one of the tools so that everybody was content with it. To make this perspective transparent, we followed the "rule of reasonableness," which we defined as an EHR configuration or tool that allowed us to get our work done, supported the delivery of quality care, provided the information we needed, prevented safety risks, and provided an EHR work- flow that we understood and completed without getting lost or frustrated. We decided that if that was the case, we would not spend the time and energy required to suggest, test, and implement changes for at least six months. This turned out to be a critical success factor. By six months, we were all accustomed to using the tools and had learned how to use them to support quality care, with little residual urge to change anything we were using. Using the rule of reasonableness worked well by moving us forward . . . and helped us avoid the kind of "perfection is the enemy of implementation" paralysis that can keep a practice from adoption and appropriate use. This is much harder than it may seem. Doctors and patients both benefit from the ability that physicians have in seeing what is wrong with something . . . While putting such "guardrails" on implementations is critical to a successful implementation, it can feel constraining, and it is important to be able to distinguish when it is best to keep people safe by having them stay inside the guardrails during an implementation and when to go "off road" in order to prevent a patient safety or regulatory "head-on collision" that an astute provider will sometimes see before others do.
—Michael H. Zaroukian, MD, PhD, FACP, FHIMSS, CMIO, Michigan State University (MSU)

Both options require significant time and user participation to understand the impact of the EHR. Here's an example of the time required.

Phase 1 design sessions probably took us close to six months. Phase two took us about three months.
—Florence Chang, MBA, CIO, Multicare

The user time commitment often requires assigning clinician and IT personnel to the project full-time and temporarily replacing them with backfill staff.

We backfilled positions. For example, we had subject matter experts from operations, clinical staff. We backfilled their positions, and application analysts.
—Florence Chang, MBA, CIO, Multicare

Prepare Software Configuration Plan

An HDO prepares a software configuration plan during the planning process. A *soft- ware configuration plan* (SCP) is a description of how an organization and vendor define, approve, make, track, and report both the initial system configuration and any subse- quent changes. The scope of configuration includes documenting and executing all required changes to the *out-of-the-box* system (e.g., list options, data, reporting) to sup- port the HDO's use of the system. This process includes four distinct steps:

1. *Identify and train the project team.* The HDO identifies key users and trains them to configure the system. The Project Team must include an interdisciplinary membership (e.g., IT analysts and clinical stakeholders).

2. *Identify and document configuration requirements* Using the detailed user requirements as a starting point, the Project Team prepares configuration requirements for the EHR supporting, for example, physician consultations, physician orders, and nursing documentation. We describe configuration requirements definition in more detail below.

3. *Complete configuration.* The HDO implements the initial software configuration and any subsequent updates.

4. *Review, confirm, and update the configuration.* The HDO reviews the completed initial configuration with a wide user audience to ensure accuracy and completeness, and updates it to reflect their needs.

For each module, there were two key players: what we called an HAC and an HIC (Health Application Coordinator and Health Information Coordinator). The HAC was the subject matter expert, the person who knew that particular operational domain, and the HIC was the person who coordinated IT.

We configured the system by having an HIC work with the corresponding HAC and together in the department in the hospital for which they were responsible. For every single application, you had the HIC who understood the guts of the application, the switches that had to be set, and the tables that had to be populated. Then you had the HAC, who understood how, for instance, a clinic operated, so that he worked with the HIC to figure out what configuration settings to make, how to populate those tables, and how to coordinate with other modules that touched it, because those tables sometimes cut across multiple applications.

—Robert Greenless, PhD, CIO–RLANRC

Define Configuration Requirements

An HDO defines the configuration requirements during the execution process. A *configuration requirement* is a description of how an organization plans to change customizable settings so the system is ready for use. The configuration must map to the workflow documented in the user requirements.

The HDO prepares configuration requirements to support how to use the new system. Documentation on configuration requirements should include a written description of added custom fields, decisions, display or processing choices, or other available options. For additional clarity, the configuration requirements may also include annotated screenshots of the vendor system showing selected options or settings. By carefully documenting each available configuration option in this way, the HDO creates a systematic *instructional manual* about the vendor system for training, testing, production use, and support. This underscores why training and support staff participates at this early stage in the project.

When preparing the configuration requirements, we suggest relying on information typically associated with use cases that includes the following:

- *Name*—The name of the process or product
- *Definition*—A description of the product created by the process and its purpose
- *Description*—A summary of the activity involved in the workflow process, including its context in patient care (i.e., *when* and *where* the activity takes place)

- *Priority*—The importance or significance of the process to caregivers or patients (e.g., high, medium, low)

- *Users*—The individuals or user roles that participate in or complete the activity

- *Pre-Conditions*—Other activities or products that the users must complete executing a specific configuration requirement (e.g., patient arrives, initial consultation completed)

- *Primary Flow of Events*—The manual and automated steps involved in completing the activity, by actor (i.e., *who* completes the step), and outcome (i.e., *what* is the result of the step). For example, a physician creating an order typically responds to a series of prompts for information about the patient and receives a series of choices based on the patient's reported condition and the treatment options available. Configuration requirements describe how these steps occur in the new system, and how the HDO must adjust the system to meet its needs.

- *Post-Conditions*—The state of the system after completing the defined steps in the system (e.g., patient views updated record via the patient portal, order presented to pharmacy via interface with pharmacy system, scheduler notified of request for return appointment, lab results available for review)

- *Alternate Options*—Differing outcomes for the activity based on decisions or choices made during the flow of events (e.g., no follow-up appointment required, request for transfer to different facility/department, reschedule appointment due to patient no-show)

- *Recommended Approach*—An analysis of the available configuration options and justification for the selected option(s), if required

- *Other Impacts*—Special considerations affecting the activity (e.g., system administrator must add or modify EHR users and permissions, and use the *comments* field for additional notes or information)

- *Assumptions*—Constraints or rules affecting the activity (e.g., both physician and nurse are present during patient examination, IT is responsible for maintaining EHR user information)

- *References*—Other related documentation, configuration settings, and so on

Configure System

An HDO completes system configuration during the execution process. This involves updating the system to reflect the setup parameters, selection lists, organization, and other options identified in configuration requirements. The output of this process is a set of test cases that verifies the configuration. A *test case* is a description of each requirement and its expected outcome from the system when a user executes it.

The HDO walks through each configuration requirement and completes the indicated changes to the system. The Project Team reviews each requirement to confirm the application performs as expected after completing a specific set of configuration changes. Despite the groundwork laid by configuration requirements, this process involves some degree of trial and error because configuration choices in one area of the application may have an unexpected impact on another. This requires revisions to one or more configuration requirements and settings to reflect optimal results across the entire application. The HDO uses the final scripts, as confirmed by the team, to create test cases to verify the configured system. Training and support personnel also use the configuration requirements as the basis for the training and support materials, respectively.

Control Software Configuration

You have to work with the users. You have to walk them through it, and say, ok, here's the configuration documentation for the decisions that you made, here's the decisions that you made in terms of the tables. Now, let's go through this application using "test patients" and let's go through it and see if it works. You find out if it works or not. You tweak this, tweak that, repeatedly. When the nursing units came up on the application the first day, there were no surprises. They knew what they were going to see.

—Robert Greenless, PhD, CIO–RLANRC

The Project Manager monitors preparing the initial software configuration and subsequent updates during the controlling process. Configuration requirements serve as a baseline for managing the software configuration similar to any other plan in the Project Management Plan. The Project Manager monitors configuration management using the control process described in integration management. For example, configuring an application typically includes adding custom fields to forms. One public sector agency we worked with was able to add the custom fields they needed, but they could not modify the application's standard reports to include this information, and an available ad hoc reporting tool provided only limited tabular, spreadsheet-style output. The vendor could only offer reporting in more usable formats in a future release.

WORKFLOW MANAGEMENT

It is hard to imagine how to configure a system such as an EHR without simultaneously considering changes to manual steps. *Workflow management* is planning, executing, and controlling the sequence of automated and manual steps that support delivery of an organization's products and services. When accomplished optimally, configuration management and workflow management work hand in hand. How you configure the software informs your desired future clinical workflow and how you design the desired future clinical workflow informs the ways in which you can configure the software. Table 4-16 displays workflow management processes and their outputs (in italics) by process group.

Prepare Workflow Management Plan

The Project Manager prepares a workflow management plan during the planning process. A *workflow management plan* is a description of how to change sequences of automated and manual steps to perform work more effectively. An HDO implementing an EHR will focus on how to configure the system and manual steps to increase patient care and quality while reducing costs.

The Project Team completes the following steps to prepare a workflow management plan:

- Define the current workflow
- Review completed configuration requirements
- Prepare a future state workflow
- Identify the gap between the current and future state
- Develop a schedule for SMEs to prepare and document workflow changes that close the gap

Preparing workflow changes occurs concurrently with configuration changes. This also includes support and training personnel participation to ensure they fully understand user needs.

Defining and modifying workflow involves identifying how an HDO's newly configured EHR system interacts with manual steps and other systems supporting service delivery. Figure 4-5 displays the relationships between workflow and other IT knowledge areas.

Initiating	Planning	Executing	Controlling	Closing
	Prepare workflow management plan *Workflow management plan*	Define workflow requirements *Workflow requirements* Perform workflow changes *Workflow changes*	Control workflow *Organizational process asset update* *Performance report* *Change request (CR)* *Project document update*	

TABLE 4-16   Workflow Management Knowledge Area by Process Group

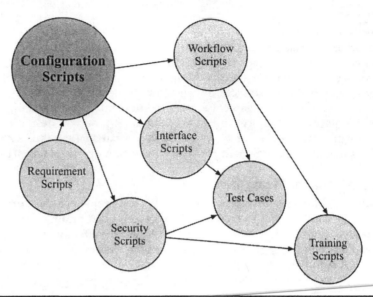

FIGURE 4-5   Workflow relationships.

Define Workflow Requirements

The purpose of workflow requirements is to define how to change work positively. This may affect job content, physician reimbursement, face-to-face communications, and productivity in an HDO. A *workflow requirement* is a description of how to reduce the number of steps, decrease the amount of time, and minimize motion (moving from place to place) during system use or manual steps.

An effective way of defining workflow requirements is to use activity diagrams. The process involves the following:

- Prepare diagrams of the current and future state in facilitated sessions with representative clinicians. For example, the current state includes computers at all nurses' stations that require preparing nursing notes at the bedside and entering this information at the station computer. The future state includes computing in each patient's room where nurses prepare their notes at the bedside.

- Conduct a gap analysis between these two states based on the number of steps, amount of time, and motion. In this example, closing the gap between the current and future state reduces the number of steps, time, and motion by eliminating preparing bedside notes and subsequently walking to the nursing station and entering them in the EHR at the nurses' station.

- Identify additional improvements (e.g., handheld, wall-mounted, or cart-based computers).

- Perform a pilot of the defined improvements and receive feedback.

- Prepare updates based on the feedback.

As with configuration requirements, we rely on the user requirement scripts and information associated with use cases when defining the workflow impact on configuration requirements and manual steps, such as the following:

- *Name*—The name of the workflow process
- *Definition*—A description of the product created by the workflow process and its purpose
- *Description*—A summary of the activity involved in the workflow process, including its context in the overall patient care workflow (i.e., *when* and *where* the activity takes place on a day-to-day basis)
- *Priority*—The importance or significance of the workflow process to caregivers or patients (i.e., high, medium, low)
- *Users*—The individuals or user roles that participate in and complete the workflow
- *Pre-Conditions*—Other workflow processes or products that prior workflow must complete before initiating this workflow (e.g., patient scheduled appointment, patient registered, initial consultation completed)
- *Primary Flow of Events*—The manual and automated steps involved in completing the workflow process, by actor (*who* completes the process) and outcome (*what* is the result of the process)
- *Post-Conditions*—The workflow state after completing a process
- *Alternate Options*—Differing outcomes for the workflow process based on decisions or choices made during the process flow (e.g., no follow-up appointment required, request for transfer to different facility/department, reschedule appointment due to patient no-show)
- *Recommended Approach*—An analysis of the available workflow options and justification for the selected option(s), if required
- *Other Actions*—Any special considerations affecting the workflow process

Perform Workflow Changes

We had three different hospitals going live at the same time. The first time when we went live was revenue cycle and EMR. We literally consolidated about 3,000 different types of workflows down to 1,200 or 1,500 workflows. This is where we really used the time to standardize our efforts, our workflow. Then from the second phase, documentation to CPOE, we started with somewhere around 2,000 workflows, and were able to get it down to about 800. So even with that effort, the day of go-live we realized we still had different ways of transferring patients.

So I think what our experience really taught us is that implementing the electronic health record really magnified the workflow process. Even though we went through the intensive effort of standardizing our processes, we still uncovered a significant amount of work after go-live. Until the system is in use and used on a day-to-day basis, you really cannot capture every detail of workflow and perform your work well with the brand new system . . .

—Florence Chang, MBA, CIO, Multicare

The Project Team makes workflow changes during the executing process. The output of this process is a workflow change. A *workflow change* is an updated configuration requirement, subsequent configuration change, and/or modification to a manual step.

Figure 4-6 displays a graphic representation of workflow before, during, and after an EHR implementation.

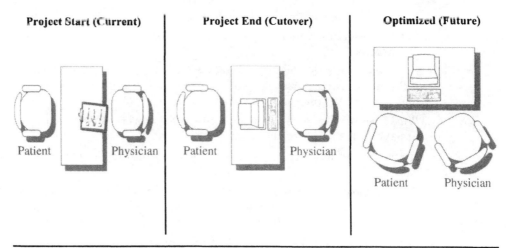

FIGURE 4-6   Workflow change.

Control Workflow

The Project Manager monitors workflow management during the controlling process. The workflow management plan serves as a baseline for managing workflow similar to any other plan in the project management plan. The Project Manager monitors workflow management using the controlling process described in integration management. For example, we worked with a long-term care hospital that examined using wall-mounted computers versus cart-based computers. During this examination, they selected the wall-mounted option. They selected this option because it minimized manual steps associated with hall traffic and maneuvering carts in patient rooms to document patient care, and tracking and charging mobile devices. While the selected option represented the best workflow approach, it involved significant additional time for regulatory approval of wall-mounted devices in patient rooms. Unfortunately, the project schedule could not accommodate this additional time. However, after further research, the hospital found they could install wall-mounted computers on freestanding closets in patient rooms without requiring time-consuming regulatory review. This allowed the hospital to employ the best workflow option without a CR or document update.

SECURITY MANAGEMENT

Security management is planning, executing, controlling, and closing system access. Table 4-17 displays security management processes and their outputs (in italics) by process group.

Prepare Security Plan

Let's say I'm a nurse that works in two different departments. I will have two different kinds of patient lists and screens, based on my logon to the system. So that means that the security team needs to make sure they have an appropriate department assigned to my logon based on the area that I work for.

You think about it, we have 8,000 employees, plus traveler nurses to support during go-live. Every single one of them needs to test the logon, and we need operations to validate that we identify all the multiple departments each individual is working for, in order to get it correct. Obviously, it takes a lot of time. Typically, you'll get that from your HR system. Lawson is our HR system, but if you don't go in and update your HR system, you don't have the most correct information either. That does require manual review by the department managers to ensure that we have the right roles for each individual, then the security folks can assign those roles accordingly. The issues that we encountered were labor intensive, and really required individual attention to configure them correctly.

—Florence Chang, MBA, CIO, Multicare

An HDO prepares a security plan during the planning process. A *security plan* is a description of how an organization will manage system access. It defines how the HDO will accomplish the following:

1. *Verify applicable standards.* Verify all applicable HDO, local, state, and federal security compliance requirements.

2. *Define configuration, testing, training, and production security.* Define security requirements to support configuration, testing, training, and production use.

3. *Implement incremental security.* Set up access to the system for subsequent system configuration, testing, training, and production use.

4. *Monitor and report compliance.* Establish methods for ongoing security monitoring, including audits and reporting (e.g., issue identification, tracking, escalation, and resolution).

The security plan will, at the end of the project, become part of security operations where it will integrate with the HDO's ongoing IT security program.

Initiating	Planning	Executing	Controlling	Closing
	Prepare security plan	Define security requirements	Control security	Conduct ongoing security compliance
	Security plan	*Security requirements*	*Organizational process asset update*	*Security audit results*
		Define security roles	*Performance report*	
		Security roles	*Change request (CR)*	
		Configure security	*Project document update*	
		Test cases		

TABLE 4-17 Security Management Knowledge Area Outputs by Process Group

Define Security Requirements

An HDO defines its security requirements during the executing process. A *security requirement* is a description of the system access specifications that an organization must support.

Like technology considerations, security issues are often the purview of specific individuals or technically oriented specialists that maintain well-established documentation, policies, procedures, and standards. For this reason, an HDO reviews its security requirements with one or two key representatives (e.g., the chief security officer or a member of his staff). This process identifies specific security policies that a new system must address, for example:

- User authentication and system access methods and restrictions by user role (e.g., nurse, physician, administrator, patient, HIM representative)
- System security monitoring and audit capabilities
- Data backup and restoration
- Compliance with regulatory standards (e.g., HIPAA standards for security, code sets, and encryption), Joint Commission safety tracking and reporting standards, use of compliance management tools, national HDO quality measures
- Compliance with technology standards [e.g., Occupational Safety and Health Administration (OSHA), National Electrical Manufacturers Association (NEMA), Federal Communications Commission (FCC), and American National Standards Institute (ANSI) compliance]

As with the detailed technical requirements described earlier, the HDO uses security requirements for soliciting, evaluating, and selecting a solution to implement. The HDO subsequently relies on these requirements during implementation to address system configuration and testing.

Table 4-18 provides an example of security requirements that an HDO may provide to a vendor.

Define Security Roles

An HDO defines security roles during the executing process. A *security role* is the list of system functions for a specific user or user type—it identifies *who* does *what* in a system. The HDO identifies the security role for each actor in the configuration requirements.

The security roles address how the HDO will configure system access by:

- Identifying user type (e.g., physician, system administrator, scheduler, department manager, patient) for each application component (e.g., orders, patient medical records, bed assignments)
- Assigning users to one or more role

An HDO defines and implements user security in progressive stages throughout the project, including:

- Configuration
- Testing
- Training
- Production

28.2. <u>Regulatory Standards</u>—*Requirements related to standards and best practices required by Federal, State, or local regulations, statutes, or laws.*
28.2.1. <u>Compliance management tools</u> (Short Answer)—*Describe the kinds of services and tools you provide to manage the operational changes and workflow improvements to comply with Joint Commission, CMS, and HIPAA standards.*
28.2.2. <u>Compliance with HIPAA data security and privacy standards</u> (Short Answer)—*Describe how the proposed security features comply with Federal (HIPAA), State, and Joint Commission health information standards for data integrity, confidentiality, auditing, and availability.*
28.2.3. <u>Core measures (HDO Quality Measures) capabilities</u> (Yes/No)—*Provides data collection capabilities to support Core Measures (HDO Quality Measures).*
28.2.4. <u>De-identification</u> (Yes/No)—*Application software provides functionality that allows users to "de-identify" individually identifiable information and comply with HIPAA requirements.*
29. <u>System Security and Control</u>—*Requirements for security, data integrity, and control of the proposed solution.*
29.1. <u>Security</u>—*Requirements related to system access control and monitoring.*
29.1.1. <u>Access level reports</u> (Yes/No)—*Provides access level reports by patient, user, and location.*
29.1.2. <u>Access restriction by user</u> (Yes/No)—*Provides functions to restrict access to specific patient records for individual users.*
29.1.3. <u>Access time out</u> (Yes/No)—*Provides a "time out" feature that automatically signs off a user if a workstation has been left unattended for a user-defined time.*
29.1.4. <u>Audit log reporting</u> (Yes/No)—*Provides audit log reporting features.*
29.1.5. <u>Audit logs for unauthorized activity</u> (Yes/No)—*Provides audit logs/error logs to detect unauthorized access or activity.*
29.1.6. <u>Clinical Context Object Workgroups (CCOW)</u> (Yes/No)—*Supports CCOW to increase interoperability between different systems for patient information access.*
29.1.7. <u>Configurable password length</u> (Yes/No)—*Permits the security administrator to specify a minimum password length that the system will enforce.*
29.1.8. <u>Electronic signature support in security</u> (Yes/No)—*Supports electronic signature.*

TABLE 4-18   Security Requirements

Configure Security

An HDO completes security configuration during the execution process. This involves updating the system to reflect the security roles. The HDO relies on its configuration requirements to complete this required set-up. The Project Team, in conjunction with HDO security personnel, reviews the configuration requirements to confirm the security roles perform as expected. The output of this process is a set of test cases that verifies security. The HDO uses the final security roles, as confirmed by the team, to create test cases and verify that they applied these roles correctly.

Control Security

The Project Manager monitors security during the controlling process. The security plan serves as a baseline for managing security similar to any other plan in the project management plan. The Project Manager also monitors security management using the control process described in Integration management. For example, we worked on a public sector project that included a SaaS implementation. The solicitation required vendors to provide results from an independent third-party security audit. The selected vendor indicated that they were in the midst of such an audit and would supply the results when they were available. The results later supplied were insufficient and did not meet due diligence requirements. Serving as Project Manager, we arranged with the chief security officer for an additional independent third-party audit. This required a CR to accommodate the cost impact. The third-party audit identified only one minor security flaw, which the vendor promptly repaired. The project implementation occurred successfully within a secure environment.

Conduct Ongoing Security Compliance

An HDO conducts ongoing security compliance management during the closing process by transferring it to operations. *Ongoing security compliance management* involves security audits of the system to ensure compliance with all security requirements. The output of this process is security audit results. A *security audit result* is a description of flaws identified during a formal evaluation of system safeguards. These flaws require correction and subsequent testing to ensure their elimination.

INTERFACE MANAGEMENT

A key component of our strategic plan was an understanding of the interfaces that would and would not be required and/or be acceptable. For example, we chose integration as we did not want interfaces within the medication process (orders, pharmacy verification, and medication administration). We knew we would have to have an admission, discharge, transfer (ADT), and billing interface to our patient registration/billing system. We also understood we would need several interfaces from existing applications for results to go into the electronic data repository. As we identified the boundaries and scope for each project, the required interfaces to implement that module were identified and planned as part of that project. The majority of our interfaces were a requirement for implementing the clinical data repository. Since then interface requirements have been adding data to the repository and new functionality (e.g., e-prescribe outbound to clearinghouse).
—Beatha Johnson, Director, Clinical Information Systems, VMMC

Interface management is planning, executing, and controlling definition, development, testing, and implementation of information exchanges between two systems. An *interface* is the exchange of information between two systems. Invariably in today's healthcare environment, an HDO will already have multiple existing HIT applications. In fact, it is likely that every HDO from the largest hospital to the smallest clinic, will have an electronic billing system, while also housing a laboratory system, pharmacy system, or human resource management system. It is rare that an HDO will elect to deploy a new HIT project to replace its entire system portfolio. It is almost certain the HDO will need interfaces with existing systems when implementing a new one. For example, if the current HIT project is an EHR implementation, with clinician documentation and CPOE, this system needs to interface with existing pharmacy, lab, and scheduling systems, and so on.

Table 4-19 shows interface management processes and their outputs (in italics) by process group.

Prepare Interface Plan

An HDO prepares an interface plan during the planning process. An *interface plan* is a description of how an organization addresses ongoing data exchanges between a new system and other existing systems.

Initiating	Planning	Executing	Controlling	Closing
	Prepare interface plan *Interface plan*	Prepare interface data map *Interface data map* Develop and test interfaces *Interface software confirmation* Enable interfaces *Interface confirmation*	Control interfaces *Organizational process asset update* *Performance report* *Change request (CR)* *Project document update*	

TABLE 4-19   Interface Management Knowledge Area by Process Group

The HDO prepares its interface plan by completing the following activities:

- *Identify Interface Scope*—Describe the number and type of data exchanges that will occur between the EHR and other third-party systems. A source to identify interfaces includes user requirement, configuration, and workflow scripts.
- *Map Data Transactions*—For each interface, identify how to represent the data in both the source and destination systems so that programmed interfaces can restructure, reformat, reinterpret, and transfer data accordingly.
- *Identify Interface Timing*—For each information exchange identified, determine the kind of required interface. Available options include the following:
  - *Batch*—The source system transmits a group of data to the destination system periodically. For example, a third-party provider of a prescription drug database may issue new updates periodically.
  - *Real-Time*—The source system transmits data to the destination system when the data becomes available. For example, a correction to a physician order prepared in the EHR automatically updates the lab system.
- *Identify Volume of Data for the Interface*—Estimate the number of records included in each data exchange and the time required to complete the exchange.
- *Identify Interface Timing*—Define staging for when to implement an interface (e.g., configuration development, testing, training, production).
- *Identify Tools for Automated Interfaces*—Identify existing or planned software applications, utilities, macros, or other tools for sharing data between the EHR and other participating systems.

Table 4-20 displays an example of an HDO's interface scope.

Transaction*	Interface**			Third-Party System***
	Trigger	Type	Direction	
Proposed system receives ADT data	A	R	D	Siemens
Proposed system sends lab orders	A	R	S	Aspyra
Proposed system receives lab results	A	R	D	Aspyra
Proposed system sends order to pharmacy system	A	R	S	Siemens
Proposed system receives transcription	A	R	D	Softmed
Proposed system transmits charges	A	B	S	Siemens

*Interface Engine will take one outbound message and format to multiple required vendor format.
**Interface:
Trigger: M—Manual user-initiated interface; A—Automatic system-initiated interface
Type: B—Batch; R—Real-Time
Direction:
S—New system will be the source of information for this transaction
D—New system will be the destination of information for this transaction
*** Third-Party System: Existing system in use at HDO

TABLE 4-20   Interface Scope

Prepare Interface Data Map

An HDO prepares an interface data map during the execution process. An *interface data map* is a description of the characteristics of each piece of information exchanged between two systems on an ongoing basis.

An interface and a conversion are very similar. Both involve sharing information between two systems. For this reason, the data conversion map in Table 4-14 also illustrates an interface data map. Conversions typically occur only once, while an interface is a recurring information exchange.

Develop and Test Interfaces

An HDO develops and tests interfaces during the execution process. The output of this process is an interface software confirmation. An *interface software confirmation* is a written acknowledgement that the option constructed or configured and tested works according to specifications. The HDO uses the interface data map prepared previously to identify the interface specifications.

HDOs have existing interface tools for sharing data between third-party systems and, for example, their EHR. These tools may include a combination of the following:

- Custom-built routines or macros that provide information to or from the new system database in one or more different source file types (e.g., SQL Server database, Excel spreadsheet, CSV text file).
- Custom-built (i.e., developed by the vendor or HDO) in-house or configured applications (e.g., a commercially available interface engine such as MQ-Series) that automatically transfer specific data in an industry-standard format between two participating systems. In the case of a standard integration engine, the application does all the data transformation, verification, and transfer based on the source and destination systems identified and the data set planned for transfer. An *integration engine* is the system infrastructure that exchanges data between different systems.
- Custom-built or standard interfaces included as part of the new system to populate its database on an as-needed basis.

The HDO tests the accuracy and effectiveness of the selected data exchange software using a sample subset of their existing data until they confirm the interface is successful.

Based on the interface timing identified in the interface plan, this activity may occur several times (e.g., during initial configuration, before testing, as part of training, at cutover). This staggered timing for interface *cutover* may require configuration changes to the interface tool to address the data sharing needs at that time. Like conversion, the HDO must test these configuration changes before implementing the interface in production.

Enable Interfaces

An HDO enables or turns on its required interfaces during the executing process. This initializes the processes and tools identified in the interface plan to perform an ongoing data exchange between the new system and other participating systems. The output of this process is an interface confirmation. An *interface confirmation* is a written acknowledgement of the accuracy and effectiveness of an interface tool and the associated data exchange.

Control Interfaces

The Project Manager monitors interfaces during the controlling process. The interface plan serves as a baseline for managing interfaces similar to any other plan in the project management plan. The Project Manager monitors interface management using the control process described in integration management. For example, HL7 is the healthcare industry standard for clinical data exchange. The HL7 Organization started in the mid to late 1980s and has subsequently produced numerous updates. There are systems, however, that are not HL7-compliant. Such non-compliant systems can be challenging when preparing and executing an interface plan. An EHR project encountered this problem, which delayed the project and required a CR to update the schedule.

I think the challenge that we had was the "one-off" systems. For example, we . . . wanted to interface with BabyStep. BabyStep is one of those systems that it's hard to write interface code for. We made it happen, but it took a lot of time and a lot of testing on both sides. It wasn't a standard interface that we had implemented in the past. We're probably the only one out there that has EPIC talking to BabyStep. That's an example of a challenge.

—Florence Chang, MBA, CIO, Multicare

TEST MANAGEMENT

> *You can never start the testing process too early, and you can never start developing your test scripts too early. That probably is one of the things that bit me in the early projects. You really need to identify a dedicated analyst who is not one of the individuals responsible for current/future state, sample build, and then proof of concept, and expect that they're going to also develop test scripts. We start testing immediately (as a means to understand what the application does and does not do) during the deep dive to understand configuration and tools so we can present the customer. You start your initial testing and script development from day one.*
>
> —Beatha Johnson, Director, Clinical Information Systems, VMMC

Test management is planning, executing, and controlling how an organization verifies that a new system meets its specifications. This involves describing how the HDO plans testing, defines test cases and data, identifies defects and reports results, corrects the defects, and establishes acceptance criteria for each kind of verification performed. Test management also includes training the parties responsible for executing tests and defines the roles of HDO and vendor personnel. Table 4-21 displays test management processes and their outputs (in italics) by process group.

Thorough testing is critical. All of the work that precedes testing is lost if the implemented system fails because of inadequate testing, as described below.

> *There was acceptance, both at the management and hospital levels, that when the application was properly tested and everybody was nodding their head yes, then it goes up. We thought we might get off schedule, but there was always a clear understanding that if the testing came back anything but correct we would not go up. We recognized that the previous project failure had been seriously understaffed in critical areas, like testing, so we brought in the right number of people at the right level.*
>
> —Robert Greenless, PhD, CIO–RLANRC

Initiating	Planning	Executing	Controlling	Closing
	Prepare test plan *Test plan*	Define test cases *Test cases* Prepare test data *Test data* Train testers *Training completion confirmation* Conduct tests *Test results* Correct defects *Test cases* Conduct regression testing *Test results*	Control testing *Organizational process asset update* *Performance report* *Change request (CR)* *Project document update*	

TABLE 4-21   Test Management Knowledge Area by Process Group

Prepare Test Plan

The HDO prepares a test plan during the planning process. A *test plan* is a description of how an organization will verify the configuration, security, conversion, and interfaces of a new system for production use. Testing focuses on all HIT components individually and together to ensure they function according to defined HDO requirements.

Testing is a highly structured sequential process as described below.

> *Testing has unit testing, and then we move into integrated testing. Integrated testing is based on scenarios, and by the way, the scenarios had been developed based on the go-live state workflow that we put in place. After the integrated testing, there are two different types of testing. In some cases, we also moved to what we called focused testing. For example, when we went live with the revenue cycle, we needed to test every single supply, every single charge associated with each supply we had in the system. We called that focused testing. And then, at the very end, there is the user acceptance testing.*

> —Florence Chang, MBA, CIO, Multicare

Testing software is an inspection process. A tester verifies one component at a time. A test plan describes this sequential and cumulative inspection process. Likewise, the Project Team inspects the system configuration, interfaces, and the conversion software before attempting to integrate them.

This plan defines the following:

- *Test Types*—Traditional software testing involves conducting an ever-widening set of inspection activities that address the following:
    - *Unit Testing*—Testing a unit of software. The Project Team may test units such as manually entered static tables, converted patient master, and physician master to verify their accuracy and completeness. This could also include:
        - *Conversion Testing*—Verifies that each required conversion of existing data to the new system performs as defined in the conversion requirements.
        - *Interface Testing*—Verifies that each required exchange of data between the new system and one or more third-party systems performs as defined in the interface requirements.
        - *Function Testing*—Verifies individual system functions (e.g., add new patient, create patient order, print pharmacy label) perform as defined in the configuration requirements.
    - *Integration/System Testing*—Tests interactions between units and verifies how they work together. This test is a run-through of the configured application to verify entire system configuration settings, application options, usability, and so on.
    - *Security Testing*—Verifies that the application meets or exceeds the standards identified in the security requirements. This is a test of the configured application by individual user role (e.g., physician, patient, nurse, HIM representative).
    - *Performance Testing*—Conducts a variety of quantitative stress tests to monitor response time. *Performance testing* is the process of verifying that the system

meets response time standards. IT conducts performance testing by simulating maximum system loads (e.g., peak simultaneous usage, and transaction and storage volumes), using third-party software tools. IT uses these tools to verify the configured system's capacity and availability to perform in excess of the HDO's requirements.

- o *Acceptance Testing*—Repeats selected tests for a pre-defined period following cutover.

- o *Regression Testing*—Re-tests the system to confirm resolution of defects. A *regression test* is a re-test of a system to verify defect correction and to confirm this did not introduce new errors. An HDO performs a regression test after correcting defects found during each test, for example, unit, integration, security, and performance tests.

- *Test Sequence*—Conducting each defined test consecutively (e.g., unit test, unit regression test, integration test, integration regression test, performance test, and performance integration test).

- *Test Environment*—A *test environment* is a system that is entirely separate from the production environment of the HDO. A *production environment* is a live system available for actual use with real instead of test data. All of the data in the test environment are separate from the actual data collected and used in patient care. This is an exact duplicate of the production environment used to test, identify, and resolve system defects and configuration issues. The HDO then migrates the tested configuration from the test environment to the production environment.

- *Test Participants*—Project Team personnel responsible for testing and the associated tools, scripts, and data. The HDO identifies additional representative users to support, review, and verify the test participants' work to complete the various tests (e.g., vendor, IT personnel, and third parties may conduct security and performance testing).

While testing is critical to success, it never identifies every defect. The ultimate *test* begins at cutover to the production environment, where you find defects you could never identify beforehand.

We identified the performance issue only when we got to a live environment and we had an extremely sick patient in our ICU, with 10 IVs running and they'd been hospitalized for a year straight. These types of patients tended to really stress the system or uncover performance problems that we hadn't encountered before. We now test with sets of patients that have more data accrued in the system. We also stress test the system with many more users on it at one time to make sure that the volume of users doesn't negatively affect performance.

—Dan Nigrin, MD, MS, CIO, Children's Hospital Boston

Define Test Cases

An HDO defines test cases in the executing process. This involves reducing a script to a specific list of activities that a tester can individually *check off* during testing. Table 4-22 displays an example of a test case used to verify the software configuration.

	Script Step	Test Result	Comments
1.1.0	**Add New User Account**	'	
1.1.1	Access My EHR		
1.1.2	From the 'Admin' pull-down menu, select 'EHR Users'		
1.1.3	The 'Account Administration' screen is displayed		
1.1.4	Click the 'Add New User' link		
1.1.5	The 'Edit Account' screen is displayed		
1.1.6	Enter the new EHR User account information: **First Name**—User's first name		
1.1.7	**Last Name**—User's last name		
1.1.8	**E-Mail Address**—User's office email address		
1.1.9	**Username**—User's account login name		
1.1.10	**Password**—User's account access password		
1.1.11	**Phone**—User's office phone number		
1.1.12	**Req. Email Notification**—Indicate whether the system notifies a user at every event in the patient care lifecycle or only at order creation or when the system requires the user's action.		
1.1.13	**Permissions**—Define the user permissions for the Order Entry, Physician Master, and Patient Master functions according to the following access levels: **Add**—The user has the ability to create new records **Update**—The user has the ability to update existing records **Delete**—The user has the ability to delete existing records		
1.1.14	**Notification Department(s)**—Select department(s) that the EHR user is responsible for managing. The user will receive notifications about patient care activity in this department or departments based on the Req. Email Notification preferences (see above). *Hold down the <control> key and click the department name to select multiple departments; then click on the arrow button to assign the department(s) to the user.*		
1.1.15	**Access to Department(s)**—Select department(s) the user should have access to. The user will only access orders, patient and physician masters, and other specific data within assigned departments. *Hold down the <control> key and click the department name to select multiple departments; then click on the arrow button to assign the department(s) to the user.*		

TABLE 4-22   Test Case

	Script Step	Test Result	Comments
1.1.16	**Account Active** **Yes**—User may access the EHR **No**—User will not have access to the EHR, but account information will remain		
1.1.17	**Can View Confidential** **Yes**—User may view patient confidential information and other patient care information marked as private or confidential **No**—User may not view confidential or protected information		
1.1.18	Click the 'Save' button		

TABLE 4-22   Test Case (*Continued*)

In addition to configuration cases, the HDO prepares scripts for security and performance testing. Two kinds of testing apply to system security, as follows:

- *White Box Testing*—Considers the internal workings of a system (i.e., the internal application code). From a security test standpoint, it determines how vulnerable the internal application code is to exploitation, tampering, or other security breaches. The results identify areas, modules, components, or code sections where potential vulnerabilities exist.

- *Black Box Testing*—Considers user access, functional restrictions based on user roles, or other configuration-established parameters controlling who can do what in the application's workflow. This puts the application through its paces from a user point of view, determining security vulnerabilities by examining each application function as the tester uses it. It does not consider the internal workings of a system.

An HDO typically relies on its IT department or a third party to conduct white box testing. The HDO focuses on verification (the software meets defined user requirements) and validation (the software is what users want), and completes thorough and complete testing to resolve issues before cutover.

While it is mathematically impossible to verify and validate every permutation of system interaction before cutover to production, an HDO conducts as much testing as feasible to reduce the risk of critical issues adversely affecting patient care and safety. This is a huge and costly, but necessary, undertaking in the healthcare industry.

We took testing very, very seriously. There were formal test plans, we spent a ton of time developing cases, and every time we had to do a test, we ran the scripts, documented the outcomes and anything that wasn't right we went back to for correction. There was commitment to make sure it was right. By virtue of the fact that we used those very thorough scripts and every single module was tested and then integration testing was done, we didn't miss much.

—Robert Greenless, PhD, CIO–RLANRC

Prepare Test Data

An HDO prepares its test data during the executing process. *Test data* is a collection of data sufficient to conduct all identified system tests and receive meaningful and accurate outcomes. Examples of test data include:

- User accounts with appropriate security role assignments
- Sample patient records
- Order templates by order type
- Values in tables (e.g., every medication, charges, option lists)
- Alerts and other notification messages and rules

The HDO loads this data before initiating each test, and may refresh or replace changes to this test data to enable completion of a subsequent test.

Train Testers

The HDO trains testers from the Project Team during the executing process. The output of this process is training completion confirmation. A *training completion confirmation* is a written acknowledgement that each trainee successfully completed a specific training course. This confirms that individuals participating in system testing received training on the purpose and content of testing and are ready to begin test activities. Verifying that the configured system meets the HDO's needs is a critical step in ensuring acceptance and ongoing use of the system.

The individuals conducting the tests need to administer each test activity and report the results consistently. Testers may include individuals who do not typically have experience with software testing. The HDO trains these test participants in the testing method described in the test plan to ensure consistency and success. This involves reviewing the content and purpose of the cases, and conducting practice tests and demonstrating results collection and reporting.

Conduct Tests

An HDO conducts tests during the executing process. This involves coordinating testers as they complete previously defined test cases. The output of this process is a set of test results. A *test result* is a reported outcome associated with completing a test case. The HDO classifies test results using a severity scale such as the following:

- *Pass (No Defect)*—The application performed as expected or desired (i.e., as defined in the test case).
- *Severity 1 (Critical)*—A *fatal* defect preventing the user from proceeding in the application (i.e., *show stopper*).
- *Severity 2 (High)*—A defect that does not prevent the user from proceeding, but causes significant delay due to the nature of the defect(s) or slow performance.
- *Severity 3 (Medium)*—A defect where a user is able to formulate a workaround.

- *Severity 1 (Low)*—A defect in, for example, placement of push buttons on a form or graphical user interface. Although these defects may not impede application functionality individually, numerous low defects may collectively qualify as a higher severity level if the volume of these defects makes it difficult to use the software.

Testing is never simple. It takes considerable insight to understand the source or root cause of defects.

Testing requires understanding of how the software configuration works but also trying to decipher whether or not the problem is with the software code itself. As with many of these big systems, you've got lots of different choices and preferences and tailoring that you can do with the software, and sometimes you can set preferences and make design decisions using the software that are not the best ones. For example, these preferences and decisions might cause system performance issues. That was one of the technical areas with some of our go-lives where we faced challenges, just in the performance of the system.

—Dan Nigrin, MD, MS, CIO, Children's Hospital, Boston

Correct Defects

An HDO prioritizes and corrects defects during the executing process. The output of this process is a set of regression test cases. After completing each round of testing, the HDO (and possibly the vendor) reviews the test results to agree upon the severity of identified defects and how to resolve them. This is an important step, as often testers perceive issues as defects; however, these issues are the result of other factors, such as the following:

- Script typos (e.g., an incorrect step that appears in place of a correct step due to a transposition during test case preparation)
- Script inaccuracies (e.g., occurrences where the script does not match the functionality in the application, because of application updates not included in the test case)
- Errors that might be functional problems, but likely occur because the test participants completed the script out of sequence (e.g., tester tried but was unable to review a patient appointment list before scheduling or confirming appointments)
- Errors that might be functional problems but likely occur because of data issues (e.g., tried to view orders on hold and none were listed because there were no orders in the system with an *on hold* status)

The HDO (and possibly the vendor) reviews each identified test result to confirm its severity. The HDO addresses defects caused by faulty or incomplete system configuration. The vendor corrects application defects caused by software logic or code errors. The vendor fixes them based on an agreed upon prioritized list of the required corrections. For example, the vendor fixes defects with a severity 1 (critical) or 2 (severe) immediately, and fixes those with severity 3 or 4 at a later date, depending on their number and overall impact to system use and performance.

Conduct Regression Testing

The HDO conducts regression testing during the executing process. The output of this process is an additional set of test results.

As with initial testing, the HDO prepares test data, conducts tests, and corrects defects during regression testing. Typically, regression testing is an iterative process. The set of scripts included in regression testing grows smaller with each iteration until the HDO or vendor addresses all defects.

Control Testing

The Project Manager monitors testing during the controlling process. The test plan serves as a baseline for managing testing similar to any other plan in the project management plan. The Project Manager monitors test management using the control process described in integration management. For example, a mid-size hospital that we worked with tested clinical systems software modified by the vendor and found numerous errors. Despite somewhat successful ongoing vendor correction, the hospital continued to find numerous defects. While the hospital was rightfully proud of their testing discipline, we suggested they were incurring unnecessary cost increases and schedule delays due to poor vendor development and testing practices. In effect, the vendor was shifting the burden of testing time and cost to their customer. We reviewed this issue with the steering committee and subsequently met with the vendor to resolve the problem. Our proposed document update prepared for the hospital and vendor reflected corrective actions, subsequently used as the basis for adjusting the project schedule without requiring a CR.

CUTOVER MANAGEMENT

Cutover management is planning, executing, and controlling the switch from existing manual and/or automated systems to a new system. It involves preparing for and monitoring the process of taking a system from test to active use. Table 4-23 displays cutover management processes and their outputs (in italics) by process group.

Prepare Cutover Plan

Planning, planning, planning! We had a formal cutover plan that we executed step-by-step per the plan. We had lots of communication throughout the hospital well in advance so they knew exactly when it was going up. We had people on every shift walking the floors from the Project Team, with the project name on their shirts. They were out there walking the floors, and the nurses, doctors, and therapists knew they were going to be there, so when they saw that red shirt, they knew this was somebody from the Project Team. If they had a question about the project, they could flag them down and get help immediately. I think that was helpful. It wasn't a matter of what number to call because there were people right there on the floor. It also helped us in terms of being able to observe things. If there was an issue someplace, we were getting first-hand, on-site feedback from somebody on the Project Team who could interpret it for us. That helped enormously.

—Robert Greenless, PhD, CIO–RLANRC

An HDO prepares a cutover plan during the planning process. A *cutover plan* is a description of how an organization prepares for and transitions from its existing manual and/or automated systems to a new system. It involves defining a methodology for facilitating and supporting each department as they switch from the old to the new system. The cutover plan addresses the following activities:

- *Identify a Cutover Team*—The HDO assembles a group of specific individuals who participate in all department transitions (IT), augmented by specific designated individuals from each transitioning user department (e.g., ED, cardiology, neurology)

- *Identify Cutover Tools and Techniques*—The HDO and vendor identify a methodology for providing user support during the cutover period (e.g., issues tracking, communications, command center, daily meetings)

- *Identify and Train Cutover Support Team*—The HDO defines key users who assist other users during cutover

Initiating	Planning	Executing	Controlling	Closing
	Prepare cutover plan *Cutover plan*	Train cutover support team *Training completion confirmation* Conduct system cutover *Successful cutover confirmation*	Control cutover *Organizational process asset update* *Performance report* *Change request (CR)* *Project document update*	

TABLE 4-23   Cutover Management Knowledge Area by Process Group

- *Prepare Cutover Schedule*—The HDO and vendor identify timing for cutover (e.g., functional, module, departmental)
- *Prepare Cutover Issue Log*—The HDO and vendor determine how to identify, track, escalate, report and resolve cutover issues
- *Conduct Readiness Review*—The HDO and vendor establish how to confirm that all system components (e.g., new system hardware and software, users, support staff) are in place and prepared for cutover
- *Deploy Production System*—The HDO and vendor establish when to switch from the old to the new system

Cutover ends with final acceptance of the system by the HDO. This is a deliverable, approved by the HDO, indicating the vendor successfully completed their project and shifted to ongoing support.

Here's an example of the details included in a cutover plan:

We had, first, a very, very good, very strong individual within our organization who does all our release management planning. He's the person who coordinated the entire cutover plan. The cutover plan included the individual tasks down to the minute of who's going to do what, two weeks prior and until the moment of go live, with individual assignment names and duration of the effort. It's about the planning—it takes a lot of time to plan every single task—and then it's about plan execution. He's the one that maintained the activities. He coordinated all the effort between teams, because there were dependencies during the entire cutover. This person is critical in this particular case for managing the timeline. That's one effort that was going on—he was coordinating all the interfaces, so on and so forth. And the other piece, at the same time, is the command center. We set up a command center, a couple of days prior, so that that there were command center directors, runners, a logistics person, a person issuing tickets. We had a communications person in the command center, we had operation leadership, and so the whole command center setup was very organized and process-driven.

—Florence Chang, MBA, CIO, Multicare

Train Cutover Support Team

The HDO trains the cutover team in the executing process. The output of this process is a training completion confirmation. This acknowledges cutover team readiness, that is, the individuals providing cutover support received training on the tools and techniques identified in the cutover plan and are ready to begin cutover activities.

The individuals supporting production users during system cutover must respond consistently to user requests, identified issues, and emergencies. The cutover team includes a combination of representative users (e.g., physicians, nurses, and other caregivers), who do not typically have cutover experience and IT staff that typically have experience providing customer service and support during this transition process. To help ensure the success at cutover, the HDO trains the cutover team in the use of the tools and techniques identified in the cutover plan. For example, this may involve reviewing the content and purpose of Frequently Asked Questions (FAQs) or typical response scenarios, conducting practice *support* calls, and demonstrating issues tracking, reporting, and resolution.

Conduct System Cutover

The HDO conducts system cutover during the executing process. This involves completing a series of activities leading up to and following a new system go-live. The output of this process is a successful cutover confirmation. A *successful cutover confirmation* is a written acknowledgement that the system is live and ready for acceptance testing. Cutover activities include the following:

- Turning on or activating required user-facing Internet or intranet web pages pointing to the new system, assuming the system is browser based
- Turning on all required interfaces between the new system and third-party systems (e.g., lab, pharmacy, scheduling)
- Initiating user and technical support
- Creating and staffing a *command center* where new system users can receive support via telephone or email as they begin to use the new system
- Sending user notifications with cutover timing, access information (e.g., user IDs, passwords, and URLs or network locations for system components), command center contact information, issue reporting procedures, and other relevant guidelines or system documentation
- Tracking, resolving, and/or escalating identified cutover issues at the command center and modifying acceptance use cases based on required adjustments or corrections to system configuration, security, or data
- Coordinating between command center and vendor representatives to resolve identified infrastructure or other system performance issues, and ensuring that vendor-provided support meets HDO expectations and contractual obligations
- Conducting acceptance tests as described in the test plan
- Updating system configuration, workflow, security, or data to accurately reflect HDO requirements or to accommodate user requests, where appropriate
- Approving acceptance of the production environment system

To clarify, before cutover you are working in a *laboratory* environment, whereas after cutover the system is in a live environment. However, remember you can never identify and resolve every issue before cutover.

Every day after we went live, we had a top 10 at 10 meeting, which was everyone from the organization coming in and talking about what were the top 10 issues within their departments. And we used a prioritization process based on weighted criteria, called "J-Lo©," named after the employees who design this prioritization process. For example, patient safety had the highest weight, and then you went to productivity, then into revenue impact, compliance, and then organization impact. Each of these had a different weight, and we scored them so that we could prioritize what were the top 10 issues we needed to address for that day. The project team, as well as the entire operation, would focus on those top 10 issues on a day-to-day basis, and during our go-live.

For example, in any of the EPIC implementations, during go-live you encounter security issues, because it's a role-driven security setup, and most people who work in clinical operations have multiple roles. With our first go-live that was the biggest challenge for our command center, to coordinate all the incoming calls and issues related to security. How to manage that appropriately? We learned from that. What we did then is as part of the testing process, right before go-live, we tested every single sign-on, every single end user sign-on before we actually went live. That became part of our go/no-go criteria.

—Florence Chang, MBA, CIO, Multicare

Control Cutover

The Project Manager monitors cutover during the controlling process. The cutover plan serves as a baseline for managing cutover similar to any other plan in the project management plan. The Project Manager monitors cutover management using the control process described in integration management. The previous example described cutover success. During a different project we reviewed the first of three hospital cutovers and uncovered numerous issues that required corrective actions (recorded in document updates) to ensure success at the remaining hospitals, including:

- *Use a Command Center*—There was limited cutover command center use before, during, and after the cutover period that hampered effective, continuous, and centralized collection, tracking, and resolution of issues

- *Cutover Issues Log Maintenance*—There was an absence of a dedicated, full-time resource to facilitate quick update and distribution of critical issues that hindered issue resolution by the cutover team

- *Command Center Reporting*—Support personnel stationed in hospital departments failed to report issues to the command center on a timely basis, increasing the number of unidentified, unreported, and unresolved issues

SUPPORT MANAGEMENT

Support management is the planning, executing, controlling, and closing technical maintenance of the system after cutover. Table 4-24 displays support management processes and their outputs (in italics) by process group.

Prepare Support Plan

The HDO prepares a support plan during the planning process. A *support plan* is a description of *who* will provide *what* technical support to users on an ongoing basis. This includes turning over project responsibility from the Project Team to technical support personnel as the system enters production use following acceptance.

This involves completing the following activities:

- *Define Support Requirements*—The HDO identifies the system support requirements
- *Identify Resources to Support the System*—The HDO and vendor identify the management structure and personnel to respond to system support issues
- *Provide Support Training*—The HDO and vendor identify and schedule system administration training for support personnel
- *Initiate Ongoing Support*—The HDO and vendor provide ongoing system support to EHR users based on defined roles and responsibilities

Prepare Support Requirements

The HDO prepares its support requirements during the execution process. A *system support requirement* is a description of what an organization and vendor will do to address issue logging, escalation and resolution, and system updates. The output of this process is a support roles and responsibilities matrix. A *support roles and responsibilities matrix* is a description of the position and function assigned to each person responsible for support.

The framework for providing support includes the following categories:

- *Technical Support*—Questions or issues from users regarding operational or technical issues
- *System Update Support*—Issues related to workflow changes, and system configuration, modifications, patches and new releases, and their impact on system use, administration, training, and support

Figure 4-7 includes an illustration of a support process flow chart.

Initiating	Planning	Executing	Controlling	Closing
	Prepare support plan *Support plan*	Prepare support requirements *Support requirements* *Support roles and responsibilities matrix* Provide support training *Training completion confirmation*	Control support *Organizational process asset update* *Performance report* *Change request (CR)* *Project document update*	Initiate ongoing support *Support tickets*

TABLE 4-24   Support Management Knowledge Area by Process Group

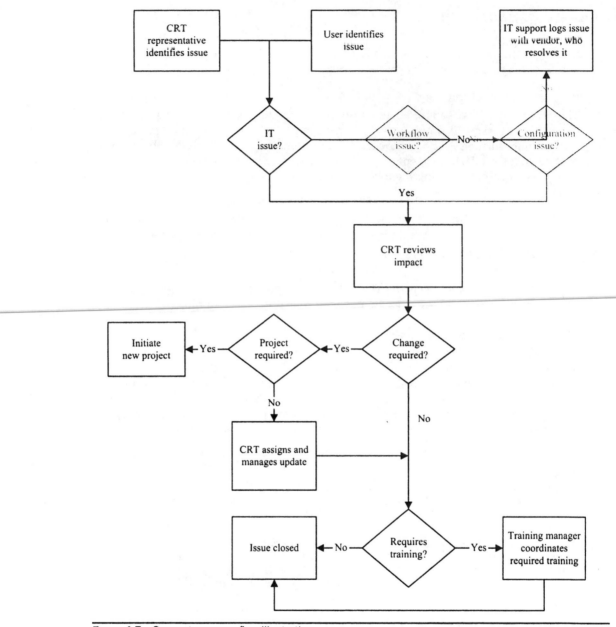

Figure 4-7 Support process flow illustration.
(The grayed-out portion of the figure represents optimization roles not typically associated with support.)

This illustration references the change requirements team. A *change requirements team (CRT)* is a group of individuals including a user, IT representative, and training department representative that works within each user department to identify needs and implement improvements on an ongoing basis. The CRT optimizes the system as described in Chapter 5. We reference the CRT in support management for the following reasons:

- Support receives issues from a variety sources. For example, a user may call support with a question about an apparent virus on his PC. Alternatively, a CRT representative may call support when working with the ED about an identified software defect.

- System support and optimization overlap. Support may receive a call or series of calls that reflect a trend about needed configuration and workflow changes. Likewise, the CRT may find software defects to refer to support. Finally, support needs to know about any workflow, configuration, or system change so they are equipped to help users when they call about a related issue.

Ultimately the CRT pre-empts the need to contact support.

Examples of system support include the following activities and events:

- Updates, patches, or replacements to system infrastructure (e.g., hardware, operating system software, database management software)
- Corrects identified application defects or errors
- Communicates planned updates to training, support, and user personnel
- Assists in understanding or finding a specific application function (e.g., advanced ad hoc reporting, filtering of patient records by specific treatment regiments)
- Resolves network and Internet connection outages
- Corrects performance delays and/or application unavailability
- Requests for restoration of backed up data
- Tracks, escalates, and resolves security-related incidents or patient safety and privacy compliance issues
- Maintains and executes disaster recovery plans (e.g., complete loss of HDO primary hosting facilities or primary HDO connection to vendor-hosted application)
- Fixes hardware failures and provides interim cutover to redundant components
- Solves workstation system and equipment problems
- Updates third-party-provided system resources
- Schedules and executes preventive maintenance and system monitoring
- Remedies unscheduled issues
- Updates system documentation and training to reflect system changes

Examples of organizations or entities involved in providing system support include HDO IT and vendor support staff. Vendor support may be available in a number of different forms, including:

- Online instructions
- Online video
- Scheduling specific training
- Technical support calls and email
- A knowledge base consisting of templates, guidelines, configurations, and other implementation, management, and technical information

Below is a description of potential support roles and responsibilities

The CIS, the Clinical Information Systems team in Information Systems, has an arm that does projects and then has an arm that does production support. The vendor contact goes through that production support team. If there's an issue identified, the customer brings that to us, and then we manage that. We identify that with the vendor, we document the information, the service request, because it's a problem. We work with the customer to get as much detail as we can. We try to reproduce the problem, we get the back end logs that the vendor may want to help them problem-solve the issue. We then work with the vendor to get the patch in that resolves it, test it, and then provide that back to the customer.

—Florence Chang, MBA, CIO, Multicare

Provide Support Training

An HDO provides support training during the execution process. The output of this process is training completion confirmation. This confirms support personnel are ready to help users during ongoing production use of the system. A system support team includes a combination of HDO and vendor staff that communicate effectively with both representative users and HDO or vendor IT staff. To ensure support is effective and successful, the HDO trains its representatives on the support team in the use of the tools and techniques identified in the support plan. This involves reviewing the content and purpose of FAQs or typical response scenarios or scripts, conducting practice *support* calls, and demonstrating issues tracking, reporting, and resolution.

An HDO should already have support procedures in place for other systems (e.g., technical support, vendor contact, system defects, patches, and releases). However, support personnel must learn about the unique configuration and associated requirements, workflow, and security associated with that new system. While training is helpful, the best way to accomplish this is by including support staff with users during configuration and workflow definition processes. Early involvement of support staff in these processes prepares them for system, workflow, and user needs after cutover.

Control Support

The Project Manager monitors support during the controlling process. The support plan serves as a baseline for managing support similar to any other plan in the project management plan. The Project Manager monitors support management using the control process described in integration management. For example, we observed support desk personnel struggling to help customers shortly after a system cutover. We met with the training manager to determine why this occurred. During this meeting, the training manager indicated that some support personnel had yet to receive training despite the notification confirming that all such personnel received and completed training satisfactorily. While we did not require a CR or document update, the training manager sent his staff to work one-on-one with support personnel during their help desk shifts until these personnel completed support training successfully.

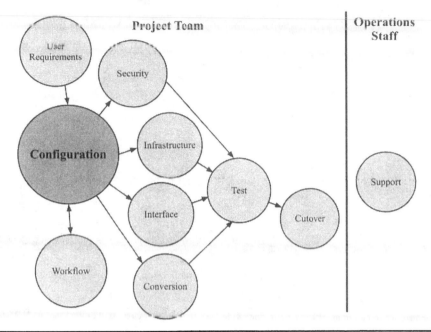

Figure 4-8 Support timing.

Initiate Ongoing Support

An HDO initiates and conducts ongoing support during the closing process. This involves providing users with post-cutover assistance on system issues and updates. The output of this process is a support ticket. A *support ticket* is a prioritized log entry of a reported system issue described in detail so support can reproduce and correct it. The HDO and vendor respond to support tickets by preparing, prioritizing, and resolving these tickets with corrective actions. Examples of corrective actions include repair of defects, configuration changes, and workload modifications. The HDO should use a CRT to review these tickets periodically to identify trends that result in configuration, workflow, training, and support updates.

Figure 4-8 displays the relationship between support, cutover, and other IT management knowledge areas.

Conclusion

This chapter described each individual IT management knowledge area. This description provided details about the processes supporting these knowledge areas and the outputs of these processes. It also included examples of analysis methods used to prepare these outputs. Table 4-25 displays all IT management knowledge area processes and their outputs by process group, with knowledge areas in bold, individual processes in normal text and outputs in italics.

The next chapter focuses on change management, with similar in-depth descriptions.

Table 4-25 IT Management Knowledge Areas by Process Group

Initiating	Planning	Executing	Controlling	Closing
User requirements	**User requirements**	**User requirements**	**User requirements**	**Security**
Prepare high-level user requirements	Prepare user requirements management plan	Prepare detailed user requirements	Control user requirements	Conduct ongoing security compliance
High-level user requirements	*User requirements management plan*	*Detailed user requirements*	*Organizational process asset update*	*Security audit results*
Infrastructure	**Infrastructure**	**Infrastructure**	*Performance report*	**Support**
Prepare high-level technology requirements	Prepare infrastructure management plan	Define detailed technology requirements	*Change request (CR)*	Initiate ongoing support
High-level technology requirements	*Infrastructure management plan*	*Detailed technology requirements*	*Project document update*	*Support tickets*
Define existing technology architecture	Prepare facility modification plan	Prepare and order equipment	**Infrastructure**	
Existing technology architecture description	*Facility modification plan*	*Equipment order confirmation*	Control infrastructure	
	Prepare system installation plan	Complete facility modifications	*Organizational process asset update*	
	System installation plan	*Site readiness confirmation*	*Performance report*	
	Security	Install equipment	*Change request (CR)*	
	Prepare security plan	*Hardware readiness confirmation*	*Project document update*	
	Security plan	**Security**	**Security**	
	Conversion	Define security requirements	Control security	
	Prepare conversion plan	*Security requirements*	*Organizational process asset update*	
	Conversion plan	Define security roles	*Performance report*	
	Interface	*Security roles*	*Change request (CR)*	
	Prepare interface plan	Configure security	*Project document update*	
	Interface plan	*Test cases*	**Conversion**	
	Software configuration	**Conversion**	Control conversion	
	Prepare software configuration plan	Prepare data conversion map	*Organizational process asset update*	
	Software configuration plan	*Data conversion map*	*Performance report*	
	Workflow	Conduct data cleansing	*Change request (CR)*	
	Prepare workflow management plan	*Data cleansing confirmation*	*Project document update*	
	Workflow management plan	Develop and test conversion solution	**Interface**	
	Test	*Conversion solution confirmation*	Control interfaces	
	Prepare test plan	Convert data	*Organizational process asset update*	
	Test plan	*Conversion confirmation*	*Performance report*	
		Interface	*Change request (CR)*	
		Prepare interface data map	*Project document update*	
		Interface data map	**Software configuration**	
		Develop and test interfaces	Control configuration	
		Interface software confirmation	*Organizational process asset update*	
		Enable interfaces	*Performance report*	
		Interface confirmation	*Change request (CR)*	
			Project document update	

Initiating	Planning	Executing	Controlling	Closing
	Cutover	**Software configuration**	**Workflow**	
	Prepare cutover plan	Define configuration	Control workflow	
	Cutover plan	requirements	*Organizational process asset*	
	Support	*Configuration requirements*	*update*	
	Prepare support plan	Configure system	*Performance report*	
	Support plan	*Test cases*	*Change request (CR)*	
		Workflow	*Project document update*	
		Define workflow requirements	**Test**	
		Workflow requirements	Control testing	
		Perform workflow changes	*Organizational process asset*	
		Workflow changes	*update*	
		Test	*Performance report*	
		Define test cases	*Change request (CR)*	
		Test cases	*Project document update*	
		Prepare test data	**Cutover**	
		Test data	Control cutover	
		Train testers	*Organizational process asset*	
		Training completion	*update*	
		confirmation	*Performance report*	
		Conduct tests	*Change request (CR)*	
		Test results	*Project document update*	
		Correct defects	**Support**	
		Test cases	Control support	
		Conduct regression testing	*Organizational process asset*	
		Test results	*update*	
		Cutover	*Performance report*	
		Train cutover support team	*Change request (CR)*	
		Training completion	*Project document update*	
		confirmation		
		Conduct system cutover		
		Successful cutover		
		confirmation		
		Support		
		Prepare support requirements		
		System support requirements		
		Support roles and		
		responsibilities matrix		
		Provide support training		
		Training completion		
		confirmation		

TABLE 4-25 IT Management Knowledge Areas by Process Group (*Continued*)

Endnotes

1. Wood, J , and Silver, D. (1989). *Joint Application Design*. New York: John Wiley & Sons Inc.
2. Miller, G. (1956). The magical number seven, plus or minus two: Some limits on our capacity for processing information. *Psychological Review, 63*(2), 81–97.
3. Anon. (2009). *Defining and Testing EHR Usability: Principles and Proposed Methods of EHR Usability Evaluation and Rating*. Chicago: The Health Information Management Systems Society.
4. Booch, G. (2005). *The Unified Modeling Language User Guide* (2nd ed.). Addison-Wesley Professional.
5. Shared Medical Systems Corporation. Retrieved June 29, 2010, from http://www.fundinguniverse.com/company-histories/Shared-Medical-Systems-Corporation-Company-History.html.
6. Brooks, J. (2009). *How to Measure SAAS Reliability*. Retrieved June 29, 2010, from http://www.eweek.com/c/a/Enterprise-Applications/Measuring-SAAS-Reliability.

CHAPTER 5

Change Management

In this chapter, we will:

- *Describe each change management knowledge area in detail*
- *Associate each change management knowledge area with processes and their outputs*
- *Define specific analysis methods associated with change management knowledge area processes and outputs*

I n the previous two chapters we defined project and IT management and their associated methodologies. Project management focuses primarily on the roles and
responsibilities of the people and teams involved in executing and managing the
project while IT management focuses on the activities and outputs involved with
designing, building, testing, and delivering the product of the project, the HIT. We
described sets of knowledge area processes and outputs for both project and IT management that the Project Manager either undertakes or assigns to specific Project Team
members. As noted in Chapter 2, we believe that both project and IT management are
important and interrelated methodologies in the successful implementation of HIT.
However, we also believe that these two methodologies alone are insufficient. In this
chapter, we describe the equally important discipline of change management, specifically managing people as they transition from paper to electronic records.

Understanding Change Management

Change management is arguably the one discipline in HIT projects that is the most
under-appreciated and underutilized. Many argue that the failure to plan and execute
change management is a major contributor to project failures even when executing
project and information IT management effectively. Two fundamental reasons may
explain this dilemma. First, change itself is incredibly challenging. Like all individuals,
healthcare workers naturally resist change. Second, the change management discipline
itself is relatively new when compared to project and IT management. As such, there
are fewer well-defined and standardized models for implementing change.

Why Do We Resist Change?

Most individuals resist change because we fear the unknown. This does not suggest that
resistance to change always means satisfaction with the current state—rather it means
that even though individuals may have significant dissatisfaction with the current state,
it is also true that the uncertainty around the unknown future brings fear, indecision,
and resistance. Change is often described as a journey, moving from a stable *now* to an

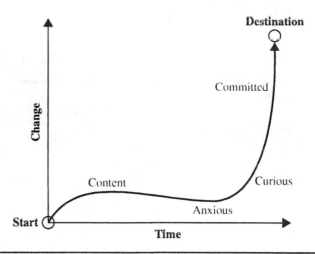

FIGURE 5-1 Change journey.

uncertain *future* in which the path between the two is unstable and possibly treacherous. Figure 5-1 displays this issue in terms of the journey, such as a sailing trip.

Once we begin our journey, we can look behind us and see the starting point. We are content knowing where we are and where we came from. Yet, at some point during this journey, we lose sight of our origin and with it the security of a known state. At the time, the destination is not yet visible, so we may have the sense that we are on an undirected journey with no one steering the ship. This state of unknown makes us anxious. The seas may be calm, but when they are not and storms arise, tossing our vessel, our stress and fear increase dramatically. Eventually we begin to see our destination on the horizon and we grow calm and curious. We often explore the future and find information that is more advantageous and appealing when compared to the current state. This occurs because it is imperative that we understand how it solves our particular problems or adds value—that is, "What's in it for me? (WIIFM)" As our anxiety diminishes, we begin to explore our imminent arrival and emerge from our journey committed to the future.

Implementing HIT, such as an EHR, involves a similar journey. Virtually every person who works in an HDO has a deep familiarity with how the organization works based on paper. With the introduction of a new paper form, a new order sheet for example, the degree of change is small and the workflow remains for the most part unchanged. An EHR, on the other hand, is a far more disruptive change. It is very difficult for individuals employed by an HDO to fully envision what their work will look like when all documentation moves from paper to on-screen.

It's hard to envision what your new world is going to look like, it's hard to envision what questions you need to ask . . . You know some people have an easier time at envisioning what the new world is going to look like, whereas others are just kind of stuck in their current work wondering how a system is going to fit into their current processes. This was and continues to be one of our biggest challenges. We addressed this by setting up the EMR on workstations, obviously in a demo environment. Lots of doctors and nurses and administrative staff could actually try the product and really get their hands dirty, so to speak.

—Dan Nigrin, MD, MS, CIO, Children's Hospital Boston

Change requires moving from our current and familiar way of doing things to an entirely new way. We fear the unknown, which starts the moment when we first learn there will be the new EHR. While we still do things the old way (e.g., use paper patient records), we cannot fully understand the new system. Our anxiety increases as the project progresses. Individuals as well as groups begin to wonder, *What does this mean for me? For us? Is my job threatened? Will our jobs change? What if I can't adapt? Will my patients suffer?* At some point, the Project Team begins to engage us in the new system, perhaps with some one-on-one training. Project Team members offer us information (e.g., confirming we will eliminate searching for missing paper patient records). Many of us begin to feel curious because we understand that using the new EHR offers advantages over the current paper-based patient record. At this point, our anxiety diminishes, our curiosity increases, and we begin the process of committing to the new system. Completing this journey successfully is, however, no small task. Not everyone follows the same path and not everyone makes it. It requires vision, leadership, true commitment, emotional intelligence, and political and practical understanding. John Kotter[1] defined several steps in this journey in which the change leaders have significant roles. The first step in his model is to enable and encourage stakeholders to see the problems the organization is facing by remaining with paper records. He refers to this process as "establishing a sense of urgency." Once people in an organization no longer feel comfortable with the current state—once they begin to believe that fundamental change in how the organization designs and delivers care is crucial to raising the level of quality, they start to feel activated and begin to move toward change—to begin the journey.

Why Do We Resist Change Management?

As described above, leading people through change is difficult. While helping an individual change is challenging, the complexity of this task compounds significantly when we tackle enterprise-level change involving dozens to thousands of people in an HDO. Implementing an EHR requires changing individual and group behaviors and requires change management.

Change management is a relatively new discipline and has only recently begun to achieve broad understanding and acceptance. Both project and IT management have professional organizations (PMI and IEEE), and both have formal methodologies (PMBOK and SWEBOK). Change management does not have this broad and formal acceptance. As such, leaders and managers within HDOs historically undervalue change management.

Lorenzi et al. offer a compelling list of reasons why people resist change management. Organizational leadership tends to resist change management because of the following properties:[2]

- *Measurability*—Both project and IT management include clearly defined objectives, tasks, and outputs. As well, these outputs are very often discretely measurable and benchmarked. For example, in project management we measure the budget of the EHR project and control for changes as the project proceeds. Likewise, in IT management we compare the user requirements to the system configuration and verify that they match. With change management, however, we rarely have such quantitative measures. It is, for example, very hard to define a metric that measures whether the EHR fully enabled our clinicians. In healthcare, measurability is paramount and if hard quantitative data are not available, we perceive less value in the process.

- *Predictability*—We can predict the likelihood of achieving project and IT management objectives. We can determine the impact of individual critical task delays on the project. Likewise, we can predict that increased system memory will enhance computer performance. Unfortunately we do not have this same level of predictability in change management. While we can coach a clinician, who is an opinion leader, on how to convince other clinicians to adopt the new EHR, we cannot predict the impact on others and their willingness to use the EHR. In addition, when the clinical users of the new system number in the hundreds or even thousands, this lack of predictability becomes that much more problematic.

- *Accountability*—We can hold the Project Manager accountable for meeting the schedule and configuring the EHR according to defined user requirements in project and IT management. However, we cannot hold the opinion leader responsible for convincing other clinicians to adopt the EHR. Far too many factors prevent us from holding this individual accountable, such as the fact that physicians are often independent contractors and not employees. Moreover, the lack of predictability and measurability makes accountability even more challenging. For an individual or team to accept the accountability for any one aspect of a project, they will likely want to know how management will measure their performance in terms of success or failure. This is problematic because change management mostly relies on qualitative measures, making it challenging to hold an individual or a team accountable.

- *Respectability*—We have long-established and standards-based project and IT management methods. Change management does not share this same widespread respect. The lack of acceptable measurability, predictability, and accountability properties underscore change management limitations, making it difficult for key stakeholders to include change management in a project and to authorize spending money and time on it.

- *Suitability*—We apply project and IT management to increase success. We know it is suitable to include these management disciplines in all IT projects. Given the uncertainty and low respectability associated with change management, it is much more difficult to prove whether it is useful. Even if it is generally suitable, it remains difficult to know which individual change management components are applicable for a project.

Table 5-1 summarizes why we resist change management.

In summary, there are many barriers to developing and implementing a strong change management methodology in HIT projects. The good news, however, is that this is changing. Change management is gaining broader understanding and acceptance. With each successive year that we develop more experience with this methodology, our positive understanding of it grows.

Properties	Project and IT Management	Change Management
Measurability	Easy	Difficult
Predictability	Strong	Weak
Accountability	Precise	Ambiguous
Respectability	Widespread	Limited
Suitability	Useful	Useless

TABLE 5-1   Why We Resist Change Management

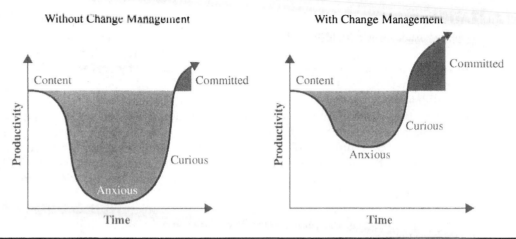

Figure 5-2 Change management cycle.

Given the reasons for resisting change management, we might logically ask what benefits change management might bring to HIT projects. Figure 5-2 describes the impact of using change management on one key factor—productivity of the users of the technology.

Anyone involved with an EHR implementation knows well that clinicians almost certainly will go through a period of decreased productivity after cutover. Using a new EHR when seeing patients, providing care, and documenting that care unavoidably slows the workflow. However, when these frontline workers are resistant to the change itself—when they do not want the new EHR—the time it takes to restore them to pre-cutover productivity increases.

However, with effective change management practices, we are better and more quickly able to bring these users from the *content* and *anxious* stages to the *curious* and *committed* perspective, which in turn significantly reduces the time of low productivity. And these positive results apply to a range of other factors (e.g., user satisfaction, user commitment, and user effectiveness).

We believe we must include change management in HIT projects, despite perceived weaknesses. We know that when we use a structured or disciplined approach for project and IT management, we increase the likelihood of HIT project success. It is only reasonable to assume that if we apply a structured approach to changing human behavior, we can also contribute to HIT project success. In fact, the more we attempt to structure change management, the more we identify how it best contributes to project success. The more we learn, the greater the likelihood a standard will emerge that we can all use to increase HIT project success.

Based on our experience, we propose a change management methodology in which we define five major components or knowledge areas:

- Realization management
- Sponsorship management
- Transformation management
- Training management
- Optimization management

REALIZATION

Realization management includes initiating, planning, controlling, and closing what a stakeholder does to achieve the fundamental objectives of the project. Table 5-2 displays realization management processes and their outputs (in italics) by process group.

Define Objectives

An organization defines project objectives during the initiating process. An *objective* is a goal or something a person or organization plans to achieve. Project initiators begin a project and define preliminary project objectives. These objectives may originate from a small formal or informal planning process. The process becomes formal when HDO leadership authorizes a feasibility analysis and business case. This includes a formal objective setting process.

Change management focuses on strategic enterprise objectives. Project management objectives focus on the project itself (e.g., maintaining within scope, staying on schedule, and keeping on budget). IT management focuses on tangible objectives (e.g., minimal system defects, fast performance time, and low downtime).

Of all the potential objectives that one might consider in HIT change management, the most fundamental are improvements in quality, an increase in patient safety, and reduction in cost of care. HIT change management focuses on changing behaviors of care providers toward these strategic objectives. One central reason that setting quality and cost objectives is so critical is that it demonstrates to HIT clinical users that, for example, the EHR will deliver measurable patient benefits. Clinical providers concentrate on the quality of care their patients receive and want to prove to their patients that their care and safety will improve through the effective use of new HIT. This is an immensely strong driver for engaging these users in the change management process (WIIFM).

Clinical folks, especially physicians and nurses, tend to respond well if you provide a clear background and basis for why you're doing things. This is especially effective if you provide data about outcomes and quality improvements. Show them, in say, journal articles and experience from folks around the country who can speak to how the new system improved their patients' care. That kind of

Initiating	Planning	Executing	Controlling	Closing
Define objectives *Objectives*	Define measurable outcomes *Measurable outcomes* Prepare outcome delivery schedule *Outcome delivery schedule* Assign responsibility for objectives *Objective responsibility list*		Control realization *Organizational process asset update* *Measurable outcome achievement* *Performance report* *Change request (CR)* *Project document update* *Achievement of an objective*	Report outcome achievement *Dashboard report*

TABLE 5-2   Realization Management Knowledge Area by Process Group

stuff resonates with them, and so as we implemented our EMR, particularly early on, we saw ourselves in an educational role to help make sure that the leadership of the organization, medical, nursing, and lay folks understood the value.

I just knew, as a physician myself, you have to do more than just tell me we're going to automate these processes and it's going to be better as a result. That just doesn't convince me, it doesn't cut it. I need to know a little bit more about why you think that, and why we're going to try and automate.

I put myself in those clinicians' shoes and thought about what they would be expecting me to show, and once we did that, I think they got on board. I think in most instances where you hear about these projects not going well, it's when they've not engaged with their clinical groups within the organization, whether it's physicians, nurses, respiratory therapists, whatever, and making sure that those groups are (a) part of the project, and (b) very well informed as to the why.

—Dan Nigrin, MD, MS, CIO, Children's Hospital Boston

Define Measurable Outcomes

An organization defines measurable outcomes for each objective during the planning process group. A *measurable outcome* is an observable result or output that an organization can demonstrate achieves an objective. Each objective has at least one measurable outcome that includes a tangible result or way to measure it. An HDO cannot determine if it achieved an objective if its related outcomes are not tangible and measurable. This often requires *tangibilizing* the intangible. For example, healthcare quality improvement is difficult to measure because it does not necessarily have a physical presence. We give it a physical dimension by defining healthcare quality improvement using specific, measurable outcomes such as reduced mortality, morbidity, infection, and/or readmission rates. The Joint Commission has numerous quality-based performance measures (e.g., Health Care-Associated Bloodstream Infections in Newborns).

The SMART analysis method helps an HDO define outcome measures. Developed by Peter Drucker as a part of Management by Objectives (MBO),[3] *SMART* is an acronym for:

- *Specific*—Well-defined and precise
- *Measurable*—Quantitative, empirical
- *Achievable*—Reasonable, attainable, and realistic
- *Relevant*—Applicable, germane
- *Time Bound*—Tied to a schedule

Ideally all objectives the organization elects to achieve should have each of the five SMART characteristics. As an example, consider the quality objective of reducing hospital-acquired infections, a well-known quality challenge that all hospitals currently face and one that may well require an EHR, CPOE, and clinical decision support to be achievable. This objective can, if defined ideally, fulfill all five SMART criteria:

- *Specific*—Hospital-acquired infections includes all clinically evident infections that do not originate from a patient's original admitting diagnosis
- *Measurable*—The hospital-acquired infection rate for all adult inpatients will decrease by half over the next 12 months, and then in half again over the next 24 months

- *Achievable*—There are organizations that recently achieved these measures
- *Relevant*—Several organizations including the Institute for Healthcare Improvement characterize this objective as centrally important
- *Time Bound*—The hospital will assess the hospital-acquired infection rate at least quarterly on an ongoing basis

An objective is SMART if it includes outcomes that determine whether the project can or did achieve the objective. Each outcome defines what the HDO plans to achieve by successfully completing the project, that is, the future state. A measurable outcome defines the value, or a basis for improvement serving as a key performance indicator (KPI).

Measuring outcome achievement may require a pre- and post-test. A *pre- and post-test* is an evaluation of conditions both before and after system implementation. An HDO collects baseline data on conditions before EHR implementation and compares this data to post-implementation conditions. Comparing data on pre- and post-project conditions helps determine whether an HDO achieves and sustains project objectives. In some cases, an HDO already has a baseline of previously measured outcomes before starting the EHR project. In other cases, an HDO must start measuring outcomes early in the project to establish a baseline before system implementation.

As another example, HDOs currently measure medication errors. They use five rights to help reduce medication errors. The *five rights* is a collection of measures that hold a healthcare practitioner accountable:

1. For giving the right drug
2. To the right patient
3. In the right dose
4. By the right route
5. At the right time

Measuring medication error rates before an EHR implementation includes mistakes associated with the condition of handwritten orders. Measuring error rates after EHR implementation includes the condition of computer-generated medication orders. The comparison of these pre- and post-project conditions measures achievement of the project objective to reduce medication error rates. Table 5-3 displays an EHR project's outcomes and indicates whether the HDO currently measures them.

Prepare Outcome Delivery Schedule

A Project Manager organizes outcomes according to a delivery schedule during the planning process. An *outcome delivery schedule* is a timetable that identifies when the project will achieve outcomes. This is consistent with the time-based dimension of SMART objectives.

It is also critical to demonstrate to involved stakeholders how the project plans to achieve objectives and their measurable outcomes. This helps to move stakeholders from uncertainty and anxiousness to curiosity and commitment. Prototyping offers an effective way of doing this. A *prototype* is a model of how the system might work. The

Objective	Measurable Outcomes	Currently Measured
Check for medication interactions—Link all patient medications and chemotherapy to an automatic crosscheck for interactions.	**Improved patient safety**—Reduce number of medical errors by eliminating illegibility issues (e.g., replacing handwritten with computer-generated documents).	Yes
Improve patient flow—Improve patient flow at the point of care in clinic by tracking and documenting patient's progress through the center including arrival, registration, laboratory, radiology, exam room, and treatment area as well as any other scheduled appointments for that day.	**Improved patient care** (Currently Measured Outcome)—Increase physician time for patient care and reduce patient wait time.	Yes
Increase timely availability of a more complete medical record—Improve the timeliness, completeness, and accuracy of medical records.	**Reduced number of month-end updates to incomplete medical records**—Measure reduction of incomplete medical records currently identified monthly and provided to physicians for completion.	Yes
	Reduced support staff records management time—Decrease hours spent by HIM personnel moving and managing paper records.	Yes
Link complexity of patient visit with suggested billing codes—Provide summary of key features in patient note necessary to document complexity of visit and appropriate selection of billing code.	**Increased revenue from patient billings**—Increase patient billings by application of most appropriate billing codes.	Yes
Merge distinct laboratory, radiology, and pathology databases—Allow clinician access to all relevant patient data without switching between multiple programs.	**Improved patient safety**—Reduce number of medical errors by eliminating illegibility issues (e.g., replacing handwritten with computer-generated documents).	Yes
	Increased availability of patient information—Improve access to key patient information by providing additional methods for information access, which will reduce phone messages, wait times, absence of relevant patient information, and so on.	Yes
	Reduced support staff records management time—Decrease hours spent by HIM personnel moving and managing paper records.	Yes

TABLE 5-3   Objectives, Measurable Outcomes Measurement Status

Objective	Measurable Outcomes	Currently Measured
Provide 24/7 clinician access to information from ALL "secured" locations—Make appropriate clinical and business information, including specific patient data, available to all authorized Cancer Center personnel 24/7 from all secure locations (e.g., home, cancer center, and HDO).	**Increased availability of patient information**—Improve access to key patient information by providing additional methods for information access, which will reduce phone messages, wait times, absence of relevant patient information, and so on.	Yes
	Reduced support staff records management time—Decrease hours spent by HIM personnel moving and managing paper records.	Yes
Provide clinical information to clinical and business management—Improve operations by providing clinical and business management with historical reporting, and providing facility information to management and clinicians to support best practice recommendations. For example, physicians and managers at one center could change their respective behaviors based on treatment information from another center, not otherwise available, leading to superior outcomes. This could contribute to standards development, internal benchmarks, improved reimbursement support, business development, encouragement for clinician creation of a learning community for continuous improvement, and so on.	**Improved patient safety**—Reduce number of medical errors by eliminating illegibility issues (e.g., replacing handwritten with computer-generated documents).	Yes
	Increased reimbursements—Improve financial results based on EHR performance incentives offered by payers.	Yes
	Optimized business decision-making—Support informed management decision-making by providing more complete, accurate, and timely information.	Yes
	Optimized provision of care—Increase the efficacy of clinical care by providing clinical management with more complete, accurate, and timely information to support decision-making.	Yes
Reduce medical errors and improve patient safety—Improve patient safety statistics (e.g., reduce incorrect lab tests, misinterpretation of orders, and incorrect drug administration).	**Improved patient safety**—Reduce number of medical errors by eliminating illegibility issues (e.g., replacing handwritten with computer-generated documents).	Yes

TABLE 5-3 Objectives, Measurable Outcomes Measurement Status (*Continued*)

Objective	Measurable Outcomes	Currently Measured
Replace physician written orders with electronic orders—Improve patient safety, reduce turnaround time, and enable electronic order checking by eliminating written orders.	**Improved patient safety**—Reduce number of medical errors by eliminating illegibility issues (e.g., replacing handwritten with computer-generated documents).	Yes
Link CPOE with automatic chemotherapy protocols—Link chemotherapy agents to standard anti-emetic regimens, modified at the clinician's request. Routinely add anti-allergy medicines for certain chemotherapy agents.	**Improved patient safety** (Currently Measured)—Reduce number of medical errors (e.g., eliminating illegibility issues and decreasing medical omissions by replacing handwritten with computer-generated documents), providing full medication list to chemotherapy pharmacist to enhance alertness to potential medication interactions, and so on. **Reduced support staff records management time** (Currently Measured)—Decrease hours spent by HIM personnel moving and managing paper records.	Yes
Promote optimal medication treatment—Optimize evaluation of medication use in oncology by regimen and not by individual drug. Having the capability to link chemotherapy regimens and associated supportive medications with medical data, cost, and so on, could provide a powerful tool that physicians could use to continuously improve their own decision-making and be able to monitor the improvements in care through measurable outcomes.	**Increased reimbursements** (Currently Measured)—Improve financial results based on EHR performance incentives offered by payers. **Optimized provision of care** (Currently Measured)—Increase the efficacy of clinical care by providing clinical management with more complete, accurate, and timely information to support decision-making (i.e., providing physicians with analysis of practices and associated outcomes).	Yes No
Provide data on a patient portal—Provide the patient with a secure method for communicating with their cancer center caregivers via secure email and allow them to see a subset of their clinical data or other linked cancer information sites.	**Increased availability of patient information** (Currently Measured)—Improve access to key patient information by providing additional methods for information access, which will reduce phone messages, wait times, absence of relevant patient information, and so on.	Yes

TABLE 5-3 Objectives, Measurable Outcomes Measurement Status (*Continued*)

Objective	Measurable Outcomes	Currently Measured
Provide comprehensive care model to prospective partner HDOs by offering an EHR solution—Provide complete information in one place to avoid fragmented care and delayed decision-making due to missing or inaccessible paper documents/film/ medical record.	**Improved patient safety** (Currently Measured)—Reduce number of medical errors (e.g., eliminating illegibility issues and decreasing medical omissions by replacing handwritten with computer-generated documents, providing full medication list to chemotherapy pharmacist to enhance alertness to potential medication interactions, and so on).	Yes
	Increased availability of patient information (Currently Measured)—Improve access to key patient information by providing additional methods for information access, which will reduce phone messages, wait times, absence of relevant patient information, and so on.	Yes
	Optimized provision of care (Currently Measured)—Increase the efficacy of clinical care by providing clinical management with more complete, accurate, and timely information to support decision-making.	Yes
Streamline information necessary for authorization of testing, chemotherapy—Provide ready access to necessary data for physicians' staff to obtain authorization for radiology studies, chemotherapy, and so on.	**Reduced support staff records management time** (Currently Measured)—Decrease hours spent by HIM personnel moving and managing paper records.	Yes
Centralize coding—Consolidate coding across all cancer centers.	**Increased coding consistency** (Currently Measured)—Standardizes recruiting and training, increases coding productivity, centralizes training, provides option for remote access for coding coverage, and so on.	Yes

TABLE 5-3   Objectives, Measurable Outcomes Measurement Status (*Continued*)

Project Team members who prepared configuration and workflow for the EHR demonstrate segments of the system in a prototype, proof-of-concept, pilot, or simulation to a broad range of stakeholders. This provides an opportunity to:

- Obtain user feedback about the configuration and workflow (e.g., it is correct or requires specific modifications)
- Build commitment and confidence in the project and how it will attain specified measurable outcomes [e.g., reduce adverse drug events (ADEs)]
- Foster constructive project participation and momentum
- Take advantage of constructive resistance where individuals refrain from using the configuration or workflow and offer improvements instead
- Reduce resistance by informing the misinformed
- Facilitate stakeholder project understanding
- Reduce stress, anxiety, and confusion

Prototypes provide compelling evidence that project changes are necessary. This is particularly important because prototypes provide direct evidence of measurable and anticipated benefits/value to project participants, increasing their commitment to and support for the project. Stakeholder sessions at regular intervals involving prototypes are also particularly important given HIT projects may take several years or longer to complete.

Identifying objectives according to an outcome delivery schedule also clarifies whom the project affects and when it affects them. An HDO will realize some benefits or outcomes immediately after implementation, while others take an extended period to achieve. For example, automated results reporting to a portal provides timely information access to physicians and patients immediately after cutover. In contrast, a clinical decision support system takes more time for physicians to collectively use and provide more complete, accurate, and timely clinical care.

> We've always done a 10% build (i.e., proof of concept) as a means to validate design decisions and future state process changes. This sample should represent 80% of what the user will experience at go-live. So for example not every location, orderable, appointment type, form is built, but a minimum of one or more representative examples of each are built. The purpose of the proof of concept is to have the user simulate and think about the new tools, modify processes, and their impact on their specific job accountabilities or work unit. The goal is to identify what we may have missed or did miss. It is also a prime opportunity to identify applications issues and bugs. Users will always find issues that an analyst doesn't, given the creative ways the user interacts with the application. This in many cases is the first time many customers have an opportunity to play with the new functionality. It is as they "figure it out" after a brief demonstration that we uncover issues, questions, and challenges.
>
> —Beatha Johnson, Director, Clinical Information Systems, VMMC

Assign Responsibility for Objectives

The executive sponsor assigns responsibility for objectives to top project leadership during the planning process. The output is an objectives responsibility list. An *objectives responsibility list* is a register of who is accountable for the achievement of each objective. The assignment process includes answering the following questions:

- Who is involved?
- Why is this important to them?
- What will they do?
- How are they going to do it?
- When will they complete it?
- How can we reward achieving it?

Objectives generally include more than one measurable outcome. Those accountable for an objective designate which key stakeholder is responsible for each outcome and measure his performance based on his achievement of it. This closely aligns project leadership with those responsible for outcome achievement.

The project sponsor may also ensure that assigned project objectives are in alignment with strategic HDO objectives and that they reinforce each other. Conflict between the two will cause confusion within the project and throughout the organization.

Control Realization

The Project Manager controls realization of project objectives and outcomes in the controlling process. The Project Manager monitors objective achievement using the control process described in integration management. For example, a state healthcare provider recently asked us to help them calculate and document whether they achieved their project outcomes. This project included a half dozen outcome measures calculated and maintained by several different parties and organizations, for example, IT, contractors, and individual departments. We assembled the information and found several discrepancies, such as missing data, different interpretations of the outcome measures, and erroneous assumptions. While we were able to assemble most of the data, we were not able to rely on the outcome measures. This resulted in a CR requiring that we assemble all of the participants to gain agreement on the definition of all measures and monitor calculation of these measures to ensure accurate and consistent reporting.

Report Outcome Achievement

The Project Manager reports outcome achievement results during the closing process. The output of this process is a dashboard report.

Fundamental to management is working toward a common goal or understanding of what an organization is trying to achieve. Aligning the organization and project participants toward a common set of measurable objectives drives everyone in the same direction.

A *dashboard report* is a written summary to management (and distributed widely) that describes the status of outcome achievement by objective. This mostly involves comparing data on pre- and post-project conditions to determine whether the HDO achieved all outcomes. This reporting process starts during the closing process and continues on an ongoing basis after project completion.

> *We were structured in our project overall. We defined the project objectives upfront and established exactly what outcomes were expected. It was easy to compare the outputs when we got there against what we originally said we set out to do.*
>
> —Dan Nigrin, MD, MS, CIO, Children's Hospital Boston

SPONSORSHIP MANAGEMENT

Sponsorship management is initiating, planning, and controlling the selection, assessment, and mentoring of a project's most senior leader. The executive sponsor project role is critical, which may seem paradoxical given the potential distance from the day-to-day project tasks. The executive sponsor is not the Project Manager. Both roles are critical, but different. One might compare these two roles to the CEO and COO of an organization. The executive sponsor's responsibilities parallel those of the CEO—to create and communicate the vision for the project to an organization's stakeholders and to ensure the Project Manager (who is similar to a COO) has the necessary resources to complete the project successfully. The Project Manager is the person responsible for day-to-day project activities. The Project Manager turns to the executive sponsor when project challenges arise that the Project Manager is unable to resolve. Table 5-4 displays executive sponsorship management processes and their outputs (in italics) by process group.

Select the Executive Sponsor

Project initiators select an executive sponsor during the initiating process. A senior HDO executive authorizes the project initiators to prepare the feasibility analysis and business case. Likewise, the senior HDO executive authorizes this same group to prepare a project charter assuming there is a recommended business case to proceed. One of the outputs, when preparing a project charter, is creation of a project steering committee and selection of the executive sponsor.

It is hard to overstate the importance of the executive sponsor to project success. It is true that the Project Manager is the person who is responsible for completing project work on a day-to-day basis, but the Project Manager faces severe project limitations if he does not have a qualified executive sponsor supporting and facilitating the Project Manager's work.

The sponsor plays a critical role. In projects that I've been the sponsor, my point of view is that I need to remove roadblocks, and get out of the way when there aren't any. The challenge is getting the clinical leadership of the organization invested and understanding why we're doing this. In many instances, I saw my role as sponsor for this initiative as educator, and not just to say "folks this is coming and it's going to turn your world upside down," but "folks this is coming, it's going to turn your world upside down but here's why we're doing it."

—Dan Nigrin, MD, MS, CIO, Children's Hospital Boston

Initiating	Planning	Executing	Controlling	Closing
Select the executive sponsor *Executive sponsor*	Assess executive sponsor *Executive sponsorship assessment results*		Control sponsorship *Organizational process asset update* *Performance report* *Change request (CR)* *Project document update*	

TABLE 5-4 Sponsorship Management Knowledge Area by Process Group

Impact Area	Scope of Change
Capability and Management	High
Clinical Workflow and Rules	High
Clinician Impact	High
Financial	High
Organization Departments and Units	High
Technology Impact	High
Patient Impact	High

TABLE 5-5 Scope of Change Analysis

The executive sponsor is an individual who has sufficient authority and influence as well as a deep understanding of the nature of change required to achieve all project objectives successfully. Defining the scope of change is an analysis method that clarifies who should be the executive sponsor, by identifying the authority and influence required to lead the project. Table 5-5 displays an example of the scope of change associated with an EHR project.

Details regarding this scope and impact of change include:

- *Capability and Management*—The impact is high because:
  - The project requires strong leadership and role-modeling throughout the HDO to encourage new system adoption
  - The amount of change caused by this project is significant in terms of HDO resource capacity
- *Clinical Workflow and Rules*—The impact is high because:
  - There are many planned changes to current clinical workflow and rules
  - These changes will standardize clinical workflow that is currently informal
  - There are widespread changes associated with new objectives and outcome measures
  - These changes will require significant training
- *Clinician Impact*—The impact is high because:
  - The project involves all clinical departments
  - Clinicians will require significant training to use the new system
  - The project includes all change types—operational (one or a few individuals), tactical (small ongoing improvements), and strategic (widespread, long-term improvements)
- *Financial Impact*—The impact is high because:
  - Project one-time costs are very high
  - Long-term, ongoing costs are also very high and widespread

- *Organization Departments and Units*—The potential impact is high because:
  - Line and reporting relationships will change
  - Roles and responsibilities will change
  - Decision-making processes will change
- *Technology*—The impact is high because:
  - A vendor will provide a significant proportion of the work (e.g., they will deliver a SaaS solution, the HDO has the infrastructure in place already)
  - The project involves significant third-party expertise and knowledge transfer
- *Patient Impact*—The impact is high because:
  - The project involves direct contact with patients
  - Patients will use a portal to communicate with their clinicians
  - Patients must learn to communicate with clinicians who use computerized patient records

HDOs may often select the CIO as the executive sponsor for an EHR project. This is generally not an optimal choice. The CIO provides significant project value and support, but the IT department is hardly a direct recipient of project value when compared to clinicians and patients. Selecting the CMO or CEO as the executive sponsor is appropriate given the widespread impact of the project (i.e., broad organizational capability requirements, extensive financial commitments, and significant patient, clinician, and IT implications).

> *Our EMR project was not led from the IT side of the organization. The patient care side of the organization led the project, all the way up to the hospital CEO, COO, and board of trustees. I think they all understood the rationale for why this project needed to happen, and they endorsed it from the get-go with very high-level backing and executive sponsorship. This started early in the project, even at the RFP stages, identifying the project scope, project charter, and then putting together a short list of potential solution partners that we would evaluate and ultimately choose.*
> —Dan Nigrin, MD, MS, CIO, Children's Hospital Boston

Assess Executive Sponsor

An organization assesses the executive sponsor during the planning process. An *executive sponsorship assessment result* is the outcome of an evaluation of an executive sponsor's actual capabilities compared to best practices.

As noted, change management is a newer discipline in healthcare organizations and the knowledge and skills the executive sponsor should possess are likely new. He may require additional training and coaching.

Few executive sponsors have prior experience in this role, and projects fail because of their poor performance. Improving an executive sponsor's knowledge and skill can occur in a number of ways, including:

- Contacting and working with peers who previously performed as an executive sponsor
- Taking a training course

- Conducting a self-assessment
- Hiring an expert to assess and mentor the executive sponsor

For example:

We needed some kind of mentoring and learning from other organizations because we didn't know what we didn't know, even within our organization. We now have multiple projects, and we have documentation on how to become an executive sponsor, what are the things that you need to do, and so forth.

It takes a lot of one-on-one conversations. I took our C-suite to another organization where I have done consulting work in the past, and had them talk at one-on-one level. Our CEO talked to another CEO, the COO talked to a COO from another organization to gain their insights and lessons learned.

We are currently hosting site visits for many organizations . . . They want to pair up with their counterpart, their CFO with our CFO, their CEO with our CEO, so they can learn how to be the executive sponsor in a project like this. Introduce and learn from others, learn from their peers.

—Florence Chang, MBA, CIO, Multicare

At a minimum, an executive sponsor should contact peers and, based on their input, conduct a self-assessment regarding the gap between the executive sponsor's own approach and best practices, to identify if they will do the following:

- Participate in the project from start to finish
- Review and approve the project feasibility analysis and business case
- Define project objectives and measurable outcomes, and assign them to project leadership
- Rely on an independent third party (e.g., a mentor), to assess their ongoing sponsorship performance
- Conduct all work ethically and require ethical behavior from others
- Approve key project personnel, such as the Project Manager
- Approve key baseline project documents (e.g., scope, schedule, budget)
- Review and approve requirements before vendor solicitation
- Approve the recommended EHR vendor
- Launch key project meetings
- Engage in project steering committee meetings, evaluate project performance, make key decisions, provide and motivate resources, constrain scope creep, address schedule constraints, resolve budget shortfalls, overcome personnel roadblocks
- Participate in key project activities, such as setting objectives and training
- Work and communicate actively and visibly at all levels of the organization, from executive management to users:
  - Solving problems
  - Demonstrating adherence to project objectives, schedule, and budget
  - Reinforcing change and managing resistance

- Manage by walking around (i.e., following a hands-on practice of visiting with and listening to managers and their staff in their work areas to receive and demonstrate a front-line understanding of HDO operations and the project impact)
- Set the direction and motivate people to achieve the project objectives

Below is a description of an example of an executive sponsor's role in an HIT project.

To enable the executive sponsors to be effective decision-makers, they must understand and agree to the project boundaries and the operational requirements to support the project. So, the initial project scope, risks, and timeline are definitely discussed with them. We usually provide a high-level demonstration of the functionality to provide the context to understand the impact to the user and process. I also invite the executive sponsors to the proof-of-concept sessions, which provide the next level of detail. Most of the executive sponsors have chosen to get involved with enough detail to allow them to go on rounds during conversion and provide a high level of assistance. They gain further knowledge by attending the same class that an end user would go to, which means they understand the functional and operational changes that will impact the nurses, support staff, and providers. When we go-live, operational meetings are put on hold. Managers and supervisors are expected to be visible and available in the work unit and actively supporting the conversion. Executive leadership makes rounds and can usually answer simple questions or find assistance. They can definitely answer the policy and practice questions that come up with any implementation.
—Beatha Johnson, Director, Clinical Information Systems, VMMC

The executive sponsor should seek training or hire a mentor to help overcome the gap identified in their self-assessment. There is generally no one who can direct the executive sponsor to undergo this assessment and subsequently seek training or mentoring. While other steering committee members may attempt to help, it is unlikely they will succeed. The Project Manager cannot do this easily because the executive sponsor is their superior. Failing to seek improvement leaves trial and error, which is too risky given how crucial this role is to project success.

Control Sponsorship
An organization controls executive sponsor performance during the controlling process. A third party (i.e., a mentor) works one-on-one with the executive sponsor monitoring to improve project leadership and management based on best practices. The mentor is an individual experienced in the executive sponsorship role.

The Project Manager monitors executive sponsorship management using the control process described in integration management. For example, a group of Project Managers responsible for EHR implementations needed our assistance. One recurring comment from several of them was that many physicians failed to attend the training. All of the Project Managers recognized training as crucial to initial system use and long-term EHR optimization.

We suggested that all physicians pass a training proficiency test confirming successful training completion before receiving an EHR user ID and password. When it was obvious to us that many Project Managers were uncomfortable with this approach, we assured them they were not responsible for resolving this issue entirely on their own, but should defer to their executive sponsors. The executive sponsor sets the project tone, and establishes project absolutes or certain things that are not negotiable. Each Project

Manager should feel comfortable carrying out these absolutes, knowing he has the backing of his executive sponsor and knowing he can rely on his sponsor to execute these absolutes when he meets resistance. The Project Manager's responsibility is to meet with his executive sponsors to request assistance in resolving this training matter.

If I had to do it all over again, what would I do differently? . . . I would talk about the kind of executive decisions that need to "be made and stood behind," to ensure that everyone has the stomach for what they're going to have to support, such as physicians having to do training and pass a competency assessment before getting an ID and password, or to have their privileges suspended if they fall too far behind in completing their work. I would make sure every leader had "skin in the game" for ensuring regular and appropriate EHR use in their units to support organizational quality and efficiency goals. I would insist that a mechanism be in place to cultivate and support clinic champions and super-users and that data mining and reporting capabilities enable robust measurement and real-time reporting of what matters. I would carefully define all of the components of EHR "Meaningful Use," describe EHR use strategies to achieve them, and then secure a commitment to holding providers and staff accountable to achieving them.

—Michael H. Zaroukian, MD, PhD, FACP, FHIMSS, CMIO, Michigan State University

TRANSFORMATION MANAGEMENT

In the previous section, we described change management activities related to selecting training and monitoring the key senior person in the HIT project, the executive sponsor. In this section, we turn attention to the project stakeholders for whom change management is important. *Transformation management* is planning, executing, and controlling the adoption of innovation by individuals or groups of stakeholders.

Healthcare organizations are unique in the range of cultures they employ. A typical hospital will have a management culture (hospital administration), a technical culture (IT department), and of course the clinical culture (nurses, physicians, laboratory technicians, to name a few). Each of these cultures has widely different factors that influence how their members accept HIT.

The quote below addresses healthcare culture. It refers to John J. Nance, a recognized aviation safety expert, decorated USAF pilot, retired Alaska Airline pilot, and professional speaker on teamwork, risk management, motivation, and so on. He is well-known for his pioneering work in human factors of flight safety and its application to patient safety.

> *Change is difficult under the best of circumstances, let alone the highly challenging environment that is healthcare, with a disruptive technology such as EHR systems. When asked to make a significant and disruptive change, even for a noble purpose, many people will in one way or another say, "We don't want to change" or "Change back."*
>
> *Navigating and leading change is about creating the rationale for near-term change, assembling a critical mass of influential stakeholders to lead change, creating and communicating the vision, and getting early positive results that can be built on and then infused into the culture. Alignment is an important component that leaders need to cultivate. I resonate with John Nance's analogy in which he describes a poorly aligned healthcare environment as a "farmers market" in which providers expect administration to give them a place to work but then exert no influence over care practices even when they are important to quality and efficiency. Such providers want to be treated as highly sought after independent vendors who can do whatever they want independent of the effect it may have on others in the system. In reality, providers in an organization are part of a team that has a shared responsibility for quality, which includes aligning itself according to the considered decisions of the organizations, physician, and business leaders according to the needs of the patients and others we serve. What we had in my internal medicine clinic was a team that operated exactly like that. We all rowed in the same direction.*
>
> —Michael H. Zaroukian, MD, PhD, FACP, FHIMSS, CMIO, Michigan State University

Table 5-6 displays transformation management processes and their outputs (in italics) by process group.

Understanding the basic concepts behind transformation can be helpful here. Successful transformation involves consensus building to ensure that an organization as a whole is committed to and ready for change. When a group engages in consensus building, it considers different opinions and then works toward achieving group agreement as the endpoint. Transformation is about supporting and achieving an objective, whereas consensus is about agreement among all participants. Transformation involves consensus; however, many project decisions are mandatory and it may not be appropriate or necessary for the group to reach agreement. For example, physicians are often

Initiating	Planning	Executing	Controlling	Closing
	Prepare change management team *Change management team* Prepare stakeholder map *Stakeholder map*	Conduct transformation *Transformation tasks* *Transformation task completion*	Control transformation *Organizational process asset update* *Performance report* *Change request (CR)* *Project document update*	

TABLE 5-6 Transformation Management Knowledge Area by Process Group

free to use their own order sets before an EHR implementation, but if one of the objectives of the EHR is to have standardized order sets, then physicians must all comply with the standardized order set after EHR implementation. If one highly respected physician resists this mandate during implementation, the Project Manager must escalate this issue to the executive sponsor. The executive sponsor meets with this physician and dictates that this is not only a project mandate, but also a medical best practice. If the executive sponsor successfully manages this situation, he may receive this physician's support, but not necessarily his agreement.

Resistance to the change that HIT brings is well-known, and the reasons are complex. Some resistance is irrational, but most is rational, based on a combination of the incentives (and disincentives) that users face. Often resistance just comes simply from a misunderstanding.

When folks push back, the knee-jerk response is to ignore them or tell them why they're not right. We tried to consciously do the opposite, to involve them more, and bring them into the tent, so to speak, because those are the people who you've really got to convince and educate and listen to for project success.

Many times, the original pushback was simply because they didn't have a complete picture. They didn't completely understand what we were planning to do, and they were going by misguided assumptions or data. Just education and a little handholding would completely win them over.

Other folks had a valid rationale for why they were pushing back. We tried to be as open minded as we could when those people would come forward, because in many instances they were right. We had to adjust project plans and functionality based on considering their points. In general, we included people who could be the most vocal opponents as much as we could. Oftentimes it's just that they're more vocal than others. A silent group is out there thinking the same things they are, and we consider it important to listen to them.

Our ICUs were a good example. For many of our go-lives, we included our intensive care units as part of the rest of the hospital's go-live, and we thought that we had taken into account their specific needs, but probably not in as detailed a way, and in an inclusive enough way. Sure enough, when we tried to go-live on our initial attempts with the rest of the hospital including our ICUs, we didn't do well. That was the case where we did have feedback from the ICUs, and we just said let's plow forward. What we did was stop our implementation there. We actually pulled back functionality and went back to our pre-cutover state for our ICUs. We just had to redouble our efforts and bring all those ICU staff more into the project than they had been, and focus on specifically adapting the system and the project overall to their needs. The experience that they have had since has been much more positive. They feel much more a part of the initiative and accepting when there are little hiccups along the way that they know we'll solve.

—Dan Nigrin, MD, MS, CIO, Children's Hospital Boston

Transformation, and by extension, transformation management is important in HIT projects for many reasons. A central one is that an HIT implementation such as an EHR highlights the workflow of each person in the clinical care team—it makes it more evident and visible to stakeholders. In the past, much of this workflow was effectively hidden from others, and limitations or failures in the workflow were therefore difficult to identify and correct. The change process that takes place in an EHR implementation makes these problems more visible, with the ideal result that involved clinicians work as a team to design new and more efficient workflows.

Prepare Change Management Team

The first step for the change manager (defined below) to undertake in this area is to assemble a change management team during the planning process. A *change management team* is a select group of representatives assembled to transition stakeholders from the current to the future state. Selecting the change management team varies, but there are some common selection criteria. The change manager can use a range of approaches to identify people who could add value to the change management team. For example, the change manager might consider:

- Participating in group meetings and identifying potential change management team members.

- Observing the organization, by walking around.

- Identifying opinion leaders. An *opinion leader* is a trusted individual who influences other people's behavior. Supportive opinion leaders increase widespread acceptance. Identifying opinion leaders involves asking who the two to three individuals are that everyone trusts. It is possible that change agents and opinions leaders are the same.

- Selecting individuals from each clinical profession. The change manager should work with the steering committee to select individuals from each clinical profession in an HDO. It is important to do this because each clinical profession plays a significant role in an EHR project.

- Obtaining supervisor approval to assign these individuals to the change management team. The Project Manager should have executive sponsor support when requesting supervisor approval.

The benefit of carefully selecting change management team members is clear:

When those clinical folks begin to tell us, yeah, this is working, we consider that probably the most important endorsement of the initiative. While the informal always happens, we consciously made sure our Project Team was extremely inclusive of clinical membership right from the get-go. From the very beginning of the project, we included lots of nurses, physicians paid to be part of the team, respiratory therapists, pharmacists, you name it. Therefore, a lot of that subjective feedback came directly from them, or from their peers to them, and then from them back into the project.

—Dan Nigrin, MD, MS, CIO, Children's Hospital Boston

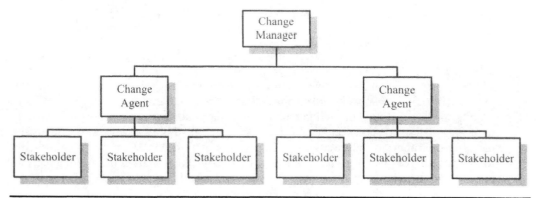

FIGURE 5-3 Change management team organization.

Figure 5-3 displays an organization chart describing a possible change management team.

The change team participants and their roles and responsibilities include the following:

- *Change Manager*—The individual responsible for initiating, planning, executing, controlling, and closing management activities that focus on transitioning stakeholders from the current to the future state. The change manager is in charge of the change management team composed of all change agents. The change manager and Project Manager may be different, given skill requirements and workload.

- *Change Agent*—Front-line advocates from throughout an organization that help stakeholders adopt the future state. Change agents exchange information between the change manager and stakeholders. Collectively change agents form the change management team.

    Change agents cannot overcome all stakeholder resistance. Some percentage of stakeholders will oppose change no matter what change agents do. The change manager and change agents will identify opponents with low influence and work with these resisters according to where they fit on a stakeholder map described below. Instances involving highly influential opponents require special attention. Change agents and the change manager identify strong advocates or opinion leaders to work with these opponents to help overcome their change resistance.

- *Stakeholders*—A *stakeholder* is an individual or group that the project affects in terms of their problems, needs, or interests. The executive sponsor, Project Manager, change manager, and change agents work together with stakeholders to transition them from the current to the future state. In HIT projects, effectively every patient and member of the HDO is a stakeholder. For example, the change management team must include patient representatives in the change management process to ensure a key beneficiary of the HIT provides input and receives support for their needs.

The ideal approach to creating a change management team is to find members that have synergistic and complementary skills and knowledge.

Prepare Stakeholder Map

Given that the number of people defined as stakeholders is very large, it is useful for the change manager to prepare a *stakeholder map* during the planning process. A *stakeholder map* is a listing of all of groups affected by the project classified according to their level of influence and support for the project. Classification is important because the change manager works with stakeholder groups differently depending on their influence and support levels. For example, a stakeholder group that is highly influential and supportive requires different time and effort when compared to a highly influential stakeholder group that is very resistant.

We borrow a concept from Everett M. Rogers,[4] who researched adopters and found that they approach a normal frequency distribution. Rogers found this very useful because he could classify adopters. Our experience suggests that stakeholders tend to follow a similar normal curve distribution. Figure 5-4 displays this distribution according to five categories:

- Very resistant
- Moderately resistant
- Neutral
- Moderately supportive
- Very supportive

The change manager takes the results of either a formal or informal stakeholder analysis and prepares a stakeholder map. Each stakeholder group classification defines the approach used to change their behavior as they transition from the current to future state. Projects perform poorly or fail if they do not classify and support stakeholder groups based on their unique needs.

The change manager prepares a stakeholder map using one or more of the following stakeholder analysis methods:

- Administering a survey
- Working in small group facilitation sessions
- Conducting interviews with stakeholders

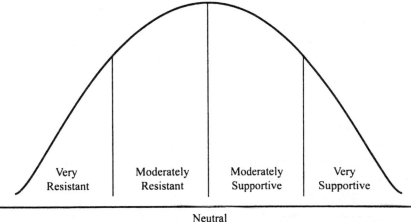

FIGURE 5-4   Stakeholder category distribution.

The change manager must carefully administer the selected analysis method because it is likely the first formal project outreach to stakeholders. The administration of the analysis method increases stakeholder awareness of planned changes and identifies their motivations.

Table 5-7 includes an example of questions included in a stakeholder analysis survey.

Stakeholders' Analysis Survey Electronic Medical Records (EMR) System Project	
SAMPLE QUESTIONS	
Respondents specify their level of agreement, likes or preferences on a five-point scale, with 1 having the least value. For example, "1=strongly agree" and "5=strongly disagree".	
IMPORTANCE	
1	What is your opinion on the importance of this EMR project to: 1) you personally, 2) your department, 3) your entire organization, 4) individual users?
2	What is your opinion on the significance of successful completion of this EMR project to: 1) you personally, 2) your department, 3) your entire organization, 4) individual users?
3	What is your opinion on the significance of failure of this EMR project to: 1) you personally, 2) your department, 3) your entire organization, 4) individual users?
4	What is your opinion on the likelihood that this EMR project will succeed: 1) due to the organization's previous successful experience with other information technology projects, 2) due to the organization's available project management expertise, 3) due to the importance of this project to the organization's future, 4) due to the benefits (e.g., improved patient safety, improved patient care), 5) due to your own interest in the success of the project?
5	What is your opinion on the level of buy-in or support for this EMR project from: 1) physicians, 2) nurses, 3) ancillary clinical services (e.g., pharmacy, lab, radiology), 4) supportive care (e.g., dietary, psychiatry, social services), 5) health information management, 6) executive director, 7) other end users?

TABLE 5-7   Example of Stakeholder Analysis Survey Questions

Stakeholders' Analysis Survey Electronic Medical Records (EMR) System Project	
INFLUENCE	
6	Do you have the administrative authority to allocate funds to support this project?
7	Do you have the informal status to influence the allocation of funds to support this project?
8	Do you have the administrative authority to assign personnel during this project?
9	Do you have the informal status to influence the assignment of personnel to support this project?
10	Do you have the administrative authority to assign additional personnel to temporarily fill in for and assume the regular responsibilities of individuals committed to this project (i.e., backfill)?
11	Do you have the informal status to influence the assignment of additional personnel to temporarily fill in for and assume the regular responsibilities of individuals committed to this project (i.e., backfill)?
12	Will you assign personnel to temporarily fill in for and assume the regular responsibilities of individuals committed to this project (i.e., backfill)?
13	Do you have the administrative authority to control the project schedule?
14	Do you have the informal status to influence the project schedule?
15	Do you have the administrative authority to control the project scope?
16	Do have the informal status to influence the project scope?
17	Do you have consensus building, negotiation, and leadership skills to support this project? If so, indicate your availability to use these skills by project phase.
18	As a potential member of the EMR system Project Team, what is your working relationship with other Project Team members associated with: 1) physicians 2) nursing, 3) ancillary services, 4) supportive care, 5) health information management, 6) executive director, 7) chief executive officer, 8) financial, 9) information technology, 10) legal?

TABLE 5-7   Example of Stakeholder Analysis Survey Questions (*Continued*)

Stakeholders' Analysis Survey Electronic Medical Records (EMR) System Project	
INFLUENCE	
19	What is your working relationship with potential EMR users associated with: 1) physicians, 2) nursing, 3) ancillary services, 4) supportive care, 5) health information management, 6) executive director, 7) chief executive officer, 8) financial, 9) information technology, 10) legal?
ENGAGEMENT	
20	Will you review regular project status reports, which may require that you conduct follow-up and report to the Project Team, advisory committee, or steering committee?
21	Will you participate in the identification, tracking, and resolution of project issues, which may require that you conduct follow-up and report to the Project Team, advisory committee, or steering committee?
22	Will you participate in weekly advisory team meetings for approximately one to two hours (e.g., to make project decisions regarding user requirements), which may require that you conduct follow-up and report to the Project Team, advisory committee, or steering committee?
23	Will you participate in weekly Project Team meetings for about one to two hours (e.g., to coordinate successful execution of project tasks by the Project Team), which may require that you conduct follow-up and report back to the Project Team, Advisory Committee, or steering committee?
24	Will you participate in other meetings for about one to two hours (e.g., to track a project budget, schedule, or quality issue and to make critical project decisions), which may require that you conduct follow-up and report to the Project Team, advisory committee, or steering committee?
COMMITMENT	
25	Will you control the project budget by performing work according to assigned budget and notifying project management when you must deviate from that budget?
26	Will you control the project schedule by performing work according to the assigned schedule and notifying management when you must deviate from that timeframe?
27	Will you control the project scope performing work according to assigned tasks and notifying project management when you must deviate from those tasks?
28	What is the likelihood that you will have other commitments (e.g., work assignments, job transfer, etc.) that may prevent you from supporting this EMR project?

TABLE 5-7   Example of Stakeholder Analysis Survey Questions (*Continued*)

This analysis method measures the degree to which stakeholders embrace change in terms of the following factors:

- *Influence*—Power the stakeholders may have that can affect project outcomes as measured by:
  - *Formal Influence*—Administrative authority conferred by an organization
  - *Informal Influence*—Unofficial leadership conferred by peers or other affected parties
- *Support*—Approve of or agree with the change as measured by:
  - *Commitment*—Degree to which stakeholders are available to participate during the project
  - *Engagement*—Willingness stakeholders have to participate in the change

The survey results become a stakeholder map. Ira Blake and Cindy Busch, in *Project Managing Change*,[5] Prentice Hall, 2009 identified a stakeholder map that displays how to approach stakeholder groups. Table 5-8 displays our stakeholder map that reflects some of their concepts.

Conduct Transformation

The change management team conducts transformation during the execution process. This process includes a set of defined and successfully executed transformation tasks. A transformation task is an activity to help stakeholder groups transition from the current to the future state. The output of this process is successful transformation task completion. Table 5-9 summarizes transformation tasks by stakeholder classification.

We categorized the types of tasks in this table by the factors defining characteristics of the stakeholder group. For example, a highly influential and supportive stakeholder or stakeholder group requires personal coaching whereas a very supportive but low influence stakeholder or stakeholder group may alternatively need informing.

Much of the prospects for successful EHR implementation and the associated organizational change management required to transform health care quality comes down to how the EHR is perceived and prioritized as a tool to achieve and continuously advance the organization's goals, rather than being the goal itself. It is important that the EHR project not be framed as an IT initiative, but rather that it is promoted and perceived as a "critical to quality" clinical initiative led by a critical mass of physicians and other clinicians aligned and rallying around organizational goals for quality and using the EHR as a tool to promote organizational and individual success. If all relevant organization leaders (executives, medical directors, managers, physicians) are not accountable for the success of the EHR project in their own units and instead are allowed to criticize and complain without practical solutions that fall within the guardrails of the EHR implementation scope, your organization may be in deep trouble.

In such cases, it isn't the EHR that is the problem, particularly when you can show it is being used effectively in some clinics but not others. Rather it is the lack of adherence to these success factors. If you don't know where you're going with the EHR implementation, if you haven't defined success and then monitored, measured, and reported everyone's performance with regard to EHR adoption

Influence	Stakeholder Role	Support				
		Very Resistant	Moderately Resistant	Neutral	Moderately Supportive	Very Supportive
High	Nurse Supervisors	•				
	Respiratory Therapists			•		
	Physicians		•			
	Nurses			•		
	Unions			•		
	HIM Managers				•	
	Pharmacist Managers					•
	Pharmacists					•
	Pharmacy Technicians					•
	Clinical Assistants	•				
	Patients				•	
	Lab Managers				•	
	Schedulers					•
	Phlebotomists				•	
	Medical Secretaries				•	
	Lab Technicians				•	
	Scheduling Managers	•				
	HIM Clerks					•
Low	Physical Therapists					•

TABLE 5-8   Stakeholder Map

and appropriate use, it's a little hard to recognize and tell people when they're out of line. Harvesting, publicly recognizing, rewarding, and disseminating the EHR best practices that evolve within your organization will help facilitate the diffusion of EHR technology throughout the enterprise, as well as infusing it deeply within your quality culture.

—Michael H. Zaroukian, MD, PhD, FACP, FHIMSS, CMIO, Michigan State University

Control Transformation

The Project Manager oversees transformation during the controlling process. The Project Manager monitors transformation using the control process described in integration management. For example, when we encounter resistance we often use storytelling. Instead of pushing a resister to comply, we tell the story of a system implementation

Influence	Task	Support				
		Very Resistant	Moderately Resistant	Neutral	Moderately Supportive	Very Supportive
High	**Coach the role models**					
	Personal coaching			•	•	•
	Personal communication	•	•	•		
	Instruct the followers					
	Storytelling*	•	•	•	•	
	Classroom training				•	•
	Virtual classroom training				•	•
	Presentations/demonstrations	•	•	•		
	Workshops	•	•	•	•	
	Self-directed training				•	•
	Inform the interested					
	Large group events	•	•	•		
	Newsletters		•	•		
	Reminders	•	•	•	•	•
	User guides				•	
	Online tutorials/help				•	
	Intranet/Internet Q&A forums	•	•	•	•	•
	Intranet/Internet FAQs/News		•	•		
	Remove the unwilling					
	Reassign within	•				
	Transfer out	•				
Low	Terminate	•				

*Storytelling—Relating to individuals based on metaphors to describe the change experience of others.

TABLE 5-9   Transformation Requirements

in a bookstore and the way in which we overcame resistance with one employee. This employee was the person responsible for selling expensive coffee table art books. All of the other departments had to sell dozens of books to equal the sale of one coffee table book. The clerk in the art department refused to use the system. We would stop by and have a friendly conversation about how he was doing and what we were doing on the project. When we implemented the system, we left him alone. The stakeholders from other departments, on the other hand, all used the system. Shortly after the implementation the clerk in the art department sought us out to brag that he was using the system and liked it. Instead of us pushing him to use the system, he looked over the fence and saw his peers having a positive experience with the new system. He felt left out and wanted to join his peers. Telling this story to resistant clinicians has had a positive effect because they too want to join their peers. This storytelling is much more effective than trying to coerce these resisters.

TRAINING MANAGEMENT

We had educators working side-by-side with us during the design. They were the ones that actually helped us define the curriculum. Because they were part of the design, build, validation, workflow analysis process, they had a much deeper understanding of how the system would function. As they went through that process, they also developed curriculum. We finished our user acceptance testing and moved into education tasks.

You usually do education in a month or two, usually two months before go-live, but we wanted to do just-in-time training. We had two different types of education: We developed eLearning modules, where you could actually log on to the system from anywhere to walk through the functionality, and then also in-classroom settings. Every single education course actually was role-based, so if you were a unit secretary, you attended unit secretary training, and spent time allocated to that kind of training. If you were a super user for the system, you went to super user training. If you were a physician, you got a certain type of training, x number of hours. Nurses would be different; the billing clerk would go through a different session, and so forth. The education really was tailored based on the individual role within the organization. Once the education was done, we were ready to go-live.

—Florence Chang, MBA, CIO, Multicare

In this change management area, we consider training management for HIT users. *Training management* is planning, executing, controlling, and closing project tasks for educating users to take advantage of workflow and system benefits. Table 5-10 displays training management processes and their outputs (in italics) by process group.

Conduct Training Needs Assessment

The change manager identifies a training manager who is responsible for overseeing training personnel as they prepare, deliver, and evaluate training required for the new system. These training personnel actively participate as part of the Project Team as they define configuration, security, and workflow requirements. Through these activities, they gain an in-depth understanding of the new system and how it supports the HDO. This knowledge makes them more effective educators who can anticipate and solve issues raised by new users during training. The training manager conducts a training needs assessment during the planning process. The output of this process is a training needs description. A *training need* is a description of the specific instructions each user requires to improve skills to use the new system and perform new workflow steps.

Initiating	Planning	Executing	Controlling	Closing
	Conduct training needs assessment	Prepare training	Control training	
	Training needs	*Training documentation*	*Organizational process asset update*	
	Prepare training plan	Conduct training	*Performance report*	
	Training plan	*Training completion confirmation*	*Change request (CR)*	
			Project document update	

TABLE 5-10   Training Management Knowledge Area by Process Group

This needs assessment is very important in that hospitals and clinics often under-resource HIT training in EHR implementations. A training needs assessment helps the training manager plan for needed training resources.

The HDO must implement training across the organization because the EMR affects virtually everyone. This is particularly challenging because the HDO must tailor the training to specific EHR roles and the unique learning style of each user . . .

We had a "no excuses" training mentality, meaning we had training available in essentially any possible modality. We had classroom training. We had trainers go out to existing departmental meetings to do training. We had web-based training that people could do either within the hospital or at home over the web. We had one-on-one training for those people who really respond best to that kind of approach. This certainly increased our training team resources, but it was well worth the investment upfront to have people well taught in how to use the system before go-live. I think that was very important to our overall success. We had a lot of staff available during the time of our go-live, command centers, phones, hotlines, people present 24/7 on our hospital floors, in our ambulatory clinic areas, to provide over the shoulder help right there at the point of care. I think that was very helpful.

—Dan Nigrin, MD, MS, CIO, Children's Hospital Boston

The training manager uses the following analysis methods to prepare and conduct a training assessment:

- Observe user behavior
- Meet with supervisors to receive their input about what training their staff requires
- Prepare a training needs assessment constructing a survey that takes into account information supplied by supervisors and helps respondents confidentially reveal their education needs (i.e., strengths and weaknesses)
- Administer the survey
- Analyze the results of the survey to determine the nature and amount of training required

Prepare Training Plan

Our training courses were also scenario based, not only role based, but scenario based on workflow. We also assigned our subject matter experts to the training. From the beginning of the project, we had clinicians, nurses, and pharmacists working on the project. They would be the ones rotating through the training sessions to supplement the workflow knowledge during training. They were not actually the ones teaching the classes, because many of them were experts in workflow in clinical operations, they were not experts in teaching. We used the teachers that actually could teach the class, but supplemented them with the clinical folks.

I think that the approach we took was unique. We had a core set of trainers who were trainers that had to go through EPIC certification, and they were the ones that actually helped us design the curriculum. When we got to the actual training, because of the number of classes that we had, we went out into the community and hired folks who had teaching credentials. It could be a sub from an elementary school, a high school, and so forth. We actually had 40–50 temporary positions. They knew it was going

to be typically a six- to eight-month engagement with us. We brought them on-site three months prior to actual training time, and then utilized their teaching capability to teach other classes.
—Florence Chang, MBA, CIO, Multicare

The training manager prepares a training plan during the planning process. A *training plan* is a description of the training target audience, their current levels of IT fluency, the training curriculum, schedule, modality, feedback, logistics, standards, deliverables, resources, and deadline. The components of a training plan template include the following:

- *Target Audience*—Training recipients arranged by course grouping (e.g., organizing trainees by courses they must complete as a prerequisite to system access)
- *Training Levels*—Classification of training by category (e.g., prerequisite, beginner, intermediate, advanced)
- *Training Modality*—Method used to deliver training including communication medium, techniques, and tools (e.g., face-to-face, online, in-situ)
- *Curriculum*—Training course title, course description, learning objectives (concise statements concerning what students should expect to learn from a specific course), course total time and time by topic, delivery method, and medium if different within a course, and course outline by day
- *Schedule*—Dates and times a course is available, including minimum and maximum class size
- *Feedback*—Method used to evaluate each individual student, course, instructor, material, and delivery method
- *Logistics*—Training supply and equipment types and quantities, and number of rooms based on capacity and location
- *Standards*—Training material and delivery design guidelines
- *Deliverable*—Output produced by course
- *Resources*—Training team roles and responsibilities for preparing, delivering, and evaluating training
- *Deadline*—Training preparation schedule

Prepare Training

The training manager coordinates the preparation of training documentation during the execution process. *Training documentation* is the set of materials used by instructors and students during training sessions. Examples of training documentation include the following:

- Frequently Asked Questions (FAQs) or other "quick" reference guides
- Videos or films for group or individual viewing
- Slides and handouts for presentations
- Workflow scripts, walkthroughs, or other scenario-based examples

- User, technical, or other technical reference manuals or guides
- Skills assessments, such as subject review guides or quizzes
- A reference knowledge base consisting of templates, guidelines, configurations, and other implementation, management, and technical information

Conduct Training

The training manager conducts training during the executing process. The output of this process is a training completion confirmation. A *training completion confirmation* is a written acknowledgement that the student successfully completed a specific training course. This confirmation includes a user ID and password. Students who fail a training proficiency exam at the end of their required courses do not receive a user ID and password until they pass the exam. Training courses vary. First, there is prerequisite skill training. *Prerequisite skill training* is a precondition users must possess before learning how to use the system. This includes, for example, how to use a PC and mouse, how to navigate the Internet using a web browser, and how to use a word processor.

Second, there is role-based training on how to use the HIT. *Role-based training* is instructing individuals according to their specific work activity. For example, physicians learn how to prepare orders because this is a role that specifically relates to their work.

The training modality also varies by role. Some users, particularly physicians, require training one-on-one by a fellow physician or nurse to help ensure success. Clinicians tend to prefer training from a contemporary, not a physician known for their IT expertise.

Table 5-11 displays an individualized training impact sheet.[6] This includes an example of individualized training and displays the following:

- The left side displays current state workflow and system steps
- The right side displays future state workflow and system steps
- The highlighting identifies the future state that is different from the current state

This approach offers many advantages. For example, it helps focus the physician on the limited number of changes that he needs to learn, which helps to reduce his anxiety over change induced by the project.

> *As a way to communicate change, we use a concept of start, stop, and continue. This document helps the user understand what they're going to start doing that is new, what they're going to stop doing, and what they need to continue to do. That's a pretty important point because most people, when you're implementing a new system, think I have to do everything differently, and you don't. You continue to do many of the things you did in your old process. It just may be with a new tool.*
> —Beatha Johnson, Director, Clinical Information Systems, VMMC

Control Training

The training manager monitors training during the controlling process. The training manager monitors training management using the control process described in integration management. For example, one of our clients had a project that was going very

WORKFLOW IMPACT

Conduct new patient consult

	Current			Future		
1	Clinical assistant receives patient arrival notification	Manual process	Flows to 2	Clinical assistant or registered Nurse receives patient arrival notification	System user process	Flows to 2
2	Clinical assistant or registered nurse completes pre-assessment questions	System user process	Flows to 3	Clinical assistant or registered nurse completes pre-assessment questions	System user process	Flows to 3
3	Registered nurse requires intervention to address patient complaints?	Manual decision	Yes flows to 4 No flows to 5	Registered nurse requires intervention to address patient complaints?	Manual decision	Yes flows to 4 No flows to 5
4	Registered nurse addresses patient complaints	Manual process	Flows to 5	Registered nurse addresses patient complaints	Manual process	Flows to 5
5	Patient or registered nurse completes self-reporting history	Manual process	Flows to 6	Patient or registered nurse completes self-reporting history	System user process	Flows to 6
6	Physician meets with new patient	Manual process	Flows to 7	Physician meets with new patient	Manual process	Flows to 7
7	Physician or registered nurse completes or updates problem list	Manual process	Flows to 8	Physician or registered nurse completes or updates problem list	System process	Flows to 8
8	Billing clerk charges patient	Manual process	Flows to 9	Proposed system sends charges to billing system	External system interface	Flows to 9
9	Physician prepares new orders?	Manual decision	Yes exits to **Create or change Orders** No terminates	Physician prepares new orders?	System decision	Yes exits to **Create or change orders** No terminates

TABLE 5-11 Individualized Training Impact Sheet

229

well. The testing demonstrated the configuration was ready, the workflow changes were complete, the conversion was done, and everyone was ready to start training. However, when initial training started, the feedback was terrible. We attended the second training round and asked Project Team members for assistance in improving training quality. We determined that because the training team was not sufficiently involved in the requirements definition and configuration sessions, they did not understand the application well enough to answer student questions beyond the training materials. Project Team members worked with the trainers intensively on how to use the system and how to translate that knowledge into effective instruction during subsequent training sessions. This did result in higher project cost, but definitely improved the training experience and subsequent system use.

OPTIMIZATION MANAGEMENT

We're now starting to use decision support to go after costly studies or costly lab assessments to present clinicians with potentially lower cost alternatives that have the same clinical utility. There are lots of things that we're finding now, and frankly, we're still scratching the surface as far as using our decision support tools. I think that's an important point for health IT implementations. It's really a long journey getting there, in fact, many of our clinicians will tell you that it's only just now, five, six, or seven years in, where they're starting to get to a completely automated system. They see for themselves, oh, this is why we did this. They see the patient's entire clinical care within one electronic system, they don't have to hunt between systems or half electronic and half on paper. They now have that fully integrated system and they're getting to that point where they are in a position where there is value and efficiency. Any organization that thinks they're going to start to see clear-cut value in just a year or two or three, they're probably fooling themselves.

—Dan Nigrin, MD, MS, CIO, Children's Hospital Boston

Optimization management is planning, controlling, and closing continued improvement of an innovation. As we defined in Chapter 1, a project is a time-limited set of activities—projects have a start and an end. With HIT projects, such as an EHR implementation, the project ends after the HDO and vendor complete an agreed-upon or contractually specified acceptance period. Optimization, however, is ongoing after the project ends. Responsibility for ongoing support and improvement rests with operations, not the Project Team. Consequently the Project Team must plan how to help operations take on this responsibility.

An HIT project eventually concludes, but configuring the system, changing the workflow, and updating the training and supporting users are ongoing. This is necessary to support changing needs, greater user familiarity with the system over time, and an evolving understanding of how the system supports and can enhance an organization's workflow.

Many of the committees formed as part of the implementation continued post project as essentially permanent ongoing committees that include technical, administrative, and clinical input. It's mostly those groups that we hear from with respect to how to improve the system.

For example, feedback came from one clinical team that continues to be involved in the project. This involves something that we call the document hierarchy. So within our EMR system, there are many text-based documents—radiology reports, discharge summaries, and so on. During our initial setup, we categorized them into different document types so that you could find what you were looking for in a certain way. Now we have more documentation online, nursing documentation, every daily physician progress note, and consultation notes. These things were not there at our initial go-live. As a result, it became unwieldy to find the document you were looking for from a user perspective. That required us to go back and essentially re-engineer our document hierarchy, which was a lot of work, but an important step and one that yielded significant improvements from a user perspective in order to use the system.

In other instances, we've actually gone back and reworked some of the implementation decisions that we originally went with; specifically to improve the way the system feels.

Another area is simply that we've got more functionality to implement still, new functionality. An example of that is our initial project scope didn't include intra-operative electronic documentation. We included the perioperative steps, but intra-operative documentation was initially out

Initiating	Planning	Executing	Controlling	Closing
	Prepare optimization management plan *Optimization management plan*		Control optimization *Organizational process asset update* *Performance report* *Change request (CR)* *Project document update*	Perform optimization *Optimization completion confirmation*

TABLE 5-12   Optimization Management Knowledge Area by Process Group

of scope. Well, now that we've finished the other components of the project, we're now going to tackle the intra-operative documentation.

These are new projects where there are incremental implementations. We actually scope these as new projects. For example, there is the Anesthesia Information Management System, the AIMS project. Within that project, we'll go ahead and budget for that backfill and so on just like we did with the previous project.

—Dan Nigrin, MD, MS, CIO, Children's Hospital Boston

Table 5-12 displays optimization management processes and their outputs (in italics) by process group.

Prepare Optimization Management Plan

The Project Manager prepares an optimization management plan during the planning process. An *optimization management plan* is a description of how an organization plans, controls, and closes continuous improvement of an innovation. The optimization management plan addresses how an organization makes updates to the system configuration, workflow, training, and support. Extensive planning, testing, and intensive monitoring occur before and during cutover. However, this process does not account for the months and years of change people experience, and the amount of system configuration, workflow, and training optimization that occurs after the system is in use.

Components of an optimization management plan include the following:

- Strategy
- Objectives
- Audience roles and responsibilities
- Configuration change procedures
- Workflow procedures
- Training procedures
- Technical support

Control Optimization

Operations oversee optimization management after project completion. For example, a large metropolitan hospital we work with implemented a new clinical application throughout their hospital and was now in the early stages of optimization. We routinely walked through the hospital to observe use of the clinical system. In one example, we found that nurses were still using paper lab order forms, supplied for backup purposes, to place orders and avoid using the system. We found this problem at a number of nursing stations. When we asked the nurses why, they responded that the paper forms were available and easy to use. We met with nursing supervisors and suggested they move the paper forms to their offices for backup, thus giving the nurses no other option but to use the new system. The hospital also provided trainers at nursing stations to support nurses as they began to use the system.

Perform Optimization

The Project Manager finishes the closing process. Optimization follows closing. It includes ongoing optimization activities performed by operational groups (e.g., nursing and physicians, workflow configuration updates, technical support, and training). The output of this is optimization completion confirmation. This confirms completion of the Project Team's role in optimization, the successful transfer of this role to operations and the beginning of operations' responsibility for ongoing optimization.

As noted in Chapter 2, a project by definition is a finite process, having a beginning and end. HIT, such as an EHR, affects and involves core clinical functions that require ongoing changes long after project completion. HDO clinical department representatives, trainers, and technical support professionals operate, maintain, and optimize this HIT system after the Project Team delivers it. The Project Team then moves on to other projects. Figure 5-5 displays the relationship between optimization, system cutover, and other change management knowledge areas.

Figure 5-6 displays an optimization process flow. As described in support management, it includes a CRT comprised of user department, IT support, and training representatives. The CRT works proactively to identify improvements on an ongoing basis to optimize use of the operational EHR.

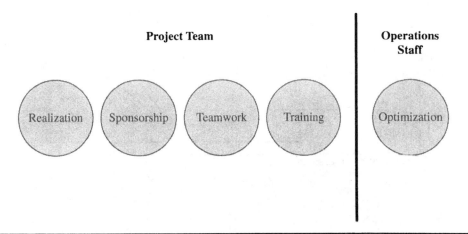

Project Team   **Operations Staff**

Realization   Sponsorship   Teamwork   Training   Optimization

FIGURE 5-5   Optimization timing.

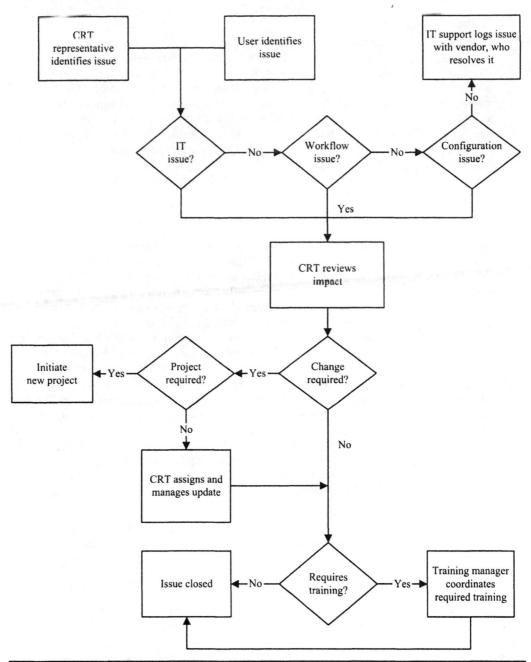

FIGURE 5-6   Optimization process flow.

Operations optimizes the system, which includes, for example:

- Configuration changes
- Workflow updates
- Prototypes of these changes
- Demonstrations to users
- Tests of the approved changes
- Training associated with these changes
- Technical support regarding the changes

I think that typically what we have done in the past is implement a project, and once it went live, that was the end of our focus. We moved on to do something else. We never optimized. Optimization terminology only came up recently as part of a project, right? If you don't do optimization, you end up with lots of workarounds, and this is what we uncovered . . . folks come up with different work-arounds. My experience through years of implementation systems is that the day of go-live, if we are utilizing 25% of the functionality that's available to us, that's a successful go-live. We had similar statistics from EPIC as well. I think many vendors will say the same thing. What that means is that the rest of the functionality really has to go through a phase of optimization. And optimization is NOT only just modifying workflow, it's education, and perhaps of course in some cases changes to the system. There are three different components, three different buckets, of optimization.

—Florence Chang, MBA, CIO, Multicare

Optimization is proactive. It includes a CRT assigned to each HDO department. This team works to anticipate, identify, and resolve issues that integrate education, IT, and service delivery before they become a reported problem.

One of the things that we have put in place now is what we call "Client Services Executives." Each unit, for example, ED or oncology, has its own Client Services Executive Team. The Client Services Executive Team is comprised of an analyst, a subject matter expert, and an educator. This three-person team works with individual units on a daily basis, proactively going out there and determining what are the issues you have and how can we help solve these issues before they result in a call into our service desk? We want to minimize the calls to the service desk, as well as the turnaround time of fixing the problem. The Client Services Executives not only help that particular unit to address the clinical application issues. If the unit has printer issues or any kind of desktop issues, the Client Services Executives will be the liaison for bringing those issues to the desktop folks, and getting the desktop folks in to solve the problem. This way, we are actually proactively going out there and working with the customers on a regular basis instead of waiting for a call coming into our service desk. That seems to work very well. The Client Services Executive Teams also help facilitate any kind of enhancements, any issues, and so forth. Our Team actually put together what we call Joint Operation Team meetings on a weekly basis to review and prioritize all the enhancements and requests, and that Joint Operation Team meeting is extremely productive. Not only do they review and prioritize requests, they also do live demos. If this is how you want to change the system, this is what it's going to look like, right there for the end user to finalize the requirements, so then the build team can go back and do the build and make changes. We don't waste time going back to get the requirements, and so forth. That seems to work very well as part of the after go-live and ongoing support to customers.

—Florence Chang, MBA, CIO, Multicare

Initiating	Planning	Executing	Controlling	Closing
Realization	**Realization**	**Transformation**	**Realization**	**Realization**
Define objectives	Define measurable outcomes	Conduct transformation	Control realization	Report outcome achievement
Objectives	Measurable outcomes	Transformation tasks	Organizational process asset update	Dashboard report
Sponsorship	Prepare outcome delivery schedule	Transformation task completion	Measurable outcome achievement	**Optimization**
Select the executive sponsor	Outcome delivery schedule	**Training**	Performance report	Perform optimization
Executive sponsor	Assign responsibility for objectives	Prepare training	Change request (CR)	Optimization completion confirmation for project
	Objective responsibility list	Training documentation	Project document update	
	Sponsorship	Conduct training	Achievement of an objective	
	Assess executive sponsor	Training completion confirmation	**Sponsorship**	
	Executive sponsorship assessment results		Control sponsorship	
	Transformation		Organizational process asset update	
	Prepare change management team		Performance report	
	Change management team		Change request (CR)	
	Prepare stakeholder map		Project document update	
	Stakeholder map		**Transformation**	
	Training		Control transformation	
	Conduct training needs assessment		Organizational process asset update	
	Training needs		Performance report	
	Prepare training plan		Change request (CR)	
	Training plan		Project document update	
	Optimization		**Training**	
	Prepare optimization management plan		Control training	
	Optimization management plan		Organizational process asset update	
			Performance report	
			Change request (CR)	
			Project document update	
			Optimization	
			Control optimization	
			Organizational process asset update	
			Performance report	
			Change request (CR)	
			Project document update	

Table 5-13 Change Management Knowledge Areas by Process Group

One example of optimization is a monthly meeting as the CRT *begins* to identify and optimize the system based on actual use of the system as opposed to testing it.

Implementing electronic health records actually is the best vehicle to standardize care across the system. If someone could actually do a good job of measuring the cost savings associated with standardization of care using electronic health record implementation, it would really be worth investigating.
—Florence Chang, MBA, CIO, Multicare

Conclusion

This chapter described each individual change management knowledge area. This description provided details about the processes supporting these knowledge areas and the outputs of these processes. It also included examples of analysis methods used to prepare these outputs. Table 5-13 displays all change management knowledge area processes and their outputs by process group, with the knowledge areas in bold, individual processes in normal text and outputs in italics.

We accomplished what we set out to do in the EMR project, but we'll never really be done.
—Dan Nigrin, MD, MS, CIO, Children's Hospital Boston

Endnotes

1. Kotter, J. P. (1996). *Leading Change.* Boston: Harvard Business School Press.
2. Lorenzi, N. M., and Riley, R. T. (2003). Organizational issues = change. *International Journal of Medical Informatics, 69,* 197–203.
3. Drucker, P. (1954). *The Practice of Management.* New York: Collins.
4. Rogers, E. M. (2003). *Diffusion of Innovations* (5th ed.). New York: Free Press.
5. Blake, I., and Bush, C. (2008). *Project Managing Change: Practical Tools and Techniques to Make Change Happen.* Financial Times/Prentice Hall.
6. Johnson, B. L., and Davis, V. R. (2004). Change management: A critical factor in EMR implementation. *For the Record, 16*(5), 32.

Integrated Methodology

T he following model is a graphical framework of our fully integrated HIT methodology. Please refer to this model while reading the book and afterward as a reference tool on each component of our methodology and how they relate to each other throughout an HIT project.

Initiating	Planning	Executing	Controlling	Closing
■ **Integration** Prepare the feasibility study and business case *Feasibility study and business case* Prepare project charter *Project charter* • **User requirements** Prepare high-level user requirements *High-level user requirements* • **Infrastructure** Prepare high-level technology requirements *High-level technology requirements* Define existing technology architecture *Existing technology architecture description* △ **Realization** Define objectives *Objectives* △ **Sponsorship** Select the executive sponsor *Executive sponsor*	■ **Integration** Prepare project management plan *Project management plan* ■ **Scope** Define scope *Scope statement* Prepare work breakdown structure (WBS) and WBS dictionary *Work breakdown structure (WBS)* *WBS dictionary* *Work package* ■ **Time** Define tasks *Task list* Sequence tasks *Task sequence* Estimate task resources *Task resource estimate* Estimate task duration *Task duration estimate* Prepare schedule *Schedule* ■ **Cost** Estimate costs *Cost estimate* Prepare budget *Project budget* ■ **Quality** Prepare quality management plan *Quality management plan*	■ **Integration** Manage project execution *Performance report* *Change request (CR)* *Deliverable* *Project document update* ■ **Quality** Perform quality assurance *Change request (CR)* *Project document update* ■ **Human Resources (HR)** Develop project team *Project team performance assessment* ■ **Communications** Distribute information *Organizational process asset update* ■ **Procurement** Select vendor *Selected vendor* • **User requirements** Prepare detailed user requirements *Detailed user requirements* • **Infrastructure** Define detailed technology requirements *Detailed technology requirements* Prepare and order equipment *Equipment order confirmation* Complete facility modifications *Site readiness confirmation* Install system *Hardware readiness confirmation* *Application readiness confirmation*	■ **Integration** Control project execution *Organizational process asset update* *Performance report* *Change request (CR)* *Project document update* Perform integrated change control *Change request (CR)* ■ **Scope** Verify scope *Deliverable completion certificate (DCC)* *Change request (CR)* *Project document update* Control scope *Organizational process asset update* *Performance report* *Change request (CR)* *Project document update* ■ **Time** Control schedule *Organizational process asset update* *Performance report* *Change request (CR)* *Project document update* ■ **Cost** Control cost *Organizational process asset update* *Performance report* *Change request (CR)* *Project document update*	■ **Integration** Close phase or project *Organizational process asset update* *Deliverable* ■ **Procurement** Perform final acceptance *Organizational process asset update* *Deliverable completion certificate (DCC)* • **Security** Conduct ongoing security compliance *Security audit results* • **Support** Initiate ongoing support *Support tickets* △ **Realization** Report outcome achievement *Dashboard report* △ **Optimization** Perform optimization *Optimization completion confirmation for project*

■ Project Management
• IT Management
△ Change Management

Initiating	Planning	Executing	Controlling	Closing
	Human Resources (HR)	**Security**	**Quality**	
	Prepare human resources plan	Define security requirements	Perform quality control	
	Human resources plan	Security requirements	Organizational process asset update	
	Acquire project team resources	Define security roles	Change request (CR)	
	Resource assignment	Security roles	Project document update	
	Communications	Configure security	**Human Resources (HR)**	
	Identify key project participants	Test cases	Manage project team	
	Project roster	**Conversion**	Organizational process asset update	
	Plan communications	Prepare data conversion map	Performance report	
	Communications plan	Data conversion map	Change request (CR)	
	Risk	Conduct data cleansing	Project document update	
	Prepare risk management plan	Data cleansing confirmation	**Communications**	
	Risk management plan	Develop and test conversion solution	Report performance	
	Identify risks	Conversion solution confirmation	Organizational process asset update	
	Risk register	Convert data	Performance report	
	Perform quantitative risk analysis	Conversion confirmation	Change request (CR)	
	Risk register update	**Interface**	Project document update	
	Perform qualitative risk analysis	Prepare interface data map	**Risk**	
	Risk register update	Interface data map	Monitor and control risk	
	Plan risk response	Develop and test interfaces	Organizational process asset update	
	Risk response plan	Interface software confirmation	Performance report	
	Procurement	Enable interfaces	Change request (CR)	
	Plan procurement	Interface confirmation	Project document update	
	Procurement plan	**Software configuration**	**Procurement**	
	Prepare solicitation	Define configuration requirements	Administer procurement	
	Solicitation	Configuration requirements	Organizational process asset update	
	User requirements	Configure system	Performance report	
	Prepare user requirements management plan	Test cases	Change request (CR)	
	User requirements management plan		Project document update	

- Project Management
- IT Management
- Δ Change Management

Initiating	Planning	Executing	Controlling	Closing
	Infrastructure Prepare infrastructure management plan *Infrastructure management plan* Prepare facility modification plan *Facility modification plan* Prepare system installation plan *System installation plan* **Security** Prepare security plan *Security plan* **Conversion** Prepare conversion plan *Conversion plan* **Interface** Prepare interface plan *Interface plan* **Software configuration** Prepare software configuration plan *Software configuration plan* **Workflow** Prepare workflow management plan *Workflow management plan* **Test** Prepare test plan *Test plan*	**Workflow** Prepare workflow requirements *Workflow requirements* Perform workflow change *Workflow changes* **Test** Define test cases *Test cases* Prepare test data *Test data* Train testers *Training completion confirmation* Conduct tests *Test results* Correct defects *Test cases* Conduct regression testing *Test results* **Cutover** Train cutover support team *Training completion confirmation* Conduct system cutover *Successful cutover confirmation* **Support** Prepare support requirements *Support requirements* *Support roles and responsibilities matrix* Provide support training *Training completion confirmation*	**User requirements** Control user requirements *Organizational process asset update* *Performance report* *Change request (CR)* *Project document update* **Infrastructure** Control infrastructure *Organizational process asset update* *Performance report* *Change request (CR)* *Project document update* **Security** Control security *Organizational process asset update* *Performance report* *Change request (CR)* *Project document update* **Conversion** Control conversion *Organizational process asset update* *Performance report* *Change request (CR)* *Project document update* **Interface** Control interfaces *Organizational process asset update* *Performance report* *Change request (CR)* *Project document update*	

- Project Management
• IT Management
Δ Change Management

Initiating	Planning	Executing	Controlling	Closing
	• **Cutover** Prepare cutover plan *Cutover plan* • **Support** Prepare support plan *Support plan* Δ **Realization** Define measurable outcomes *Measurable outcomes* Prepare outcome delivery schedule *Outcome delivery schedule* Assign responsibility for objectives *Objective responsibility list* Δ **Sponsorship** Assess executive sponsor *Executive sponsorship assessment results* Δ **Transformation** Prepare change management team *Change management team* Prepare stakeholder map *Stakeholder map* Δ **Training** Conduct training needs assessment *Training needs* Prepare training plan *Training plan* Δ **Optimization** Prepare optimization management plan *Optimization management plan*	Δ **Transformation** Conduct transformation *Transformation tasks* *Transformation task completion* Δ **Training** Prepare training *Training documentation* Conduct training *Training completion confirmation*	• **Software configuration** Control configuration *Organizational process asset update* *Performance report* *Change request (CR)* *Project document update* • **Workflow** Control workflow *Organizational process asset update* *Performance report* *Change request (CR)* *Project document update* • **Test** Control testing *Organizational process asset update* *Performance report* *Change request (CR)* *Project document update* • **Cutover** Control cutover *Organizational process asset update* *Performance report* *Change request (CR)* *Project document update* • **Support** Control support *Organizational process asset update* *Performance report* *Change request (CR)* *Project document update*	

■ Project Management
• IT Management
Δ Change Management

Initiating	Planning	Executing	Controlling	Closing
			Δ **Realization** Control realization Organizational process asset update Measurable outcome achievement Performance report Change request (CR) Project document update Achievement of an objective Δ **Sponsorship** Control sponsorship Organizational process asset update Performance report Change request (CR) Project document update Δ **Transformation** Control transformation Organizational process asset update Performance report Change request (CR) Project document update Δ **Training** Control training Organizational process asset update Performance report Change request (CR) Project document update Δ **Optimization** Control optimization Organizational process asset update Performance report Change request (CR) Project document update	

■ Project Management
• IT Management
Δ Change Management

Glossary

Activity diagram A unified modeling language (UML) graphical presentation for modeling process steps and actions.

Actor An entity (system or person) that executes an activity.

Actual cost (AC) The amount the project spent on all performed work.

Advisory committee A representative group of key individuals appointed to make project recommendations on behalf of their stakeholders (e.g., physicians, nurses, patients, and bargaining units).

Alternative scenario A major plot variation in the story that documents common secondary activities or exceptions an actor performs before achieving the desired outcome.

Application readiness confirmation A written acknowledgement provided by the vendor indicating installation compliance of all application software components according to manufacturer specified standards and readiness for configuration.

Backfill staff Personnel provided to fill positions vacated by resources assigned to the project.

Baseline A benchmark used to measure and control actual project performance.

Best-of-breed (BOB) solution A set of the most preferred software applications from a variety of different vendors.

Bidders' conference A pre-proposal meeting where vendors ask questions to clarify the intent of the RFP.

Breakeven point The point in time when the total costs of the project to date and the total dollar return or revenue are equal or where there is no net loss or gain.

Budget at completion (BAC) The total allocated budget.

Change management The discipline devoted to planning, organizing, and coordinating the resources necessary to transition individuals and groups in an organization from the current to a future state.

Change management team A select group of representatives assembled to transition stakeholders from the current to a future state.

Change manager The individual responsible for initiating, planning, executing, and controlling change management activities (e.g., realization, sponsorship, and transformation).

Change request (CR)   A formal application to modify baseline deliverables and processes.

Change requirements team (CRT)   A group of individuals including a user, IT, and training department representative that works within each user department to identify needs and implement improvements on an ongoing basis.

Communications management   Planning, executing, and controlling project information exchange required to ensure project success.

Communications plan   An organized identification of what information to collect throughout the project, who receives this information, the communications channel used with each participant or category of participant, and when to distribute it.

Configuration requirements   A description of how an organization plans to change customizable settings so the system is ready for use.

Controlling   Reviewing processes and outputs to ensure achievement of objectives according to pre-defined standards.

Conversion confirmation   A written acknowledgement of the accuracy and completeness of converted data.

Conversion management   Planning, executing, and controlling transformation and movement of data from existing manual and automated systems to the new system.

Conversion plan   A description of how an organization plans to move and/or transform data from an existing manual or automated system to a new system.

Conversion solution confirmation   A written acknowledgement that the manual, automated, or combined method used to move data from an existing source to the new system works properly within the project schedule.

Cost estimate   An approximation of expenditures required to complete a project.

Cost management   Planning and controlling costs required to complete the project within an approved budget.

Cost performance index (CPI)   A measure of how the project is performing against the budget.

Cost variance (CV)   The difference between earned value and actual costs.

Critical path   The sequence of tasks that determines the minimum time needed for project completion.

Cutover management   Planning, executing, and controlling the switch from existing manual and/or automated systems to a new system.

Cutover plan   A description of how an organization prepares for and transitions from its existing manual and/or automated systems to a new system.

Dashboard report   A written summary to management that describes the status of outcome achievement by objective.

Data cleansing   The process of identifying and resolving corrupt or inaccurate information so that it will convert properly to a new system.

Data cleansing confirmation   A written verification that completed data cleansing meets requirements for conversion and subsequent system use.

Data conversion map   An identification of the characteristics of each piece of information planned for transfer to the new system from an existing source.

Deliverable   A tangible and verifiable project output that is the result of a task or tasks.

Deliverable completion certificate (DCC)   A document that certifies completion of a project deliverable according to the work breakdown structure (WBS) dictionary.

Detailed technology requirements   An in-depth description of the equipment, and environmental and regulatory criteria (e.g., sizing and performance criteria, power, temperature, and physical space considerations), and regulatory constraints the selected vendor must support.

Detailed user requirement   An in-depth description of function and data a system must support to meet user needs.

Earned value (EV)   The value of the project work performed to date.

Earned value management (EVM)   A method of measuring project cost and schedule performance.

Equipment order confirmation   A written acknowledgement by a manufacturer that an organization is purchasing items, including their description, manufacture, model, type, and quantity.

Estimate at completion (EAC)   The total expected cost of completing the project.

Estimate to complete (ETC)   The forecasted schedule or cost to complete remaining project work.

Executive sponsor   The individual with primary responsibility for achieving the project's objectives and enabling project participants through his or her leadership.

Executive sponsorship assessment results   The outcome of an evaluation of an executive sponsor's actual capabilities compared to best practices.

Existing technology architecture description   A summary description of the systems, software, and other technical components currently supporting users that are critical to understanding the current environment.

Facilitator   An impartial person with no self-interest other than achieving the project objectives effectively and efficiently.

Facility modification plan   A description of how an organization identifies, schedules, and completes changes to its facilities to accommodate a new system.

Feasibility study and business case   A document based on research and quantification created to guide management decisions on whether or not to proceed with a project based on an assessment of its viability, costs, and benefits.

Fishbone diagram   A graphic representation that identifies and organizes a problem by cause and effect.

Five rights   A collection of measures that hold a healthcare practitioner accountable for giving the right drug, to the right patient, in the right dose, by the right route, and at the right time.

Functional decomposition   A process of breaking something down into individual components or functional parts.

Gantt chart   A bar chart that displays planned project schedule, tasks, and resources.

Hardware readiness confirmation   A written acknowledgement provided by the vendor (in a SaaS environment) or HDO (in a premise-based environment) indicating installation compliance of all equipment and hardware according to manufacturer-specified standards and readiness for configuration.

Healthcare delivery organization (HDO)   A healthcare provider (e.g., community hospital, teaching hospital, physician group, ambulatory center).

High-level technology requirements   A general description of technology constraints, and capacity and performance information required to support a proposed system.

High-level user requirements   A general description of the features and functions that a system must perform to meet user needs.

Human resources (HR) management   Planning, executing, and controlling the selection, assignment, and function of human resources—the people and teams that will work to complete the project successfully.

Human resources plan   A definition of how the Project Manager expects to acquire and assemble project staff.

Information technology (IT) management   The discipline devoted to planning, organizing, and coordinating resources to analyze, design, configure, and/or develop a system that meets user requirements.

Infrastructure   The system hardware and other physical components supporting it, and the facilities housing that equipment.

Infrastructure management   Initiating, planning, executing, and controlling requirements for the location and configuration of the physical components of a new system.

Infrastructure management plan   A description of how an organization will address the physical components of a system, including hardware components, system capacity and performance requirements, physical and environmental constraints, and changes to existing facilities.

Integrated change control   Identifying, assessing, making, and monitoring modifications to baseline project processes and outputs (e.g., to scope, time, budget, and quality).

Integrated software solution   A suite of software modules from a single vendor that support numerous functions.

Integration management   Initiating, planning, executing, controlling, and closing of all key project, IT, and change management plans, processes, and outputs required to achieve project success.

Interface   An exchange of information between two systems.

Interface confirmation   A written acknowledgement of the accuracy and effectiveness of an interface tool and the associated data exchange.

Interface data map   A description of the characteristics of each piece of information exchanged between two systems on an ongoing basis.

Interface management   Planning, executing, and controlling the definition, development, testing, and implementation of information exchanges between two systems.

Interface plan   A description of how an organization addresses ongoing data exchanges between a new system and other existing systems.

Interface software confirmation   A written acknowledgement that the interface option constructed or configured and tested works according to specifications.

Issues tracking database   A log of project questions and their answers.

IT manager   A senior IT representative who has primary responsibility for successful delivery of technology including infrastructure, security, and conversion.

Knowledge area   A field of expertise.

Lag time   The float or amount of delay one task has without causing dependent task delay.

Lead time   The amount of delay between the end of one task and the start of the next dependent task.

Mandatory qualification   An imperative condition that a vendor must fulfill to qualify for the proposed project.

Measurable outcome   An observable result or output that an organization can demonstrate achieves an objective.

Mentor   An individual who works one-on-one with an executive sponsor, monitoring to improve project leadership and management based on best practices.

Methodology   A body of methods, rules, and postulates employed by a discipline.

Milestone   An event or checkpoint to review and verify task, phase, and/or project status.

Net present value (NPV)   A formula that evaluates an investment based on the difference between the present value of cash flows in the future and the investment amount today.

Object-oriented analysis and design (OOAD)   A software engineering methodology for modeling interaction of objects or entities of interest to a system.

Objective   A goal or something a person or organization plans to achieve.

Objective responsibility list   A register of who is accountable for the achievement of each objective.

Ongoing security compliance management   Planning, executing, and controlling recurring security audits of the system to ensure continual compliance with all security requirements.

Opinion leader   A trusted individual who influences other people's behavior.

Optimization management   Planning, controlling, and closing continued improvement of an innovation.

Optimization management plan   A description of how an organization plans, controls, and closes continued improvement of an innovation.

Organizational process asset   An information source used to influence project success (e.g., policies, procedures, plans, standards, guidelines, templates, reports, lessons learned).

Outcome delivery schedule   A timetable that identifies when the project will achieve outcomes.

Output   A tangible result of a process.

Payback period   A formula that identifies the time required to recover the costs of a proposed option.

Performance report   A description of the results or the status of a situation at a certain point in time.

Phase   A specific group of tasks that occur during a distinct period.

Phase closeout   Completing a set of activities conducted within a project.

Planned value (PV)   The budgeted cost of work scheduled.

Pre- and post-test   An evaluation of conditions both before and after system implementation.

Prerequisite skill training   A precondition users must possess before learning how to use the system.

Present value table   A list of interest rates used to determine the present value of a dollar amount over time.

Primary success scenario   The main story that an actor performs from end-to-end to achieve the desired outcome without taking any alternate steps along the way.

Process   An activity conducted to produce an output.

Process group   A collection of the processes that generally occur in distinct stages of the project over time.

Procurement management   Planning, executing, controlling, and closing acquisition of goods and services necessary to support the successful project completion.

Procurement plan   A description of all the things the organization needs to purchase over the course of the project, how to secure them, and when the acquisitions occur.

Product   The information system an HIT project produces.

Production environment   A live system or system region available for actual use with real instead of test data.

Project   A short-term endeavor to achieve specific objectives.

Project budget   A prediction of maximum project costs and the baseline for managing these costs.

Project charter   A document that authorizes a project and summarizes key project elements including a project scope statement, objectives, and key stakeholders with roles and responsibilities.

Project closeout   The project completion as signed off by the steering committee.

Project document update   A change to information that is not material to baseline documents and processes.

Project initiator   A member of a small planning group responsible for starting a project.

Project library   A location for storing, organizing, and controlling key documents produced or used by the project.

Project management   The discipline devoted to planning, organizing, and coordinating resources to successfully achieve the objectives of a short-term endeavor.

Project management plan   A collection of plans for each of the other knowledge areas—scope, schedule, budget, and so on—which a Project Manager uses collectively to successfully execute, control, and close a project.

Project Manager   The individual with primary responsibility for successful project completion.

Project roster   A directory of principal individuals involved in any aspect of the project.

Project scope baseline   The approved project scope and the collection of the scope statement, work breakdown structure (WBS), WBS dictionary, and work packages.

Project team performance assessment   A gauge of team effectiveness.

Quadruple constraint   A balance of project trade-offs among the four measurable dimensions that include scope, time, cost, and quality.

Qualitative risk analysis   An assessment of vulnerability based on probability, severity, impact, and rank using subjective information.

Quality assurance (QA)   Regular, interim checks on tasks performed in the preparation of a project deliverable to ensure progress on the deliverable meets pre-defined project standards.

Quality control (QC)   The final check on a deliverable to ensure it meets pre-defined quality standards (i.e., WBS dictionary).

Quality management   Planning, executing, and controlling project processes and outputs according to approved standards.

Quality management plan   A document that defines project standards and how the project will ensure compliance with them.

Quantitative risk analysis   An assessment of vulnerability based on probability, severity, impact, and rank using objective, statistical data.

Re-baseline   A revised plan or modified benchmark reflecting changes in project conditions.

Realization management   Initiating, planning, controlling, and closing what a stakeholder does to achieve the fundamental objectives of the project.

Request for Information (RFI)   A planning solicitation to obtain information about options without contractually committing to select and acquire a product from a specific vendor.

Request for proposal (RFP)   A formal invitation to vendors to prepare a competitive response to a request according to pre-defined evaluation criteria.

Resource assignment   The designation of specific project tasks to a specific individual.

Resource loading histogram   A bar chart displaying the number of project resources according to the project schedule.

Responsibility   The control over a particular role without having to seek authorization from another party.

Return on Investment (ROI)   A formula that calculates the ratio of financial gain or loss on an investment relative to the amount of money invested.

Risk management   Planning and controlling how the project identifies and responds to potential threats to successful project completion.

Risk management plan   A description of how the project will identify, assess, and respond to potential problems threatening successful project completion.

Risk register   A log of identified risks and their rank, severity, probability of occurrence, impact, response, and party responsible for that response.

Risk register update   A change to a listed risk.

Risk response plan   A set of strategies the Project Manager, Project Team members, and other project participants may choose to apply, depending on the significance of the risk.

Role-based training   Instructing individuals according to their specific work activity.

Scenario   A story of system and actor interactions.

Schedule   An organized task list based on their sequence, duration, and resource requirements, according to a timetable.

Schedule performance index (SPI)   A measure of how well the project is performing against the planned schedule.

Schedule variance (SV)   A comparison between how much work was planned for completion and how much work was actually completed.

Scope creep   Uncontrolled additions that change what a project includes or excludes.

Scope management   Planning, executing, and controlling what a project includes and excludes.

Scope statement   A description of what the project includes and excludes.

Security audit results   The description of flaws identified during a formal evaluation of system safeguards that require correction and subsequent testing to ensure their elimination.

Security management   Planning, executing, controlling and closing system access.

Security plan   A description of how an organization will manage system access.

Security requirements   A description of the system access specifications that an organization must support.

Security roles   The list of system functions for specific users or user types (i.e., it identifies who does what in a system).

Selected vendor   The supplier chosen to deliver a service and/or product.

Service bureau   An organization providing a variety of IT services (e.g., data storage and time-share applications).

Site readiness confirmation   A written acknowledgement, issued by the vendor after a review of the modified facilities, indicating the results of modification or renovation to an organization's facilities comply with vendor infrastructure requirements.

Software as a Service (SaaS)   The delivery of application software and data to customers as an on-demand service.

Software configuration management   Planning, executing, and controlling the setup selection of vendor application options and features to meet user, technical, and security requirements.

Software configuration plan (SCP)   A description of how an organization and vendor define, approve, make, track, and report both the initial system configuration and any subsequent changes.

Software metric   A measurement of software properties, such as lines of code (LOC), function points or units of software functionality, or objects or entities of interest to a system.

Solicitation   A formal invitation to vendors to prepare a competitive response to a request according to pre-defined evaluation criteria.

Sponsorship management   Initiating, planning, and controlling the selection, assessment, and mentoring of a project's most senior leader.

Stakeholder   An individual or group that the project affects in terms of their problems, needs, or interests.

Stakeholder map   A listing of all groups affected by the project classified according to their level of influence and support for the project.

Steering committee   The body responsible for guiding or steering the project to successful completion by supporting, reviewing, and approving all project activities (e.g., resolving escalated issues, approving change requests, amending the contract, and accepting deliverables).

Storytelling   Relating to individuals based on metaphors to describe the change experience of others.

Straddle record   A record added to the old system after conversion but before cutover to the new system.

Subject matter expert (SME)   An individual with specialized knowledge about how to perform certain tasks.

Successful cutover confirmation   A written acknowledgement that the system is live and ready for acceptance testing.

Support plan   A description of who will provide what technical support to users on an ongoing basis.

Support roles and responsibilities matrix   A description of the position and function assigned to each person responsible for support.

Support management   Planning, executing, and controlling technical maintenance of the system after cutover.

Support tickets   A prioritized log entry of a reported system issue described in detail so support can reproduce and correct it.

Swim lane diagram   A grouping of activities by actor into parallel lanes similar to the lanes in a swimming pool.

System environment   A collection of hardware and software to perform certain computing activities such as development, testing, training, and production.

System installation plan   A description of the hardware, application, and system software planned for installation and configuration to support a new system, and the timing and scope of installation.

System support requirements   A description of what an organization and vendor will do to address issue logging, escalation and resolution, and system updates.

Task duration estimate   An estimate of the work period required to complete an activity.

Task list   An inventory of activities project resources must perform to produce all project deliverables.

Task resource estimate   An approximation of the type and quantity of resources required to perform an activity (e.g., people, equipment, and supplies), based on the requirements of that activity.

Task sequence   A chronological relationship between one or more activities.

Test cases   A description of each requirement and the expected outcome from the system when a user executes it.

Test data   A collection of data sufficient to conduct all identified system tests and receive meaningful and accurate outcomes.

Test environment   A system or system region that is entirely separate from the actual operations of an organization.

Test management   Planning, executing, and controlling how an organization verifies that a new system meets its specifications.

Test plan   A description of how an organization will verify the configuration, security, conversion, and interfaces of a new system for production use.

Test result   A reported outcome associated with completing a test case.

Time management   Planning and controlling the schedule required to complete the project within an approved timeframe.

Time value of money   The monetary worth of capital over a specified time.

Training completion confirmation   A written acknowledgement that each trainee successfully completed a specific training course.

Training documentation   The set of materials used by instructors and students during training sessions.

Training management   Planning, executing, and controlling project tasks for educating users to take advantage of workflow and system benefits.

Training need   A description of the specific instructions each user requires to improve skills to use the new system and perform new workflow steps.

Training plan   A description of the training target audience, their current levels of IT fluency, the training curriculum, schedule, modality, feedback, logistics, standards, deliverables, resources, and deadline.

Transformation management   Planning, executing, and controlling the adoption of innovation by individuals or groups of stakeholders.

Transformation task   An activity to help stakeholder groups transition from the current to the future state.

Transformation task completion   A written confirmation that a transformation task was successfully completed.

Unified modeling language (UML)   A graphical notation used to visualize and specify how to construct software.

User requirement   A description of a future (not current) need for a system without regard to technology (e.g., equipment).

User requirements management   Initiating, planning, executing, and controlling the identification and organization of stakeholder needs to evaluate options and acquire a solution that achieves the project objectives.

User requirements management plan   A description of how an organization plans to successfully identify and manage stakeholder system needs.

Vendor project manager   The assigned vendor employee with primary responsibility for successful implementation of the vendor product, including for example, orchestrating all vendor resources, their availability, and timing; installing the system; and ensuring the vendor sustains system support after go-live according to the contract.

WBS dictionary   A detailed description for each project component of work.

Work breakdown structure (WBS)   A hierarchical list of project deliverables organized by category (e.g., technology, clinical, training).

Work package   A description of the lowest tasks and associated components for a deliverable.

Workflow change   An updated configuration requirement, subsequent configuration change, and/or modification to a manual step.

Workflow management   Planning, executing, and controlling the sequence of automated and manual steps that support delivery of an organization's products and services.

Workflow management plan   A description of how to change sequences of automated and manual steps to perform work more effectively.

Workflow requirement   A description of how to reduce the number of steps, decrease the amount of time, and minimize motion (moving from place to place) during system use or manual steps.

Index

Note: Page numbers followed by *f* denote figures; page numbers followed by *t* denote tables.

CPSIA information can be obtained
at www.ICGtesting.com
Printed in the USA
FFOW04n1741050118
44359464-44038FF